Tribal Women

Tribal Women

Yesterday, Today and Tomorrow

Editor

S.N. Chaudhary

RAWAT PUBLICATIONS
Jaipur • New Delhi • Bangalore • Guwahati • Kolkata

ISBN 978-81-316-0665-0

Reprinted, 2017

Published by
Prem Rawat for **Rawat Publications**
Satyam Apts, Sector 3, Jawahar Nagar, Jaipur 302 004 (India)
Phone: 0141 265 1748 / 7006 Fax: 0141 265 1748
E-mail: info@rawatbooks.com
Website: www.rawatbooks.com

New Delhi Office
4858/24, Ansari Road, Daryaganj, New Delhi 110 002
Phone: 011 2326 3290

Also at *Bangalore, Guwahati* and *Kolkata*

Printed at Chaman Enterprises, New Delhi

Contents

Preface

Scheduled tribe constitutes about 8.2 per cent population in India. They are found in different pockets with high concentration in both central as well as north-eastern India. Tribal women constitute about half of their male population. In certain pockets, the condition of sex ratio is better but there are areas where condition of sex ratio is decreasing with faster rate like their non-tribal neighbours. If we see over all social status of tribal women, the picture is largely praiseworthy. In different realms of life, historically their status is independent and even better in comparison to non-tribal women as well as their male counterparts. They have enjoyed freedom in mate selection, singing and dancing, management of family life, collection of non-timber forest produce and so on. They are also credited for sustenance and continuation of number of cultural traits or indices of tribal identity. They have also played active and praiseworthy role in the management and sustenance of environmental and ecological surroundings. They have retained symbiotic relationship with most of the components of environment since long. Hence, it appears that tribal women have played crucial role in their world.

But with the passage of time and as the process of unregulated interaction between tribes with non-tribes increased, the tribal world experienced tests of both fortunes and misfortunes. Tribal women also became victims of acculturation process. New definition of development came into being. New system to regulate their life conditions was imposed by alien institutions. New state and NGO centric development schemes were introduced for the development of tribal masses. It was loudly claimed that not only because of isolation or assimilation but also integrative approach can address their problem and improve their physical and social quality of life. In addition, in the due course of time, tribal communities experienced a number of interventions made by external forces. It also experienced various types of social movements. Seasonal outmigration, popularization of consumer culture and expansion of communication and transportation system have also impacted tribal areas and tribal population. Tribal women are not an exception to this process. They are at the crossroads. Their health status, economic life, cultural practices and education status have experienced mixed taste over the time because of initiatives of different types in their life and society. How these initiatives have conditioned their socio-economic and cultural life? What is the status of their quality of life? Why it is so that only few among them have availed fruits of development and majority of them are still left out? Why it is so that even those who have availed development benefits have been forced to become dependent prone? How to improve their overall status by integrating their cultural heritage as well as new initiatives? These are some of the broad issues and questions in the light of which a two days national seminar entitled 'Tribal Women: Status, Challenges and Possibilities' was organized by Tribal Research and Development Institute, Bhopal, in collaboration with Rajiv Gandhi Chair in Contemporary Studies, Barkatullah University, Bhopal, in March 2013.

We received massive support and guidance from Shri K. Suresh (IAS), the then Director of Tribal Research and Development Institute, and Prof. Nisha Dubey, Vice-Chancellor Barkatullah University, Bhopal. At the outset, I express my thanks to both of them.

I am also extremely thankful to Shri Kuwar Vijay Shah, Minister of Scheduled Tribe and Scheduled Caste Welfare Department, Government of Madhya Pradesh, for inaugurating the seminar.

I also express my sense of gratitude and thanks to Prof. M.N. Karna, Patna and Prof. Karma Oraon, Ranchi, for delivering keynote address and valedictory address in the seminar. Number of scholars and experts, chairperson and co-chairperson of different technical sessions, chief guests in the technical sessions, paper presenters and discussants participated in the seminar. I am extremely thankful to all of them. I am also obliged and thankful to all those selected scholars who on my request revised their papers and made it available to me for publication in this volume in time. Without their cooperation, it would have been impossible to publish this book.

I am also thankful to all the researchers particularly Dr. Manish Mishra, Dr. Neeraj Kumar, Dr. Manoj Sharma, Narayan Mohanty and Bhawana Shakyawar for their continuous work, which enabled me to ensure success of the seminar as well as publication of this volume.

S.N. Chaudhary

Contributors

Anil Prasad Bandela, Assistant Professor, School of Social Work, Bastar University, Jagdalpur, Chhattisgarh.

D. Sundaram, Former Professor of Sociology, Madras University, Chennai, Tamil Nadu.

D.K. Verma, Professor, Division of SC, ST and OBC Development, Dr. Babasaheb Ambedkar National Institute of Social Sciences, Dr. Ambedkar Nagar, Mhow, Madhya Pradesh.

Debashis Debnath, Associate Professor, Indian Institute of Forest Management, Bhopal, Madhya Pradesh.

Gaya Pandey, Faculty Member, Department of Anthropology, Ranchi University, Ranchi, Jharkhand.

J.J. Roy Burman, Professor of Sociology, Tata Institute of Social Sciences, Mumbai, Maharashtra.

Karma Oraon, Professor of Anthropology, Ranchi University, Ranchi, Jharkhand.

K. Gopal Iyer, former Professor of Sociology, Punjab University, Chandigarh.

Lolita Pradhan, Research Associate, Regional Centre National Afforestaion and Eco-Development Board (RCNAEB), Indian Institute of Forest Management, Bhopal, Madhya Pradesh.

M.C. Behera, Professor, Arunachal Institution of Tribal Studies, Rajiv Gandhi University, Itanagar.

M.N. Karna, former Professor of Sociology, North Eastern Hill University (NEHU), Shillong, Meghalaya.

Madhu Nagla, Professor of Sociology, Maharshi Dayanand University, Rohtak, Haryana.

Neeta Tapan, Faculty, Department of Economics, Govt. Girls' P.G. Excellence College, Ujjain, Madhya Pradesh.

R.K. Mohanty, Reader in Sociology, Biju Patnaik State Police Academy, Bhubaneswar, Odisha.

Rahul Banerjee, Member, Dhas Gramin Vikas Kendra, Indore, Madhya Pradesh.

S.N. Chaudhary, Professor of Sociology, currently, Rajiv Gandhi Chair Professor in Contemporary Studies, Barkatullah University, Bhopal, Madhya Pradesh.

S.N. Tripathy, Professor of Economics, Gokhale Institute of Economic and Politics, Pune, Maharashtra.

Subhadra Khaperde, Member, Dhas Gramin Vikas Kendra, Indore, Madhya Pradesh.

Swapan Kumar Kolay, Associate Professor, School of Anthropology and Tribal Studies, Bastar University, Jagdalpur, Chhattisgarh.

Yatindra Singh Sisodia, Professor of Political Science, Madhya Pradesh Institute of Social Science Research, Ujjain, Madhya Pradesh.

CHAPTER 1

INTRODUCTION

S.N. Chaudhary

The status of tribal women in different important fields, particularly literacy and education, health and nutrition, politics and economy, trade and commerce, art and culture, bureaucracy, etc., cannot be understood in isolation from history, indigenous culture and non-tribal traditions like Hindu, Islamic and others. The role of enormous socio-political situations cannot also be undermined while comprehending the social status of tribal women, most of whom live in villages like their male counterparts. On the basis of a study of these inter-connected issues, it may be broadly stated that their status is mixed as well as dynamic. A section of researchers feel that much before the British invasion, the values of tribals, in general, and tribal women, in particular, especially from the standpoint of freedom from anxieties, restrictions, exploitations, etc., was progressive. Their roles and characteristics were seldom conditioned by external forces. Contemporary ecology and environment played an indispensable role in the evolution and sustenance of the high status of the local women. Women contributed to the formulation and sustenance of the economy, culture and tradition. They adapted a culture-centric system to lead an independent and peaceful life. They took part in the decision-making process relating to their life (Chaudhary: 2009). Needless to mention here that among these perspectives, culture was an effective source of sustenance and was instrumental in managing crisis situations. For example, the primitive knowledge system which historically played a crucial role in different walks of life, in turn, helped the society to sustain and overcome challenges. Many more examples of cultural traits may be underlined, which played a vital role in their life. They acquired knowledge on the basis of their experience. Commenting on the status of Baiga women, Elwin (1939) praised the exalted place of women and children in aboriginal life, its non-repressive attitude towards sex and marriage, its finely developed aesthetic sensibilities and its collective and cooperative spirit. Besides Elwin, a number of classical scholars have highlighted the advanced social status of tribal women during the nineteenth and twentieth century. For example, highlighting the status of Naga women, Haimandorf (1933) stated that most women in the other civilized parts of India may well envy the women of the Naga Hills for their high status in society and the personal freedom they enjoy. Hutton (1921) also observed that Naga women enjoy considerable freedom and high social status. They have the right to choose their husband and are never forced to marry against their will. Elwin (1961) alluded to the freedom enjoyed by Naga women and contended that they exercised significant decision-making power within their societies. Grigson (Reprint 1991) dealing with the social status of Hill Maria and Bison Horn Maria women of Bastar district of undivided Madhya Pradesh stated that, 'Daughters and sisters have no right of inheritance of their father's or brother's lands or property. For the land is really the land of the clan, and the daughters and sisters will on marriage have passed to the clans of their husbands. A widow is entitled only to maintenance, and as on her husband's death she very often becomes the wife of his younger brother, she gets her maintenance as a matter of course; if he leaves no younger brother and she does not marry again, she lives on in her late husband's house and works with other women of the family, and is maintained by their husbands. A girl whose parents die before she is married frequently goes to a married sister's house and becomes a co-wife' (p. 294). Grigson (ibid) highlighted that as a girl, she has considerable freedom both in pre-marital sexual life and in the choice of her husband, and she is fairly free to leave her husband if he ill-treats her or if he cannot beget a child. Tribal sentiment also strongly condemns wife beating. Her liking for ornament is encouraged by her parents who gradually collect beads and metal neck and arm rings, by her boy-companion presenting her with beads and carved hair-combs, and, after marriage, by her husband who respects her right to spend her earnings, however scanty it may be, from the sale of her basketry, on simple trinkets. She has the freedom to participate in tribal dances and songs, though not in religious ceremonies. In fact, her status vis-à-vis her husband is far more liberal than that of any Hindu wife. Above all, she is not exposed to the evils of child marriage and premature motherhood unlike Hindu women, as Maria headmen will vouch for (p. 295).

But as the process of interaction, or, anthropologically speaking, 'acculturation', between two unequal partners, that is, relatively more developed non-tribals, particularly from the viewpoint of material culture, and relatively less developed and relatively more isolated tribals increased, the process of assimilation also increased, and with this the status of tribals, in general, and tribal women, in particular, was gradually forced to take the back seat. The Hindu tradition influenced the tribal world with a number of its stringent practices, like the patriarchy system, right to inherit private property and religious mores, which gradually became one of the structural roots of subjugation and marginalization of tribal women. Gradually, women's access to and control over earning sources of livelihood was restricted; the degree of freedom in terms of selection of mates was limited; and over a period of time, every effort was made by the advancing acculturation to repress their identity, freedom and cultural heritage by establishing 'culture of others'. The 'culture of others' (i.e. Hinduism, Christianity, British Raj and other institutions) encouraged and forced many of them to assimilate with the non-tribal culture and tradition, and in the process, they gradually lost their original culture, both material and non-material. In other words, the induced process of development by the state and other external forces helped only a few among them to cope up with the adverse situation by availing the benefits of development, but the majority of them adapted to the institutional and non-institutional process of development for their survival. Those few who availed the benefits of the state and other institutions were forced to become dependent instead of becoming self-reliant. The ever-increasing depletion of natural resources, especially forests, as well as the emerging policies to regulate these resources in the interests of non-tribal development, forced many of them to become socially, economically and culturally marginalized in their own homeland (Chaudhary: 2010).

Tribal women were traditionally responsible for collecting firewood, fetching drinking water, nurturing children, cooking, celebrating festivals, following rituals, maintaining harmonious relations among kins and relatives and so on. According to Singh (1994), the Agaria women of Madhya Pradesh, for example, work as agricultural labourers, manage family affairs and participate in social functions. Similarly, Dhurva women manage the household, agricultural activities, basket making and collecting forest produce and fuel. The selling of surplus agricultural and forest products in the market is also their responsibility. The newly introduced process of development has restricted all these responsibilities. It is claimed that the overall result of the process of development, which strongly believes in the top-down model, especially from the standpoint of tribal women at large, is, sociologically speaking, rather inhibiting than being practical.

In most of the cases, the institutional interventions could not control marginalization and impoverization fully due to numerous external and internal constraints. In many cases, the development model left them impoverished in the long-term. Illiteracy, school drop outs, poor quality of primary education, increase in female and maternal mortality rates, inadequate institutional delivery, child marriage, scarcity in secondary and tertiary occupation sectors, shrinking control over economic resources, paucity in health and nutritional development, female infanticide particularly among tribes who are exposed to the outer world, etc., are the outcomes of the ongoing top-down or capitalistic or foreign development process.

Even civil society organizations and activists were only notionally successful or failed in restoring fundamental rights and dignity of tribal women. It is also observed (Dungdung: 2013) that in many cases, these organizations are either alien or exploitative. There are hundreds and thousands of self-help groups (SHGs) working under the guidance of NGOs in tribal areas, yet it is debatable whether the quality of their life has improved. In many remote tribal areas, it is difficult to trace the presence of an effective NGO. NGOs that claim to be engaged in capacity building are criticized for preferring to work in developed areas; if located in tribal areas, they are engaged in other types of activities, that is, those activities which ensure their own survival and development. Only those organizations which choose to protest against the functioning of the state and industrial houses in the areas are relatively closer to the heart of the tribal masses.

As a result of all these forces and in spite of the presence of the aforesaid initiatives, from the human development point of view, the status of the tribe is far inferior compared to the Scheduled Castes, and the status of tribal women is far inferior to their male counterpart. In other words, development is not to be measured in material term; rather it refers to development in terms of social, psychological and cultural aspects. It also refers to their participation in the decision-making process domestically and socially leading to their progression, liberty to say no, courage to oppose violation of their human rights and individuality and self-respect. These personalities are largely lacking in most of the tribal women, no matter where they live or what they do? Later chapters in this volume deal with these issues.

Needless to say that during the last 20 years, some new drives, especially post-globalization, have been experimented in the tribal world to accelerate the development process. Large numbers of small- and large-scale development projects have been initiated in tribal areas, which have benefitted the state, for example, power projects, industries, roads, dams, etc. However, they have apparently taken a toll on the economy, culture, society and environment at large. Due to the ongoing mammoth development projects in tribal areas, there is sizable environmental degradation. Hundreds and thousands of tribals have been relocated from their original place of living. A good many of them have lost their traditional sources of livelihood and have been forced to migrate for survival. The state has failed miserably in rehabilitating displaced tribals, most of whom are poor, illiterate and dependent as per the rehabilitation policy framed by the same government. Even if monetary compensation is provided to the displaced tribal families, their women are deprived of the benefits. Needless to say that in most of the cases, tribal women are the worst affected victims of displacement. The most serious problem is lack of food security among many tribal groups. They have been pushed towards unsafe zones. Tribals, in general, and tribal women, in particular, are the badly affected victims of this hazardous process (Chaudhary: 2013).

Many of the damages caused due to mammoth development projects such as environmental degradation are irreparable. There are different indicators of environmental degradation; they are climate change, biodiversity loss, unregulated population growth, water pollution, contamination, air pollution, green house effect, deforestation, land degradation and desertification. The existing technology is highly insufficient in reversing these damages; rather these technologies have immensely added to the ongoing degradation process. As a result, society, in general, and locals, mostly tribal women, in particular, who are supposed to cook, carry water, collect firewood and meet other fundamental requirements are the worst and immediate victims of the current top-down model of development. It is unfortunate that to overcome these problems, which are diverse in nature, today we are largely dependent on globalization and related agencies. What benefit tribal women at large have availed from these exogenous development forces? What have they gained from the expansion of markets, information technology and media revolution? And in most of the cases the answer is either frustrating or discouraging. Some of the chapters in this volume have covered these issues in detail. Due to lack of basic requirements like good quality education and technical skills, capital, risk taking capacity, absence of human resources, lack of coordination with change agents, ignorance of market mechanism and apathy on the part of village level institutions, etc., tribal women have failed badly to encounter the existing and upcoming challenges and avail the benefits of development provided by different agents of globalization (Chaudhary: 2012a). This is a serious concern from both the national development as well as national integration point of view. How to analyse and address these issues? All these issues were discussed in different technical sessions in the seminar.

Also, like other low caste women, tribal women also tirelessly work on the land of their natal and marital families but hardly a few enjoy ownership holding *patta* in their names (Chaudhary: 2011).

According to K.S. Singh (1994), Baiga women of Madhya Pradesh do not inherit parental property but a widow can inherit her deceased husband's property if she does not remarry. Bharia and other tribes also follow the same practice. Among Pando tribe, a widow enjoys rights over the property of her deceased husband in her life time provided she does not remarry. As a result, neither can women sell/mortgage land in need nor can they stop male family members from selling the land. They are also unable to obtain loan from banks and cooperative societies because technically most of them are landless, and except for some ornaments they have nothing to mortgage. Even if some of them mobilize money, due to want of banking sectors coupled with consumerism and expansion of market forces at the rural level, they are unable to save and streamline their income. Even the educated and working among them are forced by these circumstances to put up with basic human rights violations (Sachchidananda and Mandal: 1985).

Significant numbers of tribal women have become victims of human trafficking, and with the increasing trend of acculturation the cases of human trafficking are increasing day by day. The dwindling male-female ratio in certain states has led to trafficking of tribal girls for marital purpose. Tribal women bear the brunt of witchcraft even today. Some of the chapters in this volume deal with these and related issues in detail. Historically, tribals have been following the bride price system, thus, implying the higher value of tribal women. But with the entry of the dowry system of the non-tribal, gradually the social status of tribal women has been reversed and, in many cases, they are even victimized. As stated earlier, their culture is now diversified, and in this process, they have significantly lost their customary educational system, youth movement, totem system, traditional dispute redressal forums and so on. With the acquisition of various cultures, their sense of brotherhood, we-feeling and symbiotic relations with their natural resources, etc., are perhaps a thing of the past. Some of the surviving aboriginal institutions are now unable to manage the crisis situation in their life and largely caused by external forces (Chaudhary: 2012b). They have apparently lost their original personalities and adapted to the changes popularized by the state, that is, dignified life and development as promised by the state and the protest and violence as shown to them by the naxalites and other extremist movements, which have failed to ensure their development in a sustainable manner (Padel: 2013).

As for the empowerment of tribal women, it appears that it exists only in principle. Empowerment of tribal women does not simply mean their presence in secondary and tertiary sectors, regional politics and electoral representatives, particularly Gram Panchayats and formation of SHGs, but ignorance of their rights and duties, their absence in bureaucracy and trade and commerce. Even if some of them are present in these bodies and sectors, it is very difficult to say that they are empowered in terms of their access to power and prestige. Many of the women representatives have failed to discharge responsibilities entrusted upon them. Only a select few have been capable of empowering themselves. But what about majority of tribal women who are far away from development and empowerment? What about those who are highly underdeveloped as per human development indicators? Some of the chapters in this volume exclusively deal with these issues.

But the pertinent question is how to educate tribal women and make them aware of their basic rights and claims, particularly in a situation which is highly capitalistic and largely based on the top-down model of development? How to formulate policies and schemes and implement them as per their requirements? How to address the evils of society like corruption, manipulation, inclination towards materialism and market forces, growing individualism, depletion of natural resources, expansion of consumerism, increasing apathy among tribal elites—both men and women—and widening gap between aspiration and accomplishment of tribal women and young girls in particular? How to sensitize the forces of globalization operating at the village level in favour of tribal women? How to strengthen new programmes like SHGs, PESA, Forest Rights Act 2006, Panchayati Raj, MNREGA, etc., in the broader interest of tribal women? How to strengthen the interface between demand and supply? Several chapters have attempted to provide answers to these complicated issues. More specifically, some of the specific issues which have been covered in different chapters of the volume are as follows:

1. Socio-economic, cultural and health condition of tribal women in the historical and cross-cultural perspective with special mention of tribal women of Madhya Pradesh.
2. Historical and contemporary factors responsible for their inferior position in comparison to their non-tribal counterparts.
3. Process of implementation, functioning and consequences of constitutional and state level schemes for the overall welfare and development of tribal women, particularly SHGs, MNREGA, PESA, Forest Rights Act 2006 and so on.
4. The negative forces operating at both local and national level which are responsible for both underdevelopment and slow progress of tribal women.

5. Decriminalize witchcraft and sorcery, trafficking, etc., practised by tribal women and steps taken to address these problems and overall consequences of such initiatives.
6. The role of civil society organizations, extremist movements, industrial houses, development projects and local culture in the overall development or underdevelopment of tribal women.
7. Suggestions to ensure steady progress of tribal women from human rights, development and empowerment perspectives by minimizing the influence of negative forces and by maximizing the impact of positive factors so that their social status and quality of life improves in a sustainable manner and they become active partners in the development process.

In order to address the above perspectives, a two days national seminar was organized. The papers presented have been included in this volume.

II

In spite of the implementation of development projects, legal steps and protests, etc., tribal women of north-eastern states are suffering from oppression, exploitation and discrimination in different walks of life. Customary laws and patriarchy are the two major factors responsible for this state of affair. M.N. Karna observed that the situation is not better even among matrilineal tribes like Khasi, the Jaintia and the Garo who are supposedly matriarchy. They are consciously deprived of strategies that are supposed to promote their living conditions. He also warned that there is a need to comprehend reality from close quarters without which it is difficult to neutralize the negative forces responsible for the current plight.

D. Sundaram underlined the importance of the tribal–forest interface, with an emphasis on tribal women and their concerns in the historical perspective. He also examined the role of customary law with reference to their status. To him, the nature of relationship between the two was historically organic, but due to external forces there is a breakdown of the historical relationship. Attempts are being made to develop tribal women through new projects but due to the top-down model of development process comprising of unsuitable concepts of development, problems at the delivery level and lack of social capital mobilization, tribal women have miserably failed to reap the benefits of state-sponsored development programmes. Until and unless there is a bottom-up approach of development which is formulated and implemented in a holistic manner, keeping in view the concerns and implementation process of a cross section of tribal women, their development cannot be assured.

The chapter of K.G. Iyer deals with the negative impact of land acquisition and displacement of tribals from Kalinganagar, Orissa, following the POSCO project. It also examines the roles and status of civil society bodies of both local and national level in dealing with issues relating to displacement. The chapter also concentrates on merits and demerits of the 2006 rehabilitation policy of the Government of Orissa with special reference to POSCO and local tribal women.

Tribal women are subject to violence not only by the external forces but also by internal factors, and the underlying factor is mostly property. They are declared as a witch by their own kinsmen, and in order to keep ancestral property intact, they are subjected to physical and mental cruelty. The public is indifferent on this issue primarily because tribal women are generally considered as a witch or due to the biased opinion against women in general. Karma Oraon feels that in spite of the number of institutional empowerments, the status of tribal women remained at the lower ebb compared to their male counterparts. Institutional programmes like PESA, Panchayati Raj Institution, etc., have largely failed to improve the socio-economic status of tribal women.

M.C. Behera made an attempt to examine the status of tribal women of Arunachal Pradesh with the help of Lenski's sociological model named 'Status Inconsistency'. Based on case studies of the so-called successful tribal women of the state, he concluded that from their achievement their status may be high in the society but this does not mean that they are totally free from the clutches of 'ascribed status', that is, they are bound by the ascribed status. Hence, these women are caught between these two contradictions.

The social status of tribal women is heterogeneous; it differs regionally and among the tribes, however, a woman's contribution to the family and society is immense. In spite of awareness programmes by welfare groups, they are grossly denied right to both movable and immovable properties. In terms of health and nutrition, their requirements are not met. They are far away from modern health and disease management facilities which are now penetrating into many tribal villages. They are largely dependent on traditional practices, which are neither scientific nor curative in nature. This calls for, as M. Nagla says, a holistic approach to deal with these challenges and to improve their health and social condition.

Rahul Banerjee and S. Khaperde dealt with health-related issues of Bhil women in a city in Madhya Pradesh. The study is very interesting, in the sense that it has covered tribal women living in urban areas, as otherwise more than 90 per cent tribals of central India live in villages, and therefore the maximum number of studies deals with tribals living in villages. The study is theoretical as well as field based. It includes types of cloth used during menstrual period, types and awareness of reproductive health care, hygienic techniques practised in reproductive health (RH) care, their level of knowledge about health-care services meant for them and the feedback on the initiatives taken by institutions. The role of local NGOs in dealing with health care of Bhil women has also been analysed. Finally, they have concluded that in spite of the initiative measures by institutions and NGOs, neither the level of health care awareness and facilities nor the status of their health is up to the mark.

Historically, tribes of Orissa enjoyed better standards of life due to their unique cultural practices and government schemes. However, today these institutions have largely faded out. As a result, tribes are facing new challenges. One among these is the declining number of girls who undergo primary education in terms of the enrolment, retention, attendance, skill up-gradation, drop-out, non-enrolment, out of school, etc. Thus, the status of tribal girls is much inferior compared to their non-tribal counterpart. Hence, the conclusion drawn by R.K. Mohanty is very close to a number of human development reports that observe that tribals, in general, and tribal women, in particular, are at the lowest strata in the social status.

As a result of deterioration in the sources of their livelihood, S.N. Tripathy observed that a large number of tribes are today facing livelihood-related problems at the village level. Women are no exception. They seek refuge in forceful migration to non-tribal areas in search of better livelihood and survival. Unfortunately, even in their new destinations their basic rights are not protected. They are constantly exploited by contractors. Contractors pay them an advance amount back in the village, but subject them to exploitation at the place of work. They take no efforts to improve their living conditions; hence the vicious circle of exploitation continues. This calls for an integrated and holistic approach to deal with their problems. However, under the given condition, how migration may be discouraged and how their plight may be mitigated, needs to be probed thoroughly.

The overall health condition of tribal women is poor compared to other social groups. A number of factors, both historical and contemporary, are responsible for this state of affair. The five-year plans of the government have included this crisis but primarily due to lack of co-ordination between the givers and takers of the health facilities at the delivery level, the problem is still alarming. However, Neeta Tapan feels that even without addressing the structural and historical constraints, the health condition of tribal women, in particular, may be improved provided the information, education and communication (IEC) measure is implemented in favour of health management by civil societies, SHGs, etc., in the tribal villages on a consistent basis. Once the trust on the institutional measures increases, these measures are sustained, the health condition of tribal women will improve.

Joint forest management programme is one of the recent institutional initiatives, through its various provisions and schemes, to meet basic requirements of tribal women as well as to conserve forest resources. This has been intensively analysed by D. Debnath and his colleague. But two important issues, that is, what are the historical factors and conditions that determine the emergence of the JFM scheme and why is it that in spite of the functioning of this project, in the broader sense, there is neither an improvement in the health condition of tribal women nor of the forests? These questions need to be probed by analysing the interface between the forest management and tribal women. The chapter thus tries to find a solution for these two major concerns.

The chapter by S.N. Chaudhary underlines that primarily due to external forces the socio-economic status of tribal women in central India has deteriorated over a period of time since the pre-British rule. They are the first and direct victims of environmental and cultural degeneration. Various new programmes have opened up a door of opportunity for the progression of tribal women, but these welfare measures are dependent on other factors and sustainability is not guaranteed. The chapter concluded that most tribal women are victims of deprivation, even the few who have progressed economically and politically, are still not fully independent.

Y.S. Sisodia observed that in spite of the presence of a large number of tribal women in the Panchayat at all levels, as members as well as presidents, they are oppressed in terms of the social status. Their performances are suppressed, undermined or challenged. This is primarily due to the patriarchal system prevalent in the tribal world. Due to unacceptability, many innovative ideas and schemes such as PESA are forced to remain in papers. This condition prevails in Madhya Pradesh as well as in the neighbouring states of Rajasthan and Gujarat which have similar system of socio-economic conditions. Hence, neither the Panchayati Raj Institution nor women representatives of Panchayat are able to improve the status of tribal women. Even under their leadership, a number of state run programmes have failed to produce results.

D.K. Verma deals with the state of development and empowerment of Saharia women of Madhya Pradesh and Khasi women of Meghalaya. Both these categories of women represent two different socio-economic and cultural contexts. One is from the patriarchal society, while the other is from the matriarchal society. Instead of having different levels of development and empowerment, both are underdeveloped in society and they are still striving to progress. Their level of aspiration is increasing day-by-day, and in the process, state initiatives and external factors are pushing cultural factors to the back seat. The role of culture and tradition is marginalized in their life. Hence, the question in everybody's mind is, 'how will the state be able to empower them under the given socio-political context, which is market driven and capitalistic in nature?' How can one ensure their development in a sustainable manner at the cost of their tradition and culture? His chapter is an attempt to answer these questions.

It is true that Nagas are patrilineal, patriarchal and patrilocal, but their women play a significant role in their economy. They are primarily responsible for cooking, upbringing of children and live with their neighbours in harmony. Many of us are in favour of the continuation of customary law among tribes but among Nagas such law is responsible for limiting the economic progress of their women. Women do not enjoy possession of property, both movable and immovable, by inheritance either paternal or from their husband. They are not allowed to participate in social, cultural and political activities. Hence, Naga women, observed J.J. Roy Burman, are victims of gender discrimination and marginalization by their culture and value system.

There is a point of view in favour of higher social status of tribal women in comparison to tribal men. According to S.K. Kolay, women work harder, and the family economy and management totally depend on them. But in spite of this, they have no right to the property and are less paid, and even those tribal women, their number being very small, who migrate to urban areas to escape inhuman life conditions, face another kind of inhumanity and pitiable living conditions. Hence, according to him due to the number of historical and contemporary challenges, the socio-economic status of tribal women is not up to the mark.

The contribution of tribal women as construction labourers in the industrial and urban setting is not an age-old practice. However, today their number has increased due to mass construction of buildings. But in spite of their entry in new occupations, due to historical constraints, their economic status and condition have not improved, and they remain unorganized. This is explained in detail in the chapter of Gaya Pandey.

REFERENCES

Chaudhary, S.N. (ed.) (2009): *Tribal Development Since Independence*, New Delhi: Concept.

Chaudhary, S.N. (ed.) (2010): *Tribal Economy at Crossroads*, Jaipur: Rawat.

Chaudhary, S.N. (2011): "In Between Tradition and Democracy: The Status of Land Ownership to Rural Women in Madhya Pradesh". *Journal of Social and Political Studies*, Vol. II(1), June, pp. 94–106.

Chaudhary, S.N. (ed.) (2012a): *Tribal Education: Implications for Development*, New Delhi: Concept.

Chaudhary, S.N. (2012b): *In Search of Sustainable Development: Scenario in a Tribal Village of Madhya Pradesh*. New Delhi: Serials.

Chaudhary, S.N. (ed.) (2013): *Globalisation, National Development and Tribal Identity*, Jaipur: Rawat.

Dungdung, G. (2013): *Whose Country Is It Anyway?: Untold Stories of the Indigenous Peoples of India*. Kolkata: Adivaani.

Elwin, V. (1939): *The Baiga*. London: John Murray.

Elwin, V. (1961): "On Tribal Fertility in the Late Nineteenth and Early Twentieth Century India". Working Paper Series No. 98, Harvard Center for Population and Development Studies, Harvard University.

Haimendrof, C.V.F. (1933): *Naked Nagas*. Calcutta: Thacker Spink and Co.

Hutton, J.H. (1921): *The Sema Nagas*. New Delhi: Oxford University Press.

Padel, F. (2013): "Tribal Identity and Real Development in a Rapidly Globalising World". In Chaudhary, S.N. (ed.) *Globalisation, National Development and Tribal Identity*. Jaipur: Rawat.

Sachchidananda, Mandal, B.B. (1985): *Industrialization and Social Disorganization: A Study of Tribes in Bihar*. Delhi: Concept.

Singh, K.S. (1994): *The Scheduled Tribes*. Delhi: Oxford University Press.

CHAPTER 2

INTERROGATING SOCIAL OPPRESSION, ECONOMIC EXPLOITATION AND POLITICAL DISCRIMINATION: PERSPECTIVES ON THE STATUS OF TRIBAL WOMEN IN INDIA

M.N. Karna

Conventionally, the changing status of women of tribal communities has usually been examined within the broader framework of the colonial anthropological tradition. But this analysis aims to take stock of the situation by making a start to highlight the challenges and possibilities emanating from the issues of social oppression, economic exploitation and political discrimination that are being witnessed in various marginalized tribal groups. By recognizing and giving prominence to the social construction paradigm of status, it will attempt to show the relevance of a socio-political policy based on the egalitarian vision and democratic values.

I

The study of social status and its essential components has been at the centre of theoretical and conceptual discussions and policy discourses in contemporary social science. While extricating and defining the concept of status, the starting point has ordinarily been both ascribed and achieved sources of status acquired by individuals in their own groups and communities. The literature of the theme also talks about formal and informal status, functional status and scalar status. Naturally, the researchers working on the subject take different positions on different occasions and as a result there are no shared vision and unanimity on even its meaning and scope. Such a situation provides us with a freedom to transcend the received wisdom on the subject.

The status of women belonging to the various societies and groups is socially constructed, hence it is difficult and arduous to change and transform its arrangements merely through the intervention of external agency and induced policy. No similar and resembling, identical and comparable tribal groups are found in our country. They are differently placed from the points of view of location, cultural ambience and historical experiences. Consequently, the patterns and design, forces and factors of change, impact and the consequences of state policy and programmes have not been uniform and much the same. My own association with the tribal majority states of the north-eastern region of India during the last three decades amply confirms that the problems of tribal areas, in general, and women, in particular, may adequately be analysed within the conceptual frame that takes into account the three major domains of peoples life – oppression, exploitation and discrimination. This framework applies *mutatis mutandis* with the other tribal regions of the country.

Another matter of contention is that like the non-tribal society, a woman in tribal society too is briskly oppressed and decisively deprived. As marginalized communities, tribals in different parts of the country are unfavourably located within the larger non-tribal vicinity but there is no striking difference between the two sections of women. However, the geographical and ecological locale, the slow and lackadaisical pace of economic development, the growing inter-community social distance and the lack of effective mobilization of more marginalized among the marginals have made the condition more alarming in the tribal communities. It is apparently reflected in an emerging situation which now I would like to discuss.

While hierarchical inequalities are undoubtedly declining, competitive inequalities are sharply increasing both within and without this group.[1] In other words, class-like divisions are coming to light within the groups in most of the tribal communities. Likewise, class distinction in relation to the non-tribal neighbours is equally visible. What is being emphasized is not based on impression but it is broadly confirmed by empirical facts.

II

In this context, I wish to take up the issue of development strategy adopted in the country since independence and some specific constitutional and administrative measures undertaken for the tribal areas. The reference to these issues will inescapably bring to the fore the questions of identity, loss of freedom and declining control over common property resources of women. While on the one hand the state accepts the specificities of the tribal societies but when it comes to the question of human and citizenship rights of the people for ensuring welfare, creating conditions for empowering women and providing sustained development, no appropriate and out of the ordinary programmes are undertaken to achieve the goal.

Some of the crucial issues have been examined and illustrated here by turning to the situation prevailing in the tribal areas of the North-East India. Although the region is little known in central India, it comes in the news only as a problem zone. The area which is traditionally known as the region of 'seven sisters' now consists of eight states of the Indian Union after the addition of Sikkim to the North East. However, before I attempt to throw some light on the status of tribal women in this part, some general features of land and people of the region will be in order.

The North East is the only region in the country where we have 'tribal majority' states. The states of Arunachal Pradesh, Meghalaya, Mizoram and Nagaland come under this category because the population of the scheduled tribes (ST) is almost more than 70 per cent in each of these states. Even in Assam, Manipur, Sikkim and Tripura the ST population is more than the national average. These tribals are broadly divided into the Hill tribes and Plain tribes. The much-publicized matrilineal tribes, the Khasi, the Jaintia and the Garo are located in the state of Meghalaya. Mizoram, the state having the highest rate of literacy almost equal to the state of Kerala, is situated in this part of the country. The ethnic diversity is discernible in large number of ethnic groups found in various tribal majority states besides the other four states. Based on these specificities, we find different designs and patterns of status among women of these communities.

The most conspicuous aspect of this domain is the patriarchal system prevailing among the majority of tribal communities. For convenience of enquiry of the spatial variation, a few examples from the different parts of the North East have been selected to elucidate the point.

To start with Arunachal, the customary position of women in traditional Arunachal society of different tribes remain full of social drudgeries and slavery under the burden of primitive mode of production and exchange relation and a hostile geography and terrain. The monolithic patriarchal structure in almost every tribe gives the men-folk the advantage of developing their superiority over the women. The Aka society, for instance, is organized on patriarchal system with law of primogeniture and other traits of patriarchy. Although the family is ordinarily nuclear, however, polygyny is practiced by the chief and wealthy persons. Women are subjected to the drudgeries of family life and are deprived of inheritance, property rights and free and equal participation in public life.[2] Their status in the other tribes in the traditional Arunachal society is not different. While in the public life women are forced to be in the background, at home they are compelled to perform every work as a part of their duty. A primitive economy sustained by hunting, jhumming and frequent migration have also restricted the mobility of women in these communities.

The social structural reality among the tribal communities inhabiting the hill regions of Manipur also shows a very controlled nature of women's status. Tribes of the Naga and Kuki-Chin group inhabit the hill regions of the state. They are under the rule of the patriarchal system of social organization, and the father is the head of the family like most of the patriarchal societies. Naturally, the women may not have any apparent legal rights; they have just notional influence in the family. So even in social and political affairs women are able to influence decisions but only through their husbands. Among the other Naga tribes in Nagaland, the situation is not substantially different and women have high discernable status in all but name. By now it is widely known in the country that not a single woman has been elected as a member of the Nagaland State Assembly till now. Although it is not a crucial parameter to assess and judge the status of woman *per se*, it undoubtedly reflects the conventional man-centric disposition of the community concerned. In addition to this, the Naga women have no effective role to play in local secular organizations such as the Village Development Boards (VDBs) which has been constituted in the State of Nagaland by the state government and in the traditional village councils.

It is, however, a captivating fact to note that not only in the patriarchal tribal societies but also in the matrilineal communities the right to property and other social and political customary rights are unfavourable to women. The North East is one of the few regions in the country where the matrilineal system of social organization continues to be a living institution which has sustained the cultural identity of the people. All the three major communities inhabiting the State of Meghalaya – the Khasi, Jaintia and the Garo – are matrilineal and have broadly retained their customary practices and the traditional institutions of governance. These tribal communities being matrilineal, the general principle of inheritance defines the devolution of property in female lines. In the Khasi society, customarily it is the youngest daughter, *ka khadduh*, who is eligible to inherit the ancestral property.[3] But a doubt has been raised whether the youngest daughter inherits property as an *owner* or is merely its *custodian*. However, as a part of the matrilineal system, the ancestral property is managed by the eldest maternal uncle or jointly with other members who are his brothers or his sister's sons and grandsons. Naturally, such a customary practice has led to numerous misconceptions and court cases with regard to the nature and extent of ownership by the heiress of the landed property in the wake of fast changes taking place in these societies.

Like the Khasi-Pnars, the family property among the Garo also descends through the mother and not through the father. In fact, the fundamental principle of the Garo social structure is rooted in the preservation of wealth and property within the matrilineal system. Whatever a male earns or receives is actually the property of his mother or sisters. If the property is acquired after marriage, it becomes his wife's property and after her death that of her daughters. Thus in principle a female owns the entire property. First it is the mother and later the wife and subsequently the daughters. The appraisal of women's rights in property amongst the Garo thus might give an impression that the males in this society have no place so far as inheritance is concerned. Nonetheless, a closer look at the actual operation of the system renders an entirely a different story. Theoretically, the women have property rights in landed property but its use and control are substantially in the hands of the men. A man may not inherit but he has the right to control and manage his wife's property. This right has been accepted in the courts' decisions in several cases.[4]

It may be surmised at this stage of our discussion that the ownership rights in customary practices with regard to landed property bestow adequate benefits on women but their tacit exclusion from property management and from public affairs limits the power and authority they could otherwise derive from those rights. The new forces of change in social and economic domains have already started eroding women's customary rights. There is a widespread decline in land available to the community (clan land, *Ri-Raid*-community land) leading to inter-household and inter-village inequalities, and many women who had earlier usufructuary rights to community land no longer have so. Besides, in the Garo Hills, a new trend towards gifting land to sons and the emerging neolocal post-marital residential pattern is further changing the situation in this regard.

A pointed reference to the traditional tribal institutions will not be out of place here. These institutions with socio-legal power such as the village council, the regional council, the *Syiemship*, etc. are monopolized by men and they have been consistently excluding women. In the matrilineal societies, this obviously shows that in spite of men's restricted access to landownership, their rights as a gender of control over that property on the one hand and their access to public bodies on the other often enabled them to consolidate social prestige and political power. The Khasi *Syiem*, the *Nokma* among the Garo and the *Dolois* among the Jaintia still command local influence. This being the case of men's domination in the public decision-making processes provides enormous power to modify legal and customary rules.

What we have discussed so far vividly suggests that contrary to the prevailing notion, the status of tribal women is not remarkably high and has not elevated their position in terms of the social, economic and political domains of their communities. In other words, they are fettered by customary rules and regulations. They are expected to perform copious duties without accessing socially defined and conferred rights. Actually duties without rights are just hoax. We thus contest the prevailing impression about a large number of tribal groups with regard to their social fabrics. Some of these notions are the following: (1) an egalitarian nature of relationships among the members of the respective communities exists; (2) the absence of internal differentiation is found in these communities; and (3) there is no hierarchical division within the group.

It is in this context that we frequently argue that the portrayal of woman's status in the North East is more mythical and invented than authentic and real. Under the circumstances, we plead for an effective and forceful assortment of rights and privileges for women in all three major domains of life-social, economic and political which can be bestowed only through the positive intervention by a democratic state.

The fact of the matter is that the feeling of insecurity and desires to be socially and economically strong and independent are as conspicuous in tribal societies today as in any other society. By now it is apparent that in several tribal groups women are being mobilized to raise their voice against inhuman and atrocious customs associated with their life and work.[5] Many organizations of women are opposing the plan to codify customary laws and practices to give them legitimate legal force so that they are enforceable in secular law courts. Most of these established and institutionalized practices are not only unfavourable but are often hostile to women and inhibit their socio-economic progress and development.

Issues involved in the status of tribal women in India may be interrogated also within the framework of the strategy of development being adopted in augmenting the resources and correcting the instruments to ensure speedy development of the marginalized groups. It requires developing plans both at the micro- and macro-levels. While micro-level schemes and programmes have to be undertaken separately for individual tribal groups in the background of its socio-economic condition and historical experience, the macro-level planning is needed at the state level. However, the first move towards change and transformation by the modern secular institutions legitimatized by the state has more often not been resisted by a large number of tribal groups especially in the North-East India. For this reason, a sustained effort has to be made to create a mindset towards, say land reforms, both at the political and social plane. Thus, the agenda for substantial reforms has to evolve from within the community because these communities still cherish their tradition and ethnic identity. Consequently, any reform programme of long-term nature suggested from the outside is considered an imposition from the mainstream to pressurize smaller identities to assimilate to the larger whole. Agrarian reform to confer ownership right to women, for example, being a delicate issue in most of the states in the region, therefore, requires a different strategy in the light of the changing reality of the agrarian social structure. The thrust of our argument is that a comprehensive agenda for reform is needed to protect and promote the interests of the people, in general, and women, in particular.

III

Our attempt so far has been to contest the commonly held opinion about the status of tribal women in India. The prevalent perception that women in tribal society have an elevated and elated social status compared to the non-tribal women in India is not only a misrepresentation of the real-life situation but it evidently manifests a wide gap between 'impression' and 'fact'. Moreover, such a characterization has led to a lop-sided planning for the growth and development of these deprived groups. It is contended here that a proper comprehension and grasp of the issue of social status of women of various sections of the population is a subject that has both an academic and a pragmatic side. The former is usually discussed with a view that policy decisions and their effective implementation can be fruitful only if they are informed by adequate and requisite understanding of facts. The practical side, on the other hand, helps to highlight a better comprehension of the negative forces operating both at the community level and at the level of the region in which the former is located. A proper understanding of the impediments and constraints of development helps in articulating ways and means to ensure qualitative improvement in the existing status of women in tribal society by pruning and neutralizing the role of negative forces and by giving life to an ambience that takes into account the perspectives of empowerment and development.

NOTES

1. For conceptual clarity see Andre Beteille (2002). 'Hierarchical and Competitive Inequality', *Sociological Bulletin*, 51(1): 3–27.
2. See articles on M.N. Karna (1998). 'Women's movements in Assam, Arunachal Pradesh, Manipur and Meghalaya', in M.N. Karna (ed.), *Social Movements in North-East India*, New Delhi: Indus Publishing Company, pp. 43–104.
3. See M.N. Karna (2009). 'Tribal areas of Meghalaya: Land ownership of women', in Prem Chowdhry (ed.), *Gender Discrimination in Land Ownership*, New Delhi: Sage Publications, pp. 176–195.
4. *Ibid.*
5. See M.N. Karna (ed.), *op.cit.*

CHAPTER 3

TRIBAL WOMEN: STATUS, CHALLENGES AND POSSIBILITIES – A CASE STUDY OF FOREST WOMEN OF INDIAN FOREST COMMUNITY THROUGH CONCEPTUAL FRAMEWORK

D. Sundaram

Virginius Xaxa, formerly of Department of Sociology, Delhi University, and currently of Tata Institute of Social Sciences, Gauhati, has acknowledged that there is now a distinct focus on women in tribal studies, emerging out of general interest and concern with women's issues all over the world. Accordingly, as per his point of view, the value system on the concern for women governing larger Indian society has been in the process of change. With this, there has been a shift, according to him, in the image of tribal women who are thus invariably portrayed as enjoying a better social status than their counterparts in the larger Indian society. 'Tribal society in the post-Independence era', as he said further, 'has been witnessing to unprecedented change, which has been most marked in respect of culture, modes of making a living and social differentiation. Their bearing on women's status in society and gender relations has been far-reaching'.

While we agree with the version of Virginius Xaxa, it may be considered differently that there is a scope to look into the issue of the status of the tribal women within a distinct version of the dual structures, namely representational structure and the constitutive structure, within which any of the development stakeholders have to look into the issue of tribal women. According to this, women alone as a social category are of representational structure which is made up of the constitutive structures like relational inequality, as an example, between men and women called as gender relations.

Accordingly, an exercise to look into forest legislations which dispossessed the tribals, in general, and tribal women, in particular, and in the same vein, I looked into the customary law as an institutional feature of tribal community in providing healthy relational framework and also of the policy programmes of development for tribal women by the Ministry of Tribal Affairs, Government of India. All these elucidate that the legislative construction of the forest development and the policy programmes of development of tribal women are nothing but the tinkering/having a surface effect of the representational structures in which the tribal women are placed.

To begin with, when we think of the issue of tribal women and incorporating them into the development process, one cannot ignore the actual reality on women in general that the women question, their role and participation in the development process were mostly invisible. It is more appropriate if we look into the portrayal of this by a feminist, Urvashi Butalia, in India by quoting a version of an Indian journalist who said that 'he had not seen any women' for a question on him not portraying women in his writing during his survey study of a village.

This is the way of thinking and reflection of the women in development action in India. Ignoring the voice and the role of women was and is still the order of the mainstream thought of the development process.

It was the United Nations in its endeavour of the International Year of Women in 1975 that highlighted this anomalous situation of women's invisibility by stating that the policy makers did not see women as stakeholders in any of the development process. Most of these predicaments have been attributed to the flaw in the mainstream social science thought by Naila Kabeer through her book titled 'Reversed Realities: Gender Hierarchies in Development Theory' as follows:

> Reductionist theories within the mainstream social sciences have given rise to the reductionist practices and in turn reflecting the reductionist methods as far as gender issues in development.

In the context of these observations, tribal women and livelihood are the questions that are to be addressed not only from the relative point of view of the women's world but also from the point of view of legal and legislative construction and also of the policy programme for the tribal women specially of the forest women's questions in terms of their access to the resources for their livelihood. The women as such in the forest community are akin to the tribal women who have dependency on the minor forest products for their livelihood.

While this is so, the perspectives of the issue of livelihood of the tribal women, particularly of the women of the forest community as portrayed – not portrayed – in all the forest policy, legislation and management are the academic sites for elucidating the status, possibilities and challenges of tribal women. Forests in India constituting only 18% of the world's forest cover approximately 23% of the geographical area of India and happen to be the abode of majority of the India's approximate 75 million.

India's compliance with United Nations policy on forests and indigenous peoples is seriously limited by the centralization of forest management and a lack of recognition of indigenous peoples and their rights, and the situation with regard to traditional forest-related knowledge can only be understood within this wider context. Widespread resistance to state forest policy and law throughout India's history of centralized forest management has been fuelled by the fact that about 90 per cent of India's 64 million hectares of forests are under state ownership, the rest being in community and private forests. Moreover, it is predominantly the country's indigenous/tribal peoples' areas that have been declared as state-owned "forests". Also, state control over the forest land is weak and there is considerable encroachment by individuals and communities other than the tribals/indigenous people in state-owned areas. The tribal/indigenous peoples were there long before the state started encroaching on their lands and the condition of both the tribal/indigenous peoples and the forests then was far better than it is today. However, the laws enacted so far in India have largely ignored the forest dwellers and more particularly the tribal/indigenous peoples.

INDIAN FOREST LAW AND POLICY

It used to be that the forests, in ancient India, remained outside the orbit of state control and were within the domain of the forest dwellers (with omnipotent rights held by them) who were largely the tribal/indigenous people including the women living as marginalized and poorest people until the forest timber and other products became of commercial value after the advent of British in India.

During the British period, an Indian Forest Act in 1878 was passed by declaring the state as a proprietor of forests in India. The 1890 Forest Department resolution defined rights of access and uses of forest lands and of forest resources which were of traditional forest practices as 'privileges' for specific tribes which include forest women, castes, villages and organizations. With what is called today as the forest management is ultimately based on the 1927 Indian Forest Act which by itself was an outcome of the 1878 Forest Act.

Commercial exploitation and degradation of India's forests increased dramatically over a period of time, including the period after independence, with an increased control of forests by the governance mechanism by replacing the local forest dwellers and more particularly of the forest women's rights. Indeed, a National Forest Policy guidelines was formulated in the year 1952 in consonance with the increased requirement of the forest products for industrial and commercial development, as set out in the year 1952. Then the issue of conservation came and the result is that the 1980 act reasserted some of its control over forest-based resources by the government machinery. The Forest Conservation Act restricted the power of the state government over the use of forest land for non-forestry purposes without the prior approval of the central government and also prohibited unilateral decisions by the regional states on any implementation proposals. Then, the people's involvement in the development and protection of forests were thought of, for the first time, through the National Forest Policy of 1988. It stipulated that the requirements of people living in and near forests for fuel wood, fodder and small timber should be treated as the top priority and expected that the forest communities including women should be motivated to identify themselves with the development and protection of forests from which they derive benefits. The agencies for forest management are expected to engage tribal population on the preservation and conservation of the forest and its products. It was expected that all these agencies in such endeavour will provide employment opportunities for the tribal people but with no legal teeth to do so.

All of these were rhetorical in paper than in action to deal with the tribals, in general, and tribal women, in particular. All these legislative endeavours of the forest management are nothing but the truncated endeavours to the actual reality of the forest community, especially of the women in the forest community, by overlooking the constitutive structures of gender dimensions.

Accordingly, the Indian national forest law and policy is the evolution of unintended and unanticipated dispossession of the forest rights of the forest tribals including women and their livelihood as portrayed below:

1878 – *Indian Forest Act*. State is the sole proprietor of classified forest lands.

1890 – *Forest Department Resolution*. Previous rights of access and use redefined as 'privileges' for specific tribes, castes, villages and organizations.

1927 – *Indian Forest Act*. Few substantive changes over the 1878 Act. It remains the legislative basis for state forest management today. The Indian government adopted the 1927 Act after it gained independence in 1947.

1952 – *National Forest Policy*. Set out guidelines which were, for the most part, directed towards the supply of cheap timber and non-timber forest products for state-sponsored industrialization and modernization.

1976 – *Indian Forest Act*. Added to the concurrent list of the Constitution of India, Central government and states were given shared control over forest matters.

1980 – *Forest Conservation Act*. The central government reasserted some of its control over forest-based resources. The 1980 Act restricts the state government's power to de-reserve a forest, and it restricts the use of forest land for non-forestry purposes without the prior approval of the central government.

1988 – *The National Forest Policy*. Envisaged people's involvement in the development and protection of forests for the first time and never translated into law.

These forest legislations are, in one way or other, of the classic nature of dispossessions of those tribals who treat the land, or parts of it, as the only livelihood resource of the forest community. The consequence is that the forest communities, otherwise called native tribes, were driven out of these forests. Similar dispossessions continued in different form and shape which include tribal women and exclusion of them from their own cultures and landscapes and ultimately of their livelihood.

These dispossessed those who had the living in forests for a long time and familiar with all the nature of forests and find themselves in a distress over their livelihood and felt routed out of the symbiotic reality when the forest legislations and policy in the name of forest conservation afforestation had to bring the forest women and men into a mainstream of development through policy programmes which are formulated.

The tribal community and forest community were moved out and a new culture of forest management was developed by the trained forest technocrats who were brought in to manage the forests, while the native tribes were the traditional carers. These forest technocrats have a trained mind-set of top-down approach. With a disconnection for the forest tribes and with the imposed new connections with these forest technocrats, the forest community especially of the forest women community had lost livelihood of theirs who lived as tribals in the forest.

Several illustrations of such dispossessions were reported in India where the new formation of the organizational culture by the name of national parks and sanctuaries and resorts has emerged. In this context, the dispossessed forest dwellers have set fire to large areas of the forests as was seen in the areas like Kanha and Nagarhole national parks in the early 1990s. Also, what is called as insurgents – a state-constructed community of rebellions turned out from the docile forest community – have taken advantage of local resentment and have emerged as a threatening force in the larger part of forests in central and North-East India.

The technocrats of the models of conservation of forests in the name of parks, sanctuaries and resorts with the blessings of the conservation specialists with their technocratic fibre and with no social sense seldom realized how the tribal/forest community and especially the forest women are affected through the loss of their basic livelihood interest under the cloak of forest legislations.

As for the forest legislation and the livelihood strategies of the forest community with a special focus on women in forest community, a research study by Reka M. Shangpliang in her recently published research article in the *Sociological Bulletin* of Indian Sociological Society, September–December 2012 has highlighted how the women in forest who have the traditional rights over the forest minor products for their livelihood are deprived the rights in spite of the assured forest legislation of Government of India in the 2006 Scheduled Tribes and Other Traditional Forest Dwellers (Recognition of the Forest Rights) Act. So, according to Shangpliang, the development and conservation instruments of the forest legislation should be livelihood supportive for the forest women.

On the other hand, an effort to understand the issue of customary law and the status of women amidst the continued modern legal construction on forest tribes and their livelihood has found the customary law as a traditionally constituted institutional feature by the community of the forest tribes. The forest tribes are craving for getting these institutional features of customary laws restored in the context of the onslaught of modern forest legislations. This could be seen in their assertion of their quest for their traditional legal culture of their way of life. It may appear that the modern forest legislations and customary law of the forest tribes may appear to be an interface between tradition and modernity. But, in all its deeper perspectives, it can be seen that the tribal's quest for the right-based approach through customary law over all of their other needs which include their livelihood is a challenge for academic site. Particularly, it has implications from a gender perspective and asserts modern forest legislation as against the customary laws of the forest community and is against women and does harm to the forest women.

The impact of the tradition–modernity interface of the modern law on women highlights that there is a need to have a re-look into the unfinished deliberations on this subject in the making of the Constitution of India on scheduled tribes (STs) and forest community and the need for an advocacy of gender justice laws for the tribal women and also to restore the customary laws with all its positive institutional features.

Against the setting the institutional features of customary law, the methods and strategies, their organizational culture and the governance of the forest communities through local socio-cultural tradition, one could attribute them as the strong assets when compared with the modern law. The modern forest legislations have inadequate community-centric institutional features. In terms of tribal traditions which were community based and with a relatively appreciable status to women (although they were not considered equal to men on all other issues), the customary law is close to the ground reality. On the other side, modern law's individual centric ownership and by and large men-oriented with the onslaught of modern education and occupation by the Government of India's policy programmes for these forests and tribal communities reflect patriarchal features also in one form or another.

On the other hand, the common rules and sanctions by habits through customary law of the forest community are the norms, and the internal morality of a social system of the community of forests on women's issues signifies group as a factor rather than the individuals with a reflective notion that the individual's interest is safer through group approach. This cultural ethos as a customary law is a positive structure of collective way of the life and the livelihood of the forest communities which include forest women.

With this spirit of the customary law of the forest community and to use collective responsibilities characterized as a social capital in conserving the forests through a model of Joint Forest Management (JFM), a place for gender has been put in it for the forest development by the new breed of the forest technocrats with individual rights and without any legal infrastructure.

The launching of JFM without any legal or with no incorporation of customary law of the forest communities has made it into a sterile approach as far as gender issues are concerned, the fact which has been lucidly presented by Reka M. Shangpliang through her research endeavour as published in her article titled 'Forest Legislations and Livelihood Strategies: Khasi Women in Rural Meghalaya' in the *Sociological Bulletin* of Indian Sociological Society, September–December 2012.

In a different way, Prakash Kashwan has looked into JFM to highlight some other problems. One of the most important findings is that JFM has been allowed only in degraded forest, but to bring more communities under the ambit of such programmes, communities have had to actively pursue regeneration of natural forest. Furthermore, JFM requires the demarcation of boundaries between villages, often for the first time, but poor implementation has resulted in many boundary conflicts.

In this regard, the programme policy of involving the forest community of tribals has been envisaged through a scheme of community forestry in India. Ashwini Chhatre of the Centre for International Development, Kennedy School of Government, Harvard University, has acknowledged that there is significantly an increase in the forest cover in these days through a regeneration of 3.3 million hectares during 1993–2003. The result was in bringing the 21 million hectares with 13.8 million families of this increased forest cover under the JFM scheme within the philosophy of the natural resource management. But the integration of the women question has been given no place.

All these have raised the criticality of the issue of women in forest community and for lamenting the less or inadequate effort to incorporate the forest women in all the stakeholders' interest.

The research project entitled 'Empowering Women through Forestry: The Role of Indigenous Women in Forestry Development Programmes' was carried out by the CIDA-Shastri Partnership Project team that included R. Indira, the principal investigator of the project, Karim Aly Kassam of the University of Calgary, Canada, and Jayanand Derekar of Deria Village in the Joida Village in the Uttara, Kannada district, who examined 'the role of forest dependent communities in forestry development programmes with a special thrust on women. The idea of linking VFCs and SHGs to plan and implement a comprehensive forest development and conservation strategy was recommended by the project. One of the key findings of this project was that an effective VFC-SHG linkage must be established if meaningful people's participation has to be ensured.'

Through this analysis of the forest community and the forest regeneration movement, they have highlighted the fact that the invisibility of the women in all these endeavours is a fact to be pondered over.

In this regard, all pervading policy document of the Ministry of Tribal Affairs, Government of India, on gender issues of the tribal community appear to be a part-approach. The issue of bringing women into the non-forest-oriented education, skill development and employment needs to be integrated with the livelihood strategies of the forest women as marginalized tribes through the JFM philosophy. In the policy programme of the Ministry of Tribal Affairs, Government of India, there appears to be an effort of displacing the forest community of tribal women through a development endeavour called education and employment opportunities.

Ultimately, it could be envisaged that all these inclusive policy of women do require the participation of the women as was in the case of emergence of women's movement with a questioning mood in challenging the male-alone lense privilege in the development politics of everyday life of the women in the tribal community.

The focus of this paper is primarily to look into the issue of women, their livelihood, forest policy, legislation and management brings out, accordingly, the need to focus also on development programmes and gender issues as is seen in the recent Annual Report of the Ministry of Tribal Affairs, Government of India, which had a concern about the well-being of the tribes suffering due to their social and economic backwardness and relative isolation as follows:

- To ensure that ST women and girls benefit equally from general schemes.
- The development programmes also had some special schemes for the benefit of the upliftment of the tribal women in the field of education and employment to enable them to lead a life of self-confidence and dignity.

Accordingly, the annual report of the Ministry of Tribal Affairs, as presented in the Parliament, has highlighted certain schemes specifically titled as 'Gender Issues for Tribal Women and Girls' as in Appendix I.

All the policy programme for tribal women by the Ministry of Tribal Affairs, Government of India, as appended in Appendix I increasingly foster a state support to individual's development for individualized ways of life with no concern for the dictum of the customary law that the safety of individuals are in the group factor as highlighted elsewhere in this paper. In addition, the quest for getting the forest development incorporated into the market forces in the context of modernized policy programme postulates the supremacy of the patriarchal ethos over women's status.

The above presentation of the forest legislations as the evolution of dispossession of forest tribals, the quest for the common law by the forest community and the policy programme of the Ministry of Tribal Affairs, Government of India, highlight the transition of the tribals as individual oriented with a visible divergence from group interest and with no visible commitment for women as inclusive development clients/stakeholders.

In all these endeavours, the question of the emergence of women as a recognized stakeholder in the regeneration of the forest through a JFM of the natural resources as a development effort is not in any way of visible one. Accordingly, any change in the policy discourse on the inclusive policy of tribal women requires the manner in which the subalterns were negotiated within the framework of the analysis of power structure of the opposites.

In reality, we have to integrate the theories of power relating to state, market, law, and legislation and judiciary. The new breed of forest technocrats and above all the tribal community which includes tribal women will form the basis of the understanding of the problem of this seminar.

At the same time, every effort has to be taken to overlay these in the micro-regional gaze as there are diverse tribal communities with regional identity through a comparative lens that may provide us a comprehensive focus of what we know about power, community and gender relations of the existing women question in the forest community.

Thus, the rights of livelihood of tribal women in the context – as a struggle for human rights for integration to the development process – have to straddle into the prevailing dominant dimensions and activities of men. Otherwise to locate all these programmes for forest/tribal women, one needs to look into women with a shift towards gender relations between men and women on the power relations plank. It is self-evident that there is a perpetuation of gender inequality on relational perspectives between men and women. In contrary to this existing reality, the issue of the development programmes for women as is presented in the Government of India's policy note, the policy programme sees them as women-in-isolation.

There should be an effort to have the constitutional provision to converge the spirit of customary law with modern forest legislations and also to avoid the structures of dispossession of the tribals, in general, and tribal women, in particular, besides the effort of reorienting the policy programmes of development for tribal community, in general, and tribal women, in particular, from the point of view of gender relations.

Also, it will not be a far cry if we bring these to the attention of women movementalists/activists to launch a distinct tribal women movement as was done in the early sixties of the twentieth century when the women's movement was a co-event with the then protests of the International Economic Order in South, Movement for Class and Race Privileges in the Universities and Factories, Civil Rights and Black Power movements combined with the liberation struggle of Neo-Colonialism.

Finally, there is a commitment for reflexivity in the field of social sciences and humanities on women studies in India to have a shift from the pure codification knowledge into a professional skill as a requirement of the community and public use in the practice of teaching and research within universities and colleges. The relevance of which could be seen as a crucial tool of empowerment of women. Thus, it is envisaged that the knowledge sites – the universities, colleges and the research institutes – may have to have responsive commitment to integrate the knowledge on tribal women with the women studies in general as these knowledge sites are increasingly becoming under the critical scrutiny of the transformative dimensions from the point of view of the end users, i.e., the policy makers and the agents of governance, for their practical tool of empowerment arising out of the theoretical quest of the women studies discipline (which has uncovered or mainstreamed the hitherto hidden and informalized structures of human resources) to move to the arena of practice from theory for an inclusive growth in society. The cause of women studies must be a public production – a derivation of Vandana Siva and Thompson – "of a social action framework to develop rational active, many sided scientifically minded and capable of understanding and promoting a progressive view" among individuals and groups among women.

For me, the kind of public production of knowledge in the form and shape of women studies appears to be an emancipation of women from submission to the tradition – not as a revolutionary discourse but as a development discourse. All these had a turnaround in the then defined development thinking in the late 1960s which paved way for the women's emancipation from the development pill of the capitalist notion of 'universality of modernization' – a notion which is in practice in the West is good for East. So, the landmark study by a Danish social scientist Ester Boserup through her study of 'Women's Role in Economic Development' has highlighted the development action under the capitalist notion of modernization has become a liability to the envisaged improvement in the status and opportunities of women. The same framework has to be applied to the issues of development pill for tribal women.

Thus, the conceptualization of women's empowerment has to be taken up very seriously that the empowerment like modernization cannot be a universal concept. It has to be redefined in the development context and thus the empowerment is not context-free. There are diverse social set of women in question in the development contexts within which the practice of empowerment has to be deconstructed and re-constructed more as a responsive action tool to the diverse women social profile.

In this context, one cannot ignore the transformative classrooms of the Indian universities in the last four decades. The classrooms are increasingly becoming mass oriented from the elite structures of the past not only by virtue of the increase in the first-generation learners from rural hinterlands but also with increased gender equalization in access. The design of women studies programme – either as different or as integrated – should begin with the classrooms of such nature where the expectations of not only the women students but also the men students, who have new cognitive models, reflect the craving for the intellectual roots with a challenging spirit. In this context, the intellectuality of the women's empowerment to take up the knowledge production may be conditioned more by the cognitive compulsions new genre. These, when compared to the antecedent theoretical structures of the knowledge sites, have been having a quest for a new knowledge under the label of rights of human individuals, feminism, environmentalism and the governance of the development through the participatory models. In this context, the self as a creative process under the quest for modern outlook expects from the knowledge-providing structures, namely the teachers, the researchers and the universities and laboratories, to the reason-based thinking to get the tribal women empowered with autonomy in the upgradation of their status.

APPENDIX I

The policy programme of the Ministry of Tribal Affairs, Government of India, is as follows:

- A gender-specific scheme of 'Setting up Educational Complex in Low Literacy Pockets for development of Women's Literacy in Tribal Areas' was introduced in 1993–1994, was revised in 2008–2009 and renamed as 'Strengthening Education among ST Girls in Low Literacy Districts' with a concern of low female literacy among STs.
- The scheme is being implemented in 54 identified low literacy districts where the ST population is 25 per cent or more, and ST female literacy rate is below 35 per cent, or its fractions, as per 2001 census.
- Any other tribal block in a district, other than aforesaid 54 identified districts, which has scheduled tribe population 25 per cent or above, and tribal female literacy rate below 35 per cent or its fractions, as per 2001 census, are also covered.
- The areas inhabited by Particularly Vulnerable Tribal Groups (earlier known as Primitive Tribal Groups (PTGs)) and naxalite-affected areas are given priority.

- The scheme aims to bridge the gap in literacy levels between the general female population and tribal women, through facilitating 100 per cent enrolment of tribal girls in the identified districts or blocks, more particularly in naxal-affected areas and in areas inhabited by PTGs, and reducing drop-outs at the elementary level by creating the required ambience for education.
- The scheme is implemented through Voluntary Organizations (VOs)/ Non-Governmental Organizations (NGOs) and autonomous society/ institutions of state government/union territory administration.
- The scheme lays emphasis also on providing hostel facilities to enable them to attend regular schools, and wherever schools are not available within the 5 km distance, both schooling and hostel facilities may be considered.
- The revised scheme envisages the convergence with the schemes of Sarva Shiksha Abhiyan and Kasturba Gandhi Balika Vidhyalaya of Ministry of Human Resource Development.
- The policy meets the requirement of primary level students as well as middle/secondary level students and provides residential facility to ST girl students to ensure their retention in schools.
- Besides formal education, the revised scheme also takes care of skill upgradation of ST girls in various vocations.
- The revised scheme also envisages establishment of District Education Support Agency (DESA) in each low literacy district which will make efforts to ensure 100 per cent enrolment and also play the role of monitor, facilitator and support linkages with various institutions.
- As per the guidelines of the scheme, the concerns/issues affecting women should occupy central position in preparation of the projects/ schemes, including the involvement of women, right from the planning to the implementation stage.
- The projects, envisaged, that it should be so planned for substantial benefits, at least 30 per cent in proportion, are targeted for women.
- Under the scheme for construction of hostels for ST boys and girls, 100 per cent central funding is provided to states/UTs for construction of hostels for ST girls at schools, colleges, universities and vocational education levels.
- The main objective of the scheme is to promote education among ST students by providing hostel accommodation to such students who are

not in a position to continue their education because of their poor economic condition and the remote location of their villages.

- The scheme provides for the construction of new hostels and extension of existing hostel buildings for students.
- Under the scheme of establishment of Ashram schools in Tribal Sub-Plan areas, 100 per cent central funding is provided for the construction of Ashram schools for ST girls.
- These revisions were introduced from April 4, 2008, and are expected to have a profound impact on the increase in education among ST girls.
- As for the economic development is concerned, the National Scheduled Tribes Finance and Development Corporation (NSTFDC) as an apex institution under Ministry of Tribal Affairs for economic development of STs extends concessional financial assistance for income generating scheme(s)/project(s).
- The Corporation is having an exclusive scheme for economic development of STs' women titled 'Adivasi Mahila Sashaktikaran Yojana' (AMSY). Under the scheme, the Corporation provides financial assistance up to 90 per cent of the scheme/project having unit cost up to Rs. 50,000 at highly concessional rate of interest at 4% per annum chargeable from beneficiaries.
- Under AMSY during the year, as on December 31, 2010, NSTFDC sanctioned Rs. 4.16 crores for economic upliftment of 1,306 women beneficiaries and Rs. 4.63 crores for 1,784 beneficiaries under the Micro Credit Scheme.
- The Corporation also extends its financial assistance for women beneficiaries under other income-generating schemes including marketing support assistance.
- Further, the Corporation is making all endeavours to cover more women beneficiaries under NSTFDC financial assistance.
- The scheme of 'Exchange of Visits by Tribals' was introduced in 2001–2002, to enable ST below the poverty line to visit other parts of the country for a period of 10–12 days.
- The Ministry bears the entire expenditure. According to the scheme, each team/group, consisting of say 10 tribals, will include minimum 5 women.
- This enables them to broaden their perspective and also create awareness about the developments taking place in the country.

- The Ministry of Tribal Affairs introduced a scheme, 'National Tribal Award' from 2007–2008, with the objective of recognizing achievements of STs in different fields. Under individual category, one of the awardees has to be woman.
- In some of its schemes, the Ministry of Tribal Affairs takes special care to ensure 50 per cent participation of girls or women.
- In the Eklavya Model Residential Schools, for instance, 50 per cent of the seats are meant for ST girls.
- Under the Rajiv Gandhi National Fellowship scheme for M.Phil. and Ph.D., instructions have been issued to the University Grants Commission (UGC), which implements the scheme, to make efforts to award 50 per cent of the fellowships to women.
- Every year two tribals from each state/UT are invited to witness Republic Day parade in Delhi, it is ensured that each state/UT sends one woman and one man.
- Under the Special Area Programme, Special Central Assistance (SCA) to Tribal Sub-Plan (TSP) meant for community-based income generating activities for Below Poverty Line (BPL) families, the guidelines stipulated that 30 per cent of the funds are to be kept apart for 'Women Component' and to be spent for income generation activities of women beneficiaries.
- Under the scheme 'Grants under Article 275 (1) of the Constitution of India', funds are released to state governments for taking up specific projects for creation and upgradation of critical infrastructure required to bring the tribal areas at par with the rest of the country.
- It is said that all these are within the framework of the laws, development policies of Indian Constitution characterized with a democratic polity and to grant equality to women besides empowering the state to adopt measures of positive discrimination in favour of women with plans and programmes aiming at women's advancement in different spheres.
- All the programmes for the development of tribal women are basically within the spirit and philosophy of the National Commission for Women set up by an Act of Parliament in 1990 in enforcing the rights and legal entitlements of women and also within the 73rd and 74th Amendments (1993) to the Constitution of India, providing for reservation of seats in the local bodies of Panchayats and Municipalities for women, laying a strong foundation for their participation in decision making at the local levels.

- ❖ Active participation of women in the entire development process is considered essential for the overall socio-economic development. Therefore, raising the status of women, in general, and that of socially and economically backward women, in particular, is not just a moral imperative but also a strategic one.
- ❖ The major policies of the Ministry are, accordingly, aimed to ensure the overall development of both ST men and women.

However, within the STs, women often suffer from a greater disadvantage. The Ministry of Tribal Affairs, therefore, while trying achievements under schemes have coverage for women beneficiaries during 2010–2011.

CHAPTER 4

WOMEN'S PARTICIPATION IN PROTEST MOVEMENTS IN KALINGANAGAR AND POSCO

K. Gopal Iyer

INTRODUCTION

The distinguishing feature of traditional tribal society was that it was community based and had an oral code of conduct. There was no concept of private property as it is today. Victor Das (1991) states that in Jharkhand there is a peculiar affinity between arable lands and the mines. A mining company rises from the ruins of arable lands. In tribal populated regions, the women are more related to the land than their male counterparts. Thus, with the proliferation of mining companies in the region, the root cause of the exploitation of the tribal women has taken birth. The lands, which keep them occupied, are taken away by the mine owners acquired in the name of development without opening up any avenues of employment for them. Women are brought on trucks from the nearby villages by the contractors. Tribal women are attracted to such employment as it gives them ready cash. They also enjoy the daily outing. In many of the industrial centres, the employment of tribal women has led to abuses. Tribal women labourers are popularly known as rejas. As many as 47.3 per cent of the rejas are unmarried and are also the economically active earning force in their respective families. The high frequency of unmarried rejas exists because their parents delay or avoid getting their reja daughters married in time for the fear of losing a substantial income source. Their physical exploitation consists of various types of physical tortures, sexual offences, and different crimes and so on. Sometimes these exploitations lead to suicide. The greatest humiliation that the tribal rejas have to face pertains to sexual exploitation. A tribal woman's life is helpless and vulnerable. After marriage, a daughter loses her right over parental land. An unmarried daughter has the right to work on and be maintained from her family's land, but she does not inherit as a son does. A widow's usufructory right in her husband's land is similar to that of an unmarried daughter. 'She does not inherit the land but has a right to be maintained from it. The same system of male inheritance on tribal land is prevalent among the other major tribes in Jharkhand such as Mundas, Oraons, Santals, Kharias and Hos.'

Nitya Rao (2005) in his study 'Questioning Women's Solidarity: The Case of Land Rights, Santal Parganas, Jharkhand' examined the limits to collective action by women around land rights. He points out that the socially embedded nature of land as a resource and the mutuality and interdependence between men and women in the productive use of land needs to be recognized. Consequently, more than gender identities, it is other cross-cutting identities of ethnicity, education, kinship relations and marital status that both motivate women to stake their claims to land as well as oppose the claims of other women and men. Secondly, women's land claims seem to have a chance of becoming effective only if they have some male support, hence rather than aligning with other women, those who are serious in their claims seek to build alliances with men, particularly those able to influence the argument in their favour.

Walter Fernandes (2009) in his study of 'Development-Induced Displacement: Impact on Tribals' states that displacement not only deprives the family of its Common Property Resources (CPRs) but also alienates the woman from the source of her economic autonomy on which her relatively high social status was based. Women in subaltern groups had decision-making power in the family and controlled its production and economy as long as the community sustained itself on CPRs. With individual patta becoming the norm, power is transferred to the man and from him to his son. She ceases to be a decision maker and becomes fully dependent on men. However, alienation does not reduce the workload of most subaltern women because even after they are deprived of the resource base required to care for the family, the gender-based division of labour dictates that they continue to play this role. Moreover, the trauma of forced deprivation is not dealt with. One of men's coping mechanisms is drunkenness, which results in frequent wife beating. Woman was denied a job in the post-displacement phase. Women who are deprived of their sustenance have to depend on the single salary of their husbands. The women's crucial role in CPR management resulted in her relatively high status without making her equal to men. However, the law based on the eminent domain does not recognize their link with the CPRs.It allows them to be deprived of their livelihood without alternatives.

Vasudha Dhagamwar et al. made a study on 'Industrial Development and Displacement' among the people of Korba. She has studied impact of gender displacement. The process of displacement and rehabilitation has marginalized women in terms of their employment opportunities. The numbers dependent on non-land-based employment increased. The data showed a smaller number of employed women because much of the work done by them was not considered as 'work' (in its economic sense), even by the women themselves. Everyone, men and women, tend to consider a woman's work as a part of household work. Therefore, the employment statistics do not give a correct picture. Of the 235 women respondents in this category, 139 women cultivated their family land but among them only 22 women considered it to be an employment for them. This is because they were not paid any wages or emoluments. Women considered work on the family's land as a part of their household activity. Where they did paid work, such as agricultural labour, contract labour and domestic work, every woman felt that she was employed. The key factor for women considering any work as employment was income received in cash or kind. More than 75 per cent of men and women were engaged in cultivation in 1961. The scenario changed with industrialization. Women, therefore, comprised a major part of the agricultural workforce. Men had shifted to non-land-based employment after industrialization. Women strongly felt that the projects had reduced the relative value of their economic contribution. In villages facing complete dislocation, women found themselves engaged in only household chores. They also felt that they had little or no place in the new system, as they did not find employment in the industry and other related sectors. Those belonging to the lower strata had a specific problem. Their poor economic status compelled them to work as contract labourers or domestic servants in the project townships. Post-displacement, they worked as contract labourers because of their compulsions and not by choice. The fundamental crises related to fuel, water, health care, housing, sanitation and nutrition. The inadequacy of these resources affected women severely primarily because they had been the primary providers of basic needs. Poor access to or shortage of cooking fuel and water meant that women had to walk longer distances to fetch water and collect fodder and fuel wood. The absence of health facilities was emphasized the most by women, whether displaced or affected.

Sushama Sahay Prasad (1955) made a study of tribal woman labourers economic, social, sexual, psychological and physical exploitation. The tribal woman labourers were earlier called as rejas. The primary objective of taking to a particular type of job by the rejas is merely earning livelihood. The rejas are being paid in cash only. The rejas are illiterate; they hardly understand such intricacies and have to confide in their employers. Due to appalling illiteracy and ignorance among the rejas they very easily fall prey to the hands of such exploiters. The poor tribal rejas not only fall victim of exploiters in terms of inadequate and irregular wage payment, but they also have to put labour beyond the standard and prescribed working of 8 hours a day. The rejas working under them are paid less for their day's long labour. It is important to mention here that as many as 47.3 per cent of the rejas are unmarried and also the economically active earning force in their respective families. It has also been observed that the society to which the rejas belong looks at the rejas from scornful and derogatory angle because the male tribals do not prefer to marry the rejas as compared to other non-rejas tribal girls. According to this survey, 11 per cent of the rejas are divorced or separated from their husbands for different reasons. There are 33 per cent rejas who are married and 8.7 per cent are widow. The tribal rejas are being exploited physically to a great extent. Several cases of physical exploitations, especially to those rejas who have been working under contractors in brick-kiln, construction work, etc., and also to those who come from different places in India, have been observed. It has been observed that tribal rejas are taken away to different places in India by the contractors and there they live under the clutches of the contractors, sardars or other intermediaries. Tribal rejas belonging to the age groups 5–10 and 11–15 years work assiduously in brick-kilns, transportation work, construction sites, etc. Some rejas work in the form of child labour. The rejas who are engaged in construction works also have several complaints. They reported that heavy works are taken from them. But the greatest humiliation that the tribal rejas have to face pertains to sexual exploitation. Investigations by the Tripura government have revealed that some business managers and contractors in the state allegedly tortured tribal women from Bihar and treated their male counterpart as 'slaves'. In a special drive, police rescued 212 tribal labourers including 120 women mostly unmarried, allegedly brought from Bihar to Agartala for the purpose of 'immoral traffic' in the state. Psychological exploitation of the rejas emanate from all sorts of such exploitation which the tribal rejas face during the course of their day-to-day working. The rejas are psychologically depressed and agonized due to the bad behaviour of employers, associates, inmates and other peoples.

Maria Bexelius (2000) in the study on 'Protesting Violence: An Empowering Force' analyses a case study of tribal women's protests against Central Reserve Police Force (CRPF)-violence in Banpur, Orissa. Six Mahila

Mandalas have initially made village-level protests against domestic violence. Women, who have participated in the protests against the CRPF, are generally more empowered than those who have not been involved in the protests. Field findings indicate that protesting CRPF-violence had positive influence on women's political empowerment. The women, who belonged to the non-protesting, had also been organized into a women collective. Networking enhances the positive effect of organizing on women's empowerment. Mere access to a network seems to be less favourable than active involvement. Protesting CRPF-violence implied internal networking, i.e., active involvement in a network (*Matru Shakti*) linked to a mobilizing agent (*Ekta Parishad*). Those who seemed most empowered belong to a Mahila Mandala, which has been very active in earlier and/or ongoing protests. Women of Mangala Sahi have also been very active in protests over the land issue. Women of Dolagobinda Nuasahi have been continuously and actively fighting against land issue and alcoholism; they have also been leading village-level protests against the CRPF men of the village. Some of these factors have been contributing to women's empowerment. Emergence of leadership has been one favourable factor which has influenced women belonging to villages of Bhatapada, Katual and Dolagobinda Nuasahi. The protesting women belong to a Mahila Mandala which has close and regular relation with Ekta Parishad leaders who are their active supporters. Women who have been involved in the protests against the CRPF are more empowered both in the private and public sphere. Involvement in protests had positive influence on women's political empowerment. The empowerment process of the protests against CRPF have strengthened and started questioning domestic violence and protests against anti-liquor protests. Domestic violence is reportedly a serious problem in the area and it seems to be linked with men's alcoholism, as well as with patriarchy. Domestic violence takes both a physical expression in the form of wife beating and a psychological expression in the form of verbal abuse. This nature of violence is undoubtedly still a big problem as it involves alcoholism, commercial interests to protect the free sale of liquor, and the unequal power relation between the sexes in almost all villages. Adivasi women have not only been subjected to violence from the CRPF, but also the Forest Department officials have been regularly harassing the women. Simultaneously cases of rape and sexual exploitation have been taking place. The violence by forest officials declined after the protests against CRPF-violence. Women seem to be caught in a dependency trap, so deep that they do not dare risk the consequences of public protesting. Yet another problem is that of the social stigma attached to violence against women. The women's protest movement against violence in Banpur was located to rural Orissa. It could be labelled a relatively small grassroot protest, focusing on a local problem. 'The tribal identity has emerged as the predominant collective identity.'

Another study conducted by Iyer and Maharaj (1975) examines the role of tribal women in the protest movement in Jharkhand. They observe that in the struggle of Jharkhand Mukti Morcha during 1974–1976 in Dhanbad and Santal Pragana districts, the women struggled against excessive use of liquor and wife beating. Campaigns by the women against 'witch-hunting' too were taken up. In a tribal village, women often retain a large degree of control over their own labour, working essentially for themselves and their own families, at times of their own choice. Tribal women who retain their land go to market to sell their own produce. The dignity from this self-sufficiency is destroyed by displacement. Women, especially those from tribal areas, are largely dependent on common property resources for their living, but when they are relocated these are often unavailable in the new place. Women's struggles have benefited the entire community. Thus the struggle of women for economic rights is an effort to uplift the entire community. The tribal women have taken a leading role in the agrarian struggles in Jharkhand. The women play a leading role in harvesting the crop while men guard them with bows and arrows. Even in several land struggles by Jharkhand Mukti Morcha between 1974 and 1976, the women were the vanguard of the movement of forcible harvesting. They also faced the bullets of Bihar Military Police.

It is in this light that this paper discussed the protest movement of tribal women in Kalinganagar (Jajpur District) and non-tribal women in POSCO (Jagatsinghpur District) of Odisha.

PROTEST MOVEMENT OF TRIBALS IN KALINGANAGAR: DEVELOPMENT-INDUCED DISPLACEMENT

The main focus of the study here is to examine the adverse impact of globalization on account of development-induced displacement. It mainly covers the impact of globalization on the industrialization in Kalinganagar and POSCO at Jagatsinghpur. It is also attempting a comparative study of the resistance of the tribal women in Kalinganagar and the non-tribal women against POSCO at Jagatsinghpur District. The various aspects included here are the following:

- New economic policy of Government of Orissa
- Objectives, hypothesis and methodology of the study
- Timeline of Kalinganagar episode

New Economic Policy of Government of Orissa

This State of Orissa has almost 60 per cent of India's known bauxite reserve, 25 per cent of coal, 98 per cent of chromites, 28 per cent of iron ore, 92 per cent of nickel ore, 28 per cent of manganese, etc. which are enough to make profiteering private companies salivate. This had the implication of acquiring the lands of the vulnerable sections in the state and displacing them, if needed be through forceful measures. Over the years, people of Orissa have come to view the 'development' plans of the government with suspicion; they feel they are being given the short shrift. Suspicion leads to resentment and resentment leads to resistance. The police firing at Maikanch in Rayagada District that led to the loss of three tribal lives in December 2000 was still fresh in the public memory. The incident at Kalinganagar in 2006 in which 14 tribals were killed can be seen as the latest in a series of ongoing conflict between the two sides – the one favouring 'industrialization', led by the government, and the other, vulnerable section opposed to it.

The Phenomenon of Displacement has been highlighted by Padel and Das in their article 'Orissa's Highland Clearances: The Reality Gap in R&R' by emphasizing the essential ingredients. Development-induced displacement *arises out of a clash of ideologies.* On the one side, the *ideology of value systems of traditional cultures* where relationships with land and community are more important and, on the other side, an *ideology of industrialization as development,* in which market forces and swift financial profit override other values; they are antithetical to each other. This divide and rule legacy of British colonialism is bearing fruit now in *internal colonialism* being carried out through large-scale privatization of resources and alienation of huge tracts of cultivated land, by mining and construction companies, in Orissa and neighbouring states. 'Mining bauxite from these mountain tops is also an assault on the tribal religion.' Kond religion recognizes mountains as prime sacred entities and sources of life; the aluminium companies are entering the Kond region of Western Orissa being attracted due to the bauxite deposits, which are located on the summits of the high mountains; they erode the water-bearing capacity of the mountains, and thereby threaten the local Konds cultivation of millet, maize, turmeric, ginger, orange, pineapple and dozens of other food crops; the base rock of these bauxite-capped mountains are designated as Khondalite.

- ❖ It can be hypothesized in the context of Orissa that land acquisition process would be met with strong tribal resistance and would facilitate the formation of pan-tribal identity similar to Jharkhand.
- ❖ One set of issues that involves the displaced people is cultural genocide (Padel and Das, 2008). It means people die inside a soul death. The deaths at Maikanch in Rayagada District and

at Kalinganagar in Jajpur District are taken as symbolic of a collective death. Physical genocide – meaning the extermination of all members of a tribe often went alongside cultural genocide: the killing of cultures. It can be hypothesized in the context of Orissa that cultural genocide has been thrust on the tribals of Kalinganagar.

- Women's position is often badly affected due to the displacement; education, health centres and self-help groups are not provided for oustees. Lack of landownership and property rights denies women equal access to compensation. The exclusion of women from consultation and decision-making process prior to displacement and from compensation and rehabilitation packages is a matter of serious concern. In the post-displacement scenario, there is complete collapse of community and societal networks on which women have traditionally depended. This increases the vulnerabilities of women. Cases of desertion, divorce, etc. have been traced to new situations created by displacement. Women of old age, disabled, widows, with HIV AIDs, etc. are more vulnerable. Hence, mainstreaming of women in development process is an important hypothesis which would be examined in this paper.
- Over 500 arrests were made against anti-mining villagers in Kashipur up to 1999 alone (Mahapatra, 1999), and villagers attending the court every few weeks for their cases say they have to pay fees for bribes to a large range of lawyers and court officials. In this context, it is hypothesized that injustice (social cultural and economic) accentuates left extremism.

Objectives of the Study

- The adverse impact of land acquisition and development-induced displacement in Kalinganagar Industrial Complex.
- The strong resistance by the tribals in Kalinganagar would be examined in a comparative perspective to highlight the strength of the local peasant mobilization against the combined nexus of state, corporate sector and other *lumpen elements.*
- In the context of social movements, the interface between the grassroots peasant movements, civil society organizations and the left extremist groups would also be examined.
- The impact of Rehabilitation Policy will be examined in the context of the New Rehabilitation Policy 2006 of Government of Orissa

with respect to the land acquisition in Kalinganagar and POSCO. The gender mainstreaming in resettlement and rehabilitation of development-induced displacement would form an important perspective of this paper.

Timeline of Kalinganagar Episode

1992–1994 – Land Acquisition by IDCO. People initially accepted the land compensation rate without a murmur; they continued cultivating the acquired land till 1997. People displaced were rehabilitated in the colony of Trijanga and Gobarghati.

1994 – Compensation was limited to only patta holding of villagers at Rs. 33,000 per acre. Central government, on the other hand, had fixed the criteria for acquisition at Rs. 3.50 lacs per acre. Patta was not given to families cultivating government land in spite of Supreme Court Directive of January 1, 2006. IDCO had acquired 15,000 acres of private land, of which 6,900 acres were government land and 8100 acres were private lands. No patta was given for displaced families for homestead land in 1997.

June 2004 – Displaced persons wrote to the chief minister of Orissa conveying six demands including stopping further construction of industry in agriculture land.

October 7, 2005 – Tatas initiated *Bhumi Puja* which was protested by affected people – on October 25, 2005. Rabindra Jarika of Visthapan Virodhi Jan Manch was arrested on November 17, 2005; police also arrested 60 other tribal.

January 2, 2006 – Police fired on protesting tribals at Champakoila Village in which 12 persons died immediately and 37 persons injured.

January 3, 2006–March 9, 2007 – Road blocks were organized at Madhuban Chakka on the NH 200 by displaced families from their households located in the villages of Sukinda and Danagadi blocks.

DEVELOPMENT AND DISPLACEMENT IN ODISHA

Balaji and Associates (1998) estimated that in Odisha till 1995 there are as many as 79,621 families including 13,772 (17.30 per cent) scheduled tribes (STs), who have been displaced and affected by development projects. Tribal Odisha has rich mineral resources. The Government of Odisha has been taking up mining operation and setting up different industrial projects since independence. As a result of this displacement, land acquisitions have become inevitable. The magnitude of displacement due to various development projects in Odisha during the period from 1951 to 1995 is shown in Table 1.

Table 1 Scale of Displacement in Orissa between 1951 and 1995

Projects	No. of People Displaced	No. of People Rehabilitated	Percentage	No. of People Who Have Not Been Rehabilitated	Percentage
Irrigation	325,000	90,000	27.69	235,000	72.31
Factories	71,794	27,300	38.03	44,494	61.97
Mines	100,000	60,000	60.00	40,000	40.00
Others	50,000	15,540	31.08	34,460	68.92
Total	546,794	192,840	35.27	353,954	64.73

Source: Development Induced Displacement and Rehabilitation in Orissa 1951 to1995 by Dr. Walter Fernandes and Md. Asif.

Land Acquisition in Kalinganagar

The Odisha government prepared vision plan to develop the Kalinganagar Industrial Complex as one of the biggest steel hubs in Asia. The acquisition of land by IDCO for Kalinganagar Industrial Complex began in early 90s in different phases. Till now, about 13,000 acres of land have been acquired by IDCO. Of these, 6,900 acres are private land and the remaining area is said to be 'government land'. However, in reality, people have been cultivating most of these 'government land', for generations, over which they do not have patta. The land survey and settlement in the area was not done since 1928. It needs to be noted that after passing the Orissa Estate Abolition Act in 1951, the Estate of Sukinda King was vested with the government. But tenancy rights were not conferred upon the local people who were in possession of land. Even after the passing of the Orissa Survey and Settlement Act of 1958 (rules framed in the year 1962), no settlement has been done in the area. The commitments/promises made by successive governments at different times on land reforms, promising land to the landless, have never been implemented in the area. The IDCO has purchased land from people at the rate of Rs. 15,000 to Rs. 30,000 per acre in the initial phase of acquisition. Subsequently, an ex-gratia amount of Rs. 25,000 per acre has been awarded, in different phases, probably in response to people's demand for increased compensation from time to time. The compensation for land was given to only those who had patta on the land. This left a huge section of people uncompensated, as they had no patta over the land they possessed. Another section of people, who cultivated land as sharecroppers, did not receive any compensation. After acquiring land from people, IDCO has been selling the land to different industries at a much higher price.

As per the available reports, IDCO has sold land to the Tatas at Rs. 3.5 lakhs peracre which it acquired from the villagers at a nominal rate of around Rs. 45,000 to Rs. 50,000 per acre.

Table 2 List of Development Plants Wise Lands Allotted in Kalinganagar by IDCO

Name of the Plant	Area Allotted by IDCO (in acre)
Mideast (MESCO)	530
Orion	150
Maithan Ispat	100
Uttam Gala	370
NINL	2,500
Maharashtra Seamless	500
TISCO	2,400
Rohit Ferrotech	50
JINDAL	678
VISA Industries	390
Dinbandhu	100
K.J. Ispat	50

Source: ADM office, Kalinganagar.

Precipitant to Kalinganagar Massacre on January 2, 2006

During 2005, the *Visthapan Virodhi Jana Mancha* (*VVJM*) resisted all kinds of activities – like land survey, bhumi puja, levelling, boundary wall construction – relating to setting up of industries in the Kalinganagar Complex. They organized protest meetings and sit-in demonstrations in front of construction sites. In April 2005, government had issued notice to do a family survey, but the Manch decided not to cooperate with the government to do this survey as their demand for patta of their land was not met. It needs to be noted that the last family-wise survey was done in 1996. The number of family units has increased by 2004–2005.

Significance of Incidence of May 9, 2005

Among all these, the incident of May 9, 2005, assumes greater significance, in terms of culmination of simmering discontent against the administration and the companies. On May 9, hearing that the bhumi puja for Maharashtra Seamless was going to be performed, people had assembled at the site to protest and obstruct the proceedings. People were not carrying any arms. The Additional District Magistrate (ADM) of Kalinganagar came to the site to negotiate with the people. The local police were already present, to provide security to the officials of Maharashtra Seamless. The people reiterated their demands to the ADM and did not move from the place. It is alleged that the ADM, Shri Santanagopalan, in his enthusiasm, ordered lathi-charge and rushed towards the protestors, pushing some of the obstructing women to the ground. People resorted to stone pelting and the vehicle of the ADM was damaged. The ADM was beaten up in the melee, and when the Police Station In-charge of Kalinganagar tried to save the ADM he too was beaten up; both of them sustained injuries. Seeing the people's rage the police retreated from the scene that afternoon, to return later with more reinforcements. They entered the villages and went on a rampage. Fearing retaliation, most of the men folk had fled the villages and taken shelter in the surrounding hillocks. Therefore, the brunt of the police fell on the women folk and children. They were roughed up and at least 25 women were arrested. Hearing of the police terror, people from nearby villages also fled their villages and took shelter in the nearby forest. It is alleged that the melee caused the death of two children. Also, an old man, who was severely beaten up by the police, died later. On October 27, people gheraoed (encircled) the Kalinganagar Police Station protesting against the arrest of their leader Rabindra Jarika. After this incident, police have been trying to arrest the other leaders of the Visthapan Virodhi Jan Manch. On November 17, people stopped the construction work which was started by the Maharashtra Seamless Steel. Since then no further construction work took place till the date of firing. The movement was gaining momentum, and the mood of the people upbeat. Little could they foresee what was waiting in store.

On January 2, 2006, with the help of the administration, the Tatas undertook the programme of levelling the land where their plant was to come up. Top district officials, including Superintendent of Police (SP) and District Magistrate (DM), were present. People of the area had assembled to protest. Coming sporadically from several villages, their numbers had gradually swelled to 300–400, including women and children, some of them carrying bows and arrows, *tangias* (a kind of pick axe) and other traditional weapons, customarily carried by tribal people. They assembled on the adjacent fields, close to Champakoila Village. By all accounts, the mobilization of the police was massive, around 10 platoons, that is, around 300 policemen, requisitioned by the SP for overseeing the levelling of a piece of land. They had come prepared for combat, for a decisive show of strength, armed and battle ready. They had taken positions, according to unofficial police sources, divided in three contingents on three sides of the Tata establishment, which was temporarily fenced by long ropes. (Nine contingents were positioned along the rope boundary and one was 'reserve', especially meant to give protection to the top brass present.) The police had started firing and some of the agitators fell victims. In the melee one of the policemen, Gopabandhu Mohanty, slipped and fell in the hands of the fleeing tribals. He was killed by the disoriented crowd. After this, the men in uniform and gears ran amok, the officials present doing nothing to restrain them. They were seeking revenge, using the death of a colleague as an alibi. The people, frightened out of their wits, ran, as the police shot unrestrainedly from behind. Bodies, dead and injured, including women and children, lay strewn on the ground. The villagers carried some of their injured and dead people to the villages and admitted the injured into the hospital. The final count, that emerged by and by, was shocking – 1 policeman dead and 4 injured; 12 tribals dead and 37 injured – the dead, as well as the injured, included women and children.

The Peoples Union for Civil Liberty (PUCL) Team Arrived at the Following Understanding of Events

Members of three districts units of PUCL (Bhubaneswar, Cuttack and Dhenkanal) jointly constituted a fact-finding team to probe into the incident and resolved to come out with a report. The team had first visited the site of the incident and the adjoining tribal hamlets on January 11, 2006. It had subsequently made three more visits. In the course of its visit, the team had interacted with the local people, the leadership of the protesting forces, the family members of some of the deceased, the district police and civil administration, and the residents of the two rehabilitation colonies; it also visited the injured at SCB Medical Collage, Cuttack.

1. The area has a significant tribal and dalit population. The two blocks – Sukinda and Danagadi – under which the area falls, has a ST population of 36.06 per cent and 28.19 per cent and scheduled caste population of 11.89 per cent and 22.31 per cent, respectively. The ST population in the acquired area is much higher than the block average. Of the tribes, people belonging to Ho community constitute nearly 80 per cent and rest of them belongs to Munda and Santal communities. The oral history suggests that these communities came from Mayurbhanj,

Keonjher, Ranchi and Singhbhum districts in different phases in last decades of nineteenth century and early decades of twentieth century: they were settled here at the invitation of the then Sukinda King. The Madox Settlement Report 1897 also indicates about their settlement. It is also pertinent to mention that Orissa became a province only in 1936. The three villages from which people were displaced by the Tatas and the Maharashtra Seamless gave us some idea about the socio-economic profile of people.

2. No land settlement had been done since 1928, and the government has admitted this as a lapse on their part. By not conferring the tenancy rights upon the local people over the land, which has been in their possession at the time of Estate Abolition in 1951, successive governments have deprived the people of their legal rights over land and livelihood. Because of this situation, when threatened by displacement due to industrialization, people have been denied the right to claim compensation (how unjust the compensation has been is a different matter). This tantamount to deliberately neglect a marginal and deprived section of the society in conferring on them their legitimate right over their land by the government. Government must be made liable for this lapse. The PUCL team feels that timely and overdue settlement could have prevented the aggravation of the situation to such a tragic extent.
3. The government had many opportunities to allay the fears of the locals, but all along they had avoided the path of reconciliation and dialogue and, instead, took a law and order approach to the legitimate aspirations of the people. From the beginning of the conflict, the administration/government viewed the helpless tribals wanting to hold their traditional livelihood as enemies, inimical to the interest of development. The PUCL believes that such high-handedness and biases of the government towards any grassroot movement questioning the paradigms of development is the root cause of the social unrest.
4. The way the incident of January 2, 2006, was handled clearly reveals that the question of law and order was a ruse used by the government to teach a lesson to the agitators. The fact that the collective will of the local people managed to thwart some of the earlier programmes, the administration wanted to inflict exemplary retribution to break the morale of the people such that their voice of opposition is crushed once for all. The fact that women and children were not spared by the

police and agitators were shot from behind while fleeing amply indicates the 'teach a lesson mood' of the police.

The specific question posed by media was why school-going children and women taking their bath were gunned down? Tribals going away from Tata's wall-building location were shot at from behind. There was no apprehension of any assault from the Tatas. There was no FIR from anybody of Tata establishment, indicating any apprehension from any tribal to justify so heavy deployment of armed police.

Chopping Off of Sex Organs

With the chopping off of the genitals and breast of the victims, the government stands not only as a cold-blooded murderer but as a racist, sexual pervert of the worst kind. The six who were killed in custody had bayonet stabs on their face and bodies; they also had bullet wounds which were not there when they were arrested and taken in the police jeep. This proves that they were tortured before they were killed. It was only after this sequence that the police handed over their bodies to the civil surgeon and medical staff of Jajpur Town Hospital for an autopsy (according to Supreme Court directives, all killings by police should be video-taped and done in the presence of the Civil Surgeon and a Judicial Magistrate). In the firing, Sri Bhagaban Soy (25 years) of Gobarghati Village received two shots and became the first victim of police bullets. Sri Landu Jarika (29 years) of Bamiyagotha, who was by the side of Sri Bhagaban Soy, attempted to escape but he was shot and became the second victim. A group of woman and some men ran towards the two injured and as they were on their way the police started firing indiscriminately on them, shooting them. The third to fall to police bullets was Sri Sudam Barla (25 years) of Belohari Village who received bullet injuries on his head and died on the spot. A child, Gobinda Laguri (14 years), who was standing outside his house in Champakoila was hit on his chest and dropped dead. He was the fourth victim hit and the second to die on the spot. Ms. Janga Jarika (27 years) was on her way to bathe at the village pond when she was hit and died on the spot. She is a mother of four small children, two girls Bonita (6 years) and Menka (3 years) and two boys, Madhu (9 years) Bijay (7 years). She was the fifth victim hit and the third to die on the spot. As they were running away, the police continued to fire on them. This is corroborated by the fact that many of the dead and injured have received bullet injuries showing that the bullets penetrated from the back. Most of them did not rush to their homes but into the forest in order to save their lives. On seeing them run away policemen chased them and continued with their targeted firing. A policeman, Gopa Prasad Mohanty, who had entered the crowd and started hurting the people with rifle and bayonet was beaten to death by the people. The villagers who did not run away started taking their dead and injured. But the police stopped them and started arresting all of them. But the villagers managed to rescue 14 of their injured people. Both the parties proceeded towards the Jajpur Town Hospital 40 km away. Some of the villagers took their injured to the Cuttack Medical College Hospital 90 km away. Besides the 14 injured, the villagers managed to take hold of four of their dead relatives and bring the bodies to their village. Police repression continued till the late night and went to the extent of preventing them from taking the injured to hospital.

When the relatives were preparing the bodies for the cremation ceremonies, they saw that both fists of all six victims were cut off. Those close saw that the genitals of all four men were cut off and the breasts of the two women. At the foundation-laying ceremony of Messrs. Maharashtra Seamless Ltd. on May 9, 2005, near Khuranti Village, the people had organized a sit-in protest. On that day, same government team, consisting of District Collector and District Superintendent of Police and ADM broke up the sit-in by beating up demonstrators and then resorting to firing – this time with rubber bullets. It was followed but a raid on the villages and consequent arrest of 40 people, which included 25 women, 14 children and a 70-year-old man. Among them was a mother with a 15-day-old infant. The infant was separated from his/her arrested mother who was nursing him. Two toddlers in Gadpur Village and two sick people in Chandia Village died as there was nobody left in their families to care for them.

Controversial Compensation

Following the massacre, on January 3, 2006, the State Chief Minister Naveen Patnaik announced a meagre ex-gratia of Rs. 1 lakh to immediate kin of each of the deceased and free medical expenses to those injured in the police firing. The compensation package further added insult to the injuries. Later, the chief minister announced to further increase the ex-gratia to 5 lakhs to the family members of each firing victims while and ex-gratia of Rs. 50,000 to each injured person besides bearing all the expenses of their treatment. Moreover, Chief Minister Patnaik promised a job in the government offices or public enterprises to an adult member from each bereaved family. However, the kin of all the 13 police-firing victims, under the banner to *Vistapan Virodhi Janamanch*, had rejected the government's offer of ex-gratia.

Table 3 Victims Killed on the Spot and Through Hospital Neglect

Name of the Victim	Age	Spot Where Killed	Status
Ms. Janga Jarika	27	Baligotha	4 children
Gobinda Laguri	14	Champakoila	Student
Shri Sudam Barla	25	Belohari	Unmarried
Mrs. Deogi Tiria	NA	Champakoila	3 children
Shri Rangalal Munduya	40	Baligotha Hospital	Single
Shri Rama Ch Jamuda	NA	Bamiyagotha Hospital	2 children
Ms. Ati Jamuda	32	Police custody	Unmarried
Sri Bana Badara	35	Police custody	5 children
Sri Rama Gagarai	35	Police custody	5 children
Sri Landu Jarika	29	Police custody	2 daughters
Sri Bhagaban Soy	25	Police custody	Unmarried
Ms. Mukta Bankiri	30	Police custody	Unmarried
Mr. Sudam Barla	50	Policy firing	Married
Mr. Shyam Gagrai	35	AIIMS, New Delhi	Married

Source: Fieldwork and SDM office

The Immediate Aftermath

With the four dead bodies that could not be recovered by the police, and which remained in the custody of the shell-shocked tribals, the people, under the banner of VVJM, Sukinda, sat on a dharna at Madhuban Chhaka, on the NH-200. As the shock and grief gave way to outrage and a new resolve to thwart the designs of the government, the ever-swelling numbers of agitators blocked the highway, with seven-point demands. After the remaining bodies were handed over to the families, on January 4, 2006, mass cremation was held at Ambagadia Village. (The place of cremation got renamed as Veer Bhumi.) It was discovered that out of the bodies handed over by the police, five had their palms chopped off. This added to the outrage and anger.

Development and Displacement

The number of total displaced families during 1996 was 679, which increased to 1,400 by 2007. The three villages from which people were displaced by the Tatas and the Maharashtra Seamless gave us some idea about the socio-economic profile of people.

Table 4 Socio-Economic Profile of the Displaced Persons from Three Villages

Name of the Village/ Panchayat	No. of Households	% of ST Population	% of SC Population	Literacy Rate	% of Cultivator Labour	% of Agricultural Labour
Chandia	331	85.9	2	37.6	41	36.2
Gobaraghati	558	88.8	2.1	53.5	16	37.7
Gadaput	140	97.8	0	46.7	43	13.5

Source: Fieldwork and District Statistical Hand Book

The majority of the displaced are apparently tribals and a small section belongs to scheduled castes. Lower middle class and marginal peasants constitute nearly 60 per cent to 70 per cent of the population and a majority of them, though in possession of land, have no patta (Record of Rights). A small section of people have land ranging between 15 acres and 60 acres. A sizable number of people are sharecroppers, cultivating the land of absentee landlords of the area.

Displacement and Rehabilitation

According to official data, 814 families have been displaced, so far, in Kalinganagar. The above data shows that only 35 per cent of the displaced persons were rehabilitated and the majority of remaining 65 per cent were not rehabilitated which is apparently great source of injustice and also a cause for discontent and anguish.

Status of Rehabilitation in Gobarghati Colony

Only 120 families (18.78 per cent) out of a total of 639 families (displaced from the villages, Khandiapusi, Madhapur and Sarangpur by the) Neelachal Ispat Nigam Limited (NINL) are residing in the colony. Rest of the families (about 70 per cent of the total displaced) who have not come to settle in the colony have opted for Rs. 50,000 as cash compensation in lieu of 10 decimal homestead land at rehabilitation colony. A large section of the displaced families chose not to come to the resettled colony because of lack of livelihood in the vicinity. Even people who had received compensation money for their land could not buy land as land price suddenly increased many times in the surrounding areas, due to the prospects of industrialization. Of the people staying in the colony, only 25 families have got employment in NINL. The remaining families go to work in the stone crushers, earning Rs. 40–50 per day; they daily cover a distance of 14 to 15 km.

Table 5 The Status of Homestead Land and Employment Provided by Different Companies in Kalinganagar Till 2012

Provision of Homestead Land and Jobs for the Displaced Families				
Name of the Industry	**No. of Displaced**	**Provision of 10 Decimal Homestead Land**	**Provided Rs. 50,000 for Those Not Availing Homestead Land**	**No. of Persons Provided Direct Employment**
NINL	639	131	508	182
MESCO	53	53	–	47
Jindal	60	51	8	Nil
Visa	23	3	20	Nil
Rohit	12	Nil	12	Nil
Common Corridor	28	Nil	28	Nil
Total	815	238 (29.20)	576(70.67)	229(29.00)

Source: ADM Office, Kalinganagar.

Note: The above data shows that only 29.20 of the displaced persons availed the homestead rights and the rest preferred cash amount of Rs. 50,000. The percentage given employment was restricted to only 29 per cent.

There is no other work opportunity available in the nearby areas. These displaced families, although living as daily wage earners, have not been considered as Below Poverty Line (BPL) families. For 120 families, five tube wells have been installed and two of them are not working. Inside the colony, roads are also of murram (Sheer red-soiled pebbles) and get washed away in the rainy season. There is one primary school in the colony. The next higher school is at a distance of 5–6 km. Electricity connection has been provided up to the colony but people are not in a position to get connection. There is no Primary Health Centre (PHC) in the colony. The nearest PHC is at about 20 km from the colony. The displaced families, although resettled since 1997, have not been provided with patta for their homestead land. Instead, an 'Intimation Slip for Settlement of Land' has been issued from the Office of Tahsildar, Sukinda, with the instruction that 'transfer not possible without the prior permission of the Revenue Officer'.

New Rehabilitation Policy of Orissa Government 2006

New Rehabilitation Policy of Orissa Government 2006 has been acclaimed as more broad based to minimize the discontent of displaced persons. The author had the occasion of visiting Kalinganagar during 2012. Between 2006 and 2012, a lot of changes had taken place in the mind-set of local tribals, police personnel, district administration and the corporate managements. This was apparently a phase of transition from agitation to rehabilitation. Tatas promised to adopt humanitarian approach for resettling the displaced families. A visit to the rehabilitation colony presented a subdued mind-set of the tribals who had received the enhanced compensation and rehabilitation package from the district administration. As per the new policy of 2006 in the industrial project and mining project, onetime cash assistance of Rs. 5 lakhs was fixed for displaced families who lost all land including homestead land.

Provision for granting of free homestead land of 1/10th acre in the resettlement habitat to each displaced family is 'subject to availability' of land. In lieu of the homestead land, Rs. 50,000 shall be given. The policy also provides for house-building assistance Rs 1.5 lakhs for each displaced family. Furthermore, a monthly maintenance allowance of Rs. 2,000 is to be provided to each displaced family for one year. The policy gives special benefits to displaced tribal and indigenous families, including preferential allotment of land. Tata Steel reportedly started implementing the same and provided jobs to 29 displaced from Kalinganagar, who were trained in welding technology by the steel company. As on November 22, 2006, more than 300 affected families were relocated from Kalinganagar industrial area. According to a release issued by Tata Steel, displaced families would be allotted 1/10th acre of land. Each family will get Rs. 1.5 lakhs for building houses and a maintenance allowance of Rs. 2,000 per month for one year. It also has the provision of mainstreaming the women by providing land rights to those who have attained the age of 35 years. The author observed during field work in February–March 2012 that the houses being built by the tribal families also consisted of 20 cents area; these belonged to the families who were benefitted due to the presence of adult males and females above 35 years; they had built larger houses in the extended area due to the new provision of mainstreaming the women. There was apparently greater satisfaction among the families who accepted the new rehabilitation scheme. There were still some sections of tribals who did not benefit due to absence of ownership of patta land. This was the situation during March 2012.

The Worst Instance of Brutality – Medha on Kalinganagar

The brutal massacre of the people in Kalinganagar was criticized by most of the social activists and political parties. Iron lady of humanitarian activism, Medha Patekar had come down heavily on Orissa Chief Minister Naveen Patnaik after a visit to Kalinganagar massacre site on February 11. He has certainly erred, she felt. If not he, who shall be held responsible for the cold-blooded murder of 12 illiterate tribal citizens who did not do any crime other than calling upon the state to protect their fundamental rights over howsoever tiny might be their plots of land, she asked. To tell the least, this is the worst instance of brutality that a government in free India has ever perpetrated on its innocent, illiterate and forest-dependant people. The government shall attract attention of the world community to this brutality, declared Medha. The police raided the tribal habitations in the night and arrested 26 women in blatant violation of all legal norms and human rights, she reminded. Oppression has been going on relentlessly since then. In an act of barbarism, five bodies handed over to the relatives after post-mortemhad their palms chopped off from their wrists. The doctors at Jajpur Hospital sought to justify chopping off the hands on the ground that they had cut off the palms to take fingerprints as the faces had been completely disfigured by bullets. The consent of the relatives of the deceased was not taken. In addition, relatives of the six victims taken for post-mortem alleged that there was no Protection of Democratic Rights and the genital organs of all six, including a woman, had been chopped off or mutilated during post-mortem. Dr. B.D. Sharma (2006) in his book 'People's Revolt in Kalinga Nagar' has observed that the Kalinganagar episode is a great human tragedy and is a result of the state remaining totally unconcerned about the people's side, their fears and aspirations. What is worse is that the state has refused to learn from the experience in Rourkela, Kashipur, etc. The state government has been extremely cautious in dealing with the situation. Collector and SP were replaced. A judicial inquiry has been ordered. The CM has preferred not to visit the area. Even Smt. Sonia Gandhi and the union home minister visited the villages without state security. CM has come round to the view that there is need for all party consensuses about future course of development, especially about industries in tribal areas.

Anti-POSCO Agitation in Jagatsinghpur District (Odisha)

As is now well known, the Government of Orissa and Pohang Steel Company (POSCO), Republic of Korea, signed a Memorandum of Understanding (MoU) on June 22, 2005, for setting up an Integrated Steel

Plant in Jagatsinghpur District, Orissa, affecting eight villages of three Gram Panchayats of Kujang Tahsil, i.e., Dhinkia, Gadakujanga and Naogaon. The attempts by the district administration to acquire land have been thwarted by strong local opposition starting in early 2006, primarily by the POSCO Pratirodh Sangram Samiti (PPSS) that spearheads the movement against POSCO. In response to this resistance, the state government has been using the tactic of the abuse of the criminal system to file numerous false criminal complaints against all persons resisting the object, including members of the PPSS, leading to threats of arrest perpetually hanging over them.

The biased nature of the police and their actions becomes evident from the targeting of villagers resisting the POSCO project on the one hand, and their refusal, on the other hand, to initiate any criminal action against goons and other persons perpetrating violence on these villagers. About 230 cases had been filed implicating about 1,500–2,000 villagers resisting POSCO between 2006 and 2012. Most of the complaints have left the number of accused open-ended, which allows the police to implicate any person in any case, despite not being specifically named therein. A large number of these cases have been filed by government officials during times of peaceful demonstrations by the members of the PPSS. Shri Abhaya Sahu, the Chairman of the PPSS, was arrested on two occasions and has over 50 cases registered against him, including cases when he was not present in the villages on the day of the alleged offence. Manorama Kathua, President of Women's Wing of the PPSS, aged about 29 years has several cases filed against her and has been unable to apply for bail due to financial constraints and has not left the village in 6–7 years. These are just few instances of arbitrary actions of the police which include failure to take any action against hired goons and the police. The state on the other hand has turned a blind eye to offences committed against these villagers, and in fact, in some instances, has almost protected the offenders. In a shocking incident of police high-handedness, 65-year-old Smt. Satyabati Swain was arrested in September 2011, when her son Shri Ranjan Swain was beaten by hired goons resulting in grave injuries. The police refused to register a complaint in regard to the attack on Ranjan Swain and instead arrested his mother.

The impact of police actions has been disastrous due to the filing of cases and warrants against almost 2,000 persons. It has resulted in the targeting of entire villages, who are under constant threat of arrest and have not left the villages in 6–7 years, and whenever they do leave, are constrained to do so surreptitiously. In many cases, entire families have been implicated; resulting in none of them leaving the village for years. The inability to leave the village has resulted in a complete lack of access to medicines or any medical treatment to the villagers. A team of doctors who visited these villages found that at least 30 women needed urgent medical intervention, else their condition would deteriorate. Most arrests of persons took place when villagers were compelled to leave the village to visit the doctor requiring medical assistance. The inability to leave the village and maintain business ties has adversely impacted the trade which is the major source of livelihood for them The government has taken other forms of coercive action and terminated government employees for having protested against the POSCO Project, including Shri Babaji Charan Samantara, who worked as postmaster in Dhinkia for 28 years and Shri Kailash Chandra Biswas employed as a high school peon, at the Government School, Dhinkia, for over 20 years. Over the last eight years, the government has made innumerable attempts to break the struggle against POSCO by employing various arm-twisting tactics. However, what is perhaps the greatest betrayal of the state against its own people is the use of the criminal system to implicate villagers in a large number of false cases to intimidate them, instil fear in them and break them into submission. The state is using every underhand trick in the book to counter the legitimate and peaceful voices of dissent.

In the light of the above, the concerned intellectuals and activists have made the following demands:

1. The government should withdraw all the criminal cases foisted on villagers of POSCO-affected villages and other members of PPSS.

2. Cases must be immediately registered in regard to the violence perpetrated against the villagers of POSCO-affected villages.
    a) Against police officials in regard to the violence on May 15, 2010, at Balithut circle.
    b) Against hired goons in regard to the violence on December 14, 2011, during the peaceful protest against the construction of the coastal road connecting Paradip Port to the proposed site of the POSCO Steel Plant.

3. The government should immediately conduct an enquiry into the abuse of the criminal system to target villagers and take necessary action against all officials who are involved in the filing of false cases against villagers resisting the POSCO Steel Plant. The government should respect and protect the constitutional rights of the villagers to protest and conduct itself in a democratic manner abuse of the criminal system and filing false cases to curb dissent against the POSCO Steel Plant in Orissa. As is now well known, the Government of Orissa

> and Pohang Steel Company (POSCO), Republic of Korea, signed a Memorandum of Understanding (MoU) on June 22, 2005, for setting up an integrated steel plant of a total capacity of 12 million tonnes per annum in Jagatsinghpur District, Orissa. The integrated steel plant includes a captive power plant and a captive minor port and was to be located on the north-western bank of the Jatadharmohan River creek, 12 km south of the Paradeep Port requiring a total of 4,004 acres of land, which would affect eight villages of three Gram Panchayats of Kujang Tahsil, i.e., Dhinkia, Gadakujanga and Naogaon. However, the attempts by the district administration to acquire land have been thwarted by strong local opposition starting in early 2006, primarily by the POSCO Pratirodh Sangram Samiti (PPSS) that spearheads the movement against POSCO. The PPSS has its base in Dhinkia Gram Panchayat, wherein three of the villages, namely Dhinkia, Govindpur, and the hamlet village of Patna, are being affected by the proposed steel plant. A number of reports and documents have been brought out in regard to the social and environmental impacts of the project and the rights of the people over the forest land which they have been cultivating for generations. In response to this resistance, the state government has used several tactics to tire out the movement. One of the tactics is the abuse of the criminal system to file numerous criminal complaints against all persons resisting the project, including members of the PPSS leading to threats of arrest perpetually hanging over them.

There were about 230 cases that had been filed implicating about 1500–2000 villagers resisting POSCO between 2006 and 2012. About 15–20 of these cases had been filed in the months of November and December 2012. We were informed by the representatives of the movement and the advocates concerned that 1 case of murder, 16 cases of dacoity and over 100 cases of attempt to murder had been filed so far against villagers of the affected areas. Of the cases that had been filed against them, the complainant in about 70 per cent of the cases was government officials. Fifty-seven persons have so far been arrested by the police and have been released on bail. At the time of our visit, two villagers from Dhinkia Village, namely Shri Alok Swain and Bhibuna Mahapatra, were in prison having been arrested on December 8, 2012, and December 9, 2012, respectively. Both of them had gone for the last rites of Shri Abhaya Sahu's mother. While one of them was arrested, the other had been injured in a road accident and was arrested while he had gone for treatment. Shri Babli Raut, belonging to the scheduled caste community from Govindpur Village, was arrested from Balthur, when he had gone to receive medical treatment; 23 cases had been filed against him.

Protest Movement against POSCO and Women's Participation

The police started entering the area around midnight and the massive swelling in their ranks was noticed by the villagers at around 2 a.m., early in the morning on February 3, 2013. The villagers then alerted others and rushed to the dharna (sit in) and human chain site. The police started their attack at around 4 a.m., targeting the women and children who were standing in the frontlines of the human chain, thinking that their presence would make the police act a little humanely at least. This, however, did not deter the police force; they (all male) attacked the women injuring many of them. Even more brutally, they reportedly swung little children accompanying their mothers in air. They then arrested several villagers and whisked them away to some unknown location. The assault, however, did not deter the villagers, and many more of them reached the protest site amidst growing tension. The situation turned almost into a warlike one. The police started breaking down the betel vines and cutting trees. The unarmed villagers faced a 12-platoon strong police force armed to teeth.

In the early hours of February 3, 2013, 12 platoons of armed police entered Govindpur Village under proposed POSCO project area and started beating people to pave the way for acquiring land. The news of police entering the area before sunrise spread like wild fire and hundreds of men, women and children gathered there and resisted the forceful acquiring of their land. People squatting there appealed to the armed police, district administration and Odisha Industrial Infrastructure Development Corporation (IDCO) officers not to render them landless and homeless and allow them to live with dignity. They shouted slogans that they want to live like human beings, not landless beggars. But the adamant district administration with the help of the armed police started beating the unarmed people blue and white.

The beating of unarmed peaceful agitators, women and children by IDCO officer Sangram Mohapatro was shown live in different TV channels. This was the scene at Govindpur. Under the leadership of PPSS Chairman Abhaya Sahu and Secretary Sisir Mohapatra, thousands of protesting people gathered at Dhinkia-Patnahat Village and condemned the police brutality and the inhuman action of the district administration. Bibhu Prasad Tarai the local MP along with hundreds of protestors seized the Dhinkia-Govindpur route and squatted on the road. After discussion with the MP the police force was withdrawn in the evening. But again on February 4, 2013, morning the police brutality was repeated and betel vines were destroyed by force. Hundreds of women and school-going children lined-up before the armed police force and resisted. Police and the district administration did not deter. Forcible destroying of betel vines and felling of trees continued with the help of hired goondas and hoodlums. State leaders of five political parties namely CPI, CPI(M), Socialist Party, RJD and Forward Bloc rushed to the spot and condemned the police brutality and rendered their all-out support to the peaceful agitators. At the same time at the capital city Bhubaneswar, these five political parties took a procession and held *rasta roko* at Raj Mahal Square protesting the police brutality.

Congress leaders including former MLA Umesh Swain, state spokesperson Arya Kumar Gyanendra and former IG of Police Batta Krushna Tripathy visited the spot and condemned the police brutality and forceful land acquisition. They declared support of the Congress party to the agitating people. On February 5 also the acquiring of land by force for POSCO continued with the armed police force resorting to inhuman atrocities let loose on the children and the women agitators, injuring many. Abhaya Sahu, Chairman of PPSS, started hunger strike demanding the withdrawal of armed police forces from the proposed site, putting a full stop to forceful acquiring of land and release of all arrested innocent people. Hundreds joined him in support. It may be recalled here that the MoU signed by the state government with the POSCO steel major for the proposed POSCO project is already outdated since June 10, 2010. The said MoU was signed in 2005 June. After its expiry, it was not renewed again. In the absence of a valid MoU already 60,000 trees have been felled by the district administration. It has targeted felling of some 1 lakh both fruit-bearing and non-bearing trees till the end of July. According to a survey, there are still more than 5 lakh trees – both fruit-bearing and non-bearing – in the proposed POSCO project area. This area comes under highly cyclone-prone environment. These trees are the natural protectors of cyclone. During the 1999 Cyclone, 10,000 human beings lost their lives. Out of them 6,000 unfortunate people belonged to Erasama and Kujang area only. This is a cyclone-prone seashore area of the Jagatsinghpur District. The felling of trees in such huge number will not only create health hazards in the area but also worsen the environmental conditions. People from all walks of life, in general, and environmentalists, in particular, have condemned this act of the state government which jeopardizes the natural environmental condition.

Green Tribunal's Rejection

In 2012, when the Government of Odisha was acquiring land for the proposed POSCO project, nearly 8 lakh trees were felled arbitrarily. *The National Green Tribunal* rejected the environment and forest permission granted to POSCO project. There were restrictions in felling of trees, land acquiring and supply of water to POSCO. In view of the green tribunal's rejection of the permission, an environmental expert team was constituted and asked for investigation and report. The report is yet to come. But the haste the district administration has shown in acquiring the land for POSCO by passing all laws of the land and strictures is highly questionable and tantamount to contempt of tribunal's orders. Not only that there is no resettlement and rehabilitation, development decisions for the land-loosing people in the Resource Planning and Development Commission (RPDCA) meeting of the district. In this background, the forceful acquiring of land by the district administration is totally arbitrary and contrary to the established laws of the land; it is argued by intellectuals and people from all walks of life. The state government which claims to have a peaceful industrial policy time and again has resorted to this brutal attack on unarmed peaceful agitators and acquiring land forcefully by using armed police and hired goondas. This is being condemned by all the political parties of the state. It may be recalled that due to opposition and resistance by the people of the proposed area the land acquisition was stopped. But again from February 3, 2013, the district administration has resorted to police brutality by attacking the people and injuring them. Even the children and women are not spared. PCC State President Niranjan Patnaik demanded that the project should be established peacefully. The government has betrayed and applied force to acquire the land. People of the proposed project are opposing and sent a memorandum to the Governor of Odisha to shift the POSCO Project from the area. Likewise the BJP State President Juel Oram also condemned the state government action and said that the state government has committed criminal offence by sending police force in the dead night and attacking unarmed people, children and women. This is completely undemocratic and unlawful.

More than a thousand armed police besieged the Gram Panchayat of Dhinkia on February 3, 2013, in Jagatsinghpur District of Orissa to crush the resistance to the POSCO Steel Plant. For the entire day, thousands of people sat in the heat, where several people (including children) and even two policemen fainted. At noon, the district collector declared their protest 'unlawful' and subsequently loudspeakers blared threats about use of tear gas, lathi charges, 'those engaging in unlawful protests being dispersed' continuously for four hours. Efforts were made to divide the protesters as well. The protesters remained firm. Eventually, perhaps afraid of the heavy media presence and unable to break the will of the people, the police withdrew. The people have left some of their number on guard, fearful of the police returns at anytime.

Resistance by Women of Govindpur and Dhinkia of Police High-Handedness

At 4 a.m. on Sunday, February , 2013, nearly 400 policemen surrounded the entry points to the villages of Govindpur and Dhinkia in the Jagatsinghpur District of Odisha. The two villages are among the last hurdles to the steel major POSCO's $12 billion project in the state. As dawn broke, the police lathi-charged the villagers who had gathered at the spot, injuring over 25, mostly women and children. However, the land acquisition was stalled on February 7, following mounting criticism of the police action. This was the latest in the Odisha government's attempts to restart work on the mega steel project that has met stiff public opposition in the state, since its inception in 2005. After initial obstacles in the land acquisition process, POSCO had scaled down its demand from 4,000 acres to 2,700 acres. The government acquired 2,000 acres between 2005 and 2011. The remaining 700 acres have to be acquired from Govindpur and Dhinkia villages – mostly forested areas. Despite the village councils passing resolutions under the Forest Rights Act to not hand over any land for industrial purposes, the villagers allege that the government has been attempting to take the land by force. Soon after the district administration declared it would acquire the remaining 700 acres, the residents of the two villages started protesting. 'Children were kicked around like footballs by the police and some even got hit by lathis,' says Prashant Paikray, spokesperson for an anti-POSCO outfit. Although the government claimed that the land acquisition, which started earlier this month, was peaceful, television footage showed state officials, including Land Acquisition Officer Sangram Mohapatra, hitting protesters with lathis. The police action came as a surprise early on February 3,though tension had been prevailing in the area for the preceding 20 days when about 200 policemen, later increased to 400, were stationed near the POSCO transit camp, 2 km away from Govindpur Village. After dispersing the protesters, the police entered Govindpur Village and started destroying the betel vines, before going on a manhunt for anti-POSCO leaders like Abhaya Sahu and Manorama Khatua of the PPSS. Mostly frail women, old and young, stood up to the blows that the police rained on them with canes, some of them stripping partially in protest. Several of them were injured in the lathi-charge but the undeterred women of Govindpur and Dhinkia villages threatened to strip en masse if the police are not withdrawn from their area immediately. As the world celebrates Women's Day, these village women are engaged in a bitter tussle with the administration to stop land acquisition for the POSCO Steel Project. They also want the five platoons of police still deployed at the site of the proposed mega project in Jagatsinghpur District withdrawn.

The state government had resumed land acquisition, which involves clearing betel plantations in the villages. The drive began only hours after three anti-POSCO protesters were killed in a bomb attack. The activists allege that supporters of the POSCO Plant were behind the attack. The women who clashed with the police belong to the PPSS, which has spearheaded the anti-POSCO agitation for the last eight years. They said hundreds of them would strip if their demands are not met. The government says it has acquired about 2,000 acres of land in the region in 2011 and needs to acquire another 700 acres, mostly in Govindpur area, for the project. It says the villagers have agreed to the land acquisition. But the villagers deny this and the stand-off has continued for some time now, with the administration being forced to abandon land acquisition activities every now and then. But POSCO is not having a smooth run. The anti-POSCO movement is gearing up again against land acquisition. The POSCO struggle has now acquired strategic importance for other industries and corporate groups that face public agitation for destroying forests. The nude protests by women have caused temporary setback to the land acquisition for POSCO project.

At least 31 people, including women, were booked for protesting in a semi-nude condition against South Korean steel major POSCO's plant in Odisha's Jagatsinghpur District. Some of the women allegedly entered a prohibited area, took off their clothes and clashed with police in Govindpur Village, about 120 km from here. At least 15 people, including five police personnel, were injured in the clash. Police have registered cases against 31 people. A case has also been registered against PPSS Chairman Abhaya Sahu for abetting the incident. Terming semi-nude protest by some women during anti-POSCO agitation as 'unfortunate', the Odisha government expressed concern over support from certain political parties and NGOs to such activities. Rout, the Local MLA, held five political parties CPI, CPI-M, Forward Bloc, RJD and Samajwadi Party responsible for the anti-POSCO agitation since 2005. He pointed out that the government is acquiring its own land in illegal possession of certain villagers and not an inch of private land is being acquired. Police sources in Jagatsinghpur District said a handful of elderly women while being chased away from the prohibited area tried to disrobe in public. Hundreds of women from Odisha's Govindpur and Dhinkia villages are locked up in a bitter battle with the state government over the acquisition of land for the POSCO Steel Project. A large number of women from all age group clashed with police and some stripped partially protesting the acquisition of land for the controversial POSCO Steel Project. These women, who were caned by the police on duty, have also threatened to intensify their stir and strip en masse if the government fails to stop acquiring land for the project. These anti-POSCO women protesters have also demanded the urgent withdrawal of police from their area. These women protesters want the government to immediately withdraw five platoons of police still deployed at the site of the proposed mega project in Jagatsinghpur District. What further sparked the protest was the tragic killing of three anti-POSCO protesters in a bomb attack. The anti-POSCO activists have alleged that supporters of the POSCO plant were behind the attack. The injured were mainly women. The protestors alleged that the police fired teargas shells and made a lathi-charge on them, which was denied by the police. The police said they had requested the family members to receive the bodies at the time of post-mortem and while accepting them after inquest. 'But you are neither receiving the notices nor coming forward to perform the last rites'. Three activists of anti-POSCO brigade were killed at Patna Village while allegedly making explosives. CPI National Secretary, M.P.D. Raja led a demonstration by anti-POSCO agitators, mostly children and women, demanding complete withdrawal of police force from the proposed plant site areas in Odisha's Jagatsinghpur District. Raja, who flayed 'midnight entry by the police' into Govindpur Village in a bid to facilitate acquiring of land, led the demonstration as it neared Govindpur-Mangala Chhak where police set up a temporary camp. A large number of activists from CPI, CPI(M), Forward Bloc, Samajwadi Party, RJD and members from different NGOs also participated in the demonstration. The supporters and activists of opposition Congress and BJP also joined the gherao agitation led by D. Raja. Meanwhile, all the schools in Dhinkia and Govindpur villages remained empty for the fifth consecutive day as children took part in the stir. Social activist Swami Agnivesh visited Govindpur Village the next day to express solidarity with the agitating people. The CPI-backed PPSS leader Abhaya Sahu's fast also entered the third day. 'I will continue fast till complete withdrawal of force from the area,' Sahu said raising question on the legal status of the land acquisition for a foreign company signs 'a valid MoU'. The police raid followed an FIR which accused one of the petty industrialist being the instigator of the December 14 clash between the anti-POSCO brigade and the contractor group, leaving one dead and 25 injured. The FIR was filed by one Mounabati Das, an activist of the PPSS. Police have already arrested a local Congress leader Jayant Biswal in this connection. A construction firm worker was killed and two others injured when clashes broke out near Dhinkia Village in the district between villagers and workers over construction of a road.

'The blood stained soil will inspire many more children of the village. They and their mothers and sisters will take a pledge to protect this soil. POSCO will never become a reality here.'

Ignoring the prohibitory orders more than 3,000 villagers and leaders of a variety of social movements and political parties gathered in a meeting at Dhinkia to protest the murders and the land grabbing and repression they have suffered while still in shock after the bombing. They called for an immediate halt to the land acquisition. The rally was attended by CPI, CPM, Samajwadi Party, RJD, Forward Bloc, Congress, Aam Aadmi Party, RPI, CPI-ML (Ram Chandra Group), CPI-ML (Kahnu Sahnyal Group), Jan Badi Lekhaka Sangh, All India Revolutionary Women's Organization, HAL Bistapita Andolan, Basti Surakshya Mar ha, etc. A number of women disrobed themselves as a desperate peaceful protest against the brutal repression and war waged on their villages. Many women were beaten with sticks by the police and more than 60 were injured in total. These pictures from an Odiya newspaper tell part of the story:

The police arrested the top anti-POSCO leader Abhaya Sahu, which has triggered tension in Jagatsinghpur District as thousands of villagers blocked roads and sealed entry points to the site of the proposed steel project. People have installed wooden barricades in the villages of Dhinkia, Govindpur, Mahara and Patna and they are keeping round-the-clock vigil to prevent entry of any company and government officials to the proposed site. District Superintendent of Police S.S. Dev Dutta Singh said that the anti-POSCO leader was wanted in several cases including in a dowry death case and in a case of atrocity against the members of scheduled caste. Sahu claimed 28 persons sustained injuries after being attacked by lathi wielding people, who raided the area near Mahal under Dhinkia Panchayat and attacked the villagers, including women and children. Opposing construction of the 10-km long road along the coast from the oil refinery on the sea beach up to the proposed POSCO site, PPSS supporters have been sitting on dharna at Mahal ever since the foundation stone for the same was laid in August. But the protesters won this round – after four days the state government suspended the operation until after a session of the state's parliament that ends in March.

Killings and repression by police but anti-POSCO struggle remains defiant.

On March 2, 2013, in Patna Village, Dhinkia, a group of activists were taking refuge in the house of a fellow activist after being hunted by police forces for three days for their anti-company activities. Suddenly an explosion was heard and some went out to see what it was. Another bomb was thrown at them and four people were critically injured. Three died soon after from their injuries while the fourth was able to get to hospital and his life was saved. They were Manas Jena, Nabin Mondal (brother of Dula Mondal who was also recently killed) and Narahari Sahu – three key activists against the POSCO plant which threatened their land and families. Nabin Mondal had recently filed an FIR against IDCO Officer Sangram Mohapatra for another violent attack on the village on February 3, 2013. Laxman Paramanik who was taken to hospital was in critical condition.

The sister of Manas Jena was in tears of sadness, rage and disgust at the death of her brother who was killed by bombing. The police have refused to accept the FIR on the killing filed by family members of the victims, but they did accept an FIR against the victims and survivors including PPSS leader Abhaya Sahu on false charges of conspiracy.

Police later gave statements to the media claiming that the three activists were in fact making a bomb which exploded and killed them. This version of events has been carried by the Indian newspapers and TV. Following the killings, the district administration put prohibitory orders on the whole Patna area, trying to prevent villagers and activists from meeting to arrange rallies objecting to the murders. Meanwhile, the land acquisition was ramped up as local officials used the prohibition to push through land grabbing without the usual activist opposition; 22 betel vine plantations had already been destroyed by March 5, 2013. Despite this enormous repression 3,000 villagers and supporters gathered on March 6, 2013, to cremate the bodies of the martyrs and protest against the brutality of POSCO and the state police, who worked hand in glove with the company.

The POSCO movement has been violently repressed. The police, state agencies and the company goondas have repeatedly attacked villagers, made false arrests, abused women and killed local activists. Several of the villages in Govindpur are under constant police occupation. During February 2013, the villages were stormed by armed police and villagers were beaten and abused. POSCO is yet to get environmental clearance, mining lease, water source allocation, renewal of lease or settlement of claims under the Forest Rights Act, yet hand-in-hand with the state government it continues to grab land and harass villagers. But none of this has been enough to deter the defiant villagers.

POSCO project noted social activist Medha Patkar that the government should honour the wishes of people and scrap the POSCO project. 'The project, ever since it was initiated, has only brought state repression, police atrocities and host of other problems for the villagers', she said and pointed out 'the project having been rejected in the Gram Sabha should not be imposed on the people'. The Orissa High Court on Friday declined to grant interim stay on acquisition of forest land by state government for the POSCO Steel Project in Jagatsinghpur District. The court however ordered status quo to be maintained on private lands falling in the project area till disposal of the case.

The dream project of Odisha government has become a nightmare for the people living in the proposed POSCO project area. The conflict between industrial development and livelihood has brought the state and people face to face. In such a situation, it may not become an easy sail either for POSCO or the protesting people to arrive at any logical conclusion.

CONCLUSION

This paper highlights women's participation in protest movements in Kalinganagar and POSCO. The objectives of the study were the following:

- The adverse impact of land acquisition and development-induced displacement in Kalinganagar Industrial Complex.
- The strong resistance by the tribals in Kalinganagar.
- The interface between the grassroots peasant movements, civil society organizations and the left extremist groups.
- The impact of Rehabilitation Policy is examined in the context of the New Rehabilitation Policy 2006 of Government of Orissa with respect to the land acquisition in Kalinganagar and POSCO. The gender mainstreaming in re-settlement and rehabilitation also forms an important perspective of this paper.

The following hypotheses has also been examined in this study:

- Land acquisition process would be met with strong tribal resistance in Kalinganagar and would facilitate the formation of strong tribal identity.
- One set of issues that involves the displaced people is cultural genocide (Padel and Das 2008) and this phenomenon has been examined in Kalinganagar tribal movement.

IDCO had allotted 7,818 acres to 12th Industrial Plants in Kalinganagar. The precipitant to Kalinganagar Massacre was the initial acquisition of land in Kalinganagar from the tribals in every low rate extending from Rs. 15,000 to Rs. 30,000. Due to people demand an ex-gratia amount of Rs. 25,000 per acre was awarded by mid-90s. The compensation for land was given to only those who had patta on the land. This left a large number of tribal who had cultivated the land generationally without patta. IDCO have been selling the land to different industries at a much higher price, i.e., at Rs. 3.5 lakhs per acre. This was perceived as great injustice by the tribals. The simmering discontent of the tribals prompted them on May 9, 2005, to resist the Bhumi Puja which was to be conducted by the industry, namely, Maharashtra Seamless. The police resorted to force and arrested 25 women. The police also arrested other leaders of Vishtapan Virodhi Jan Manch on November 17, 2005. On January 2, 2006, the Tata Steel Industry undertook the programme of levelling the land of the plant; this was protested by over 400 tribals including women and children. The mobilization of the police was massive, and the police firing led to the massacre of 14 tribals including women and children which was almost similar to cultural genocide. The police brutality included the chopping of sex organs of the women. The forceful land acquisition culminated in colossal human disaster which sends the message that the lands should not be acquired without the consent of the affected people.

The forceful land acquisition culminated in colossal human disaster which sends the message that the lands should not be acquired without the consent of the affected people. The tribal movement at Kalinganagar got wide support from various civil society organizations including the left extremists. The stiff resistance of the tribals was instrumental in the announcement of New Rehabilitation Policy 2006 of Odisha government, which has been acclaimed as more broad based to minimize the discontent of displaced persons. The tribals by 2011–2012 were gradually reconciling to the path of transition from agitation to rehabilitation. The companies including Tatas adopted Humanitarian Approach for resettling the displaced families. Such a transformation could take place because of strong tribal movement leading to the massacre of 14 tribals. The New Rehabilitation Policy 2006 of Odisha government was also gender friendly as women of 35 years and above were entitled to be recognized as a separate unit for compensation. The author could witness in 2012 that woman tribal beneficiaries were actively engaged in constructing their houses. The Tatas were also extending full cooperation in extending treatment to the needy tribals in the hospital. These measures had a tranquilizing effect on the tribal and non-tribal workers. The atmosphere was conducive to the normal working of the difference industries.

The government and POSCO singed an MoU on Jun 22, 2005, for setting up integrated steel plants in Jagatsinghpur District. The IDCO was facilitating the acquisition of over 4,000 acres of land for setting up their plant. The land was to be acquired from three Panchayats of Kujang Tahsil, i.e., Dhinkia, Gadakujanga and Naogaon. The attempts by the district administration to acquire land were strongly resisted by the villagers and particularly by women folk. The state government has been using brutal police force to suppress the agitation led by women, men and children from 2005 to 2013. The agitation was led by PPSS under the leadership of its president Shri Abhaya Sahu. During the course of nine long years of struggle, the local police force of Jagatsinghpur District had filed 230 cases implicating about 1500–2000 villagers among whom the majority were women. Shri Abhaya Sahu the president of PPSS was arrested on two occasions and has over 50 cases registered against him. Besides this, Manorama Kathua, President Women's Wing of the PPSS, was also arrested; she is aged 29 years and has several cases filed against her. The villagers have been unable to apply for bail due to financial constraints and are also confined to the village for the past 6 to 7 years. These are just few instances of arbitrary actions of the police which include failure to take any action against hired goons and the police. Many women have been severely injured without any medical treatment reaching them. The state on the other hand has turned a blind eye to offences committed against these villagers, and in fact in some instances, has almost protected the offenders. A team of doctors who visited these villages found that at least 30 women needed urgent medical intervention, else their condition would deteriorate. The district administration has been able to forcefully acquired 2,000 acres between 2005 and 2011. The district administration is still trying to acquire another 700 acres from the villages of Govindpur and Dhinkia. The courage and bravery of the women needs to be applauded to prevent the POSCO Plant from operationalizing. The district administration and the Odisha government have deliberately deprived the villagers from giving pattas to the government land in which they have been tilling the betel vine crop for last 50 years. The police, state agencies and the company goondas have repeatedly attacked villagers, made false arrests, abused women and killed local activists.

REFERENCES

Bexelius, Maria (2000). *Protesting Violence – An Empowering Force? A Case Study of Tribal Women's Protests against CRPF-Violence in Banpur, Orissa, India*, Sweden: University of Uppsala.

Das, Victor (1992). *Jharkhand Castle over the Graves*, New Delhi: Inter-India Publication.

Dhagamwar, Vasudha, et al. (2002). *Industrial Development and Displacement– The People of Korba*, New Delhi: Sage Publications.

Fernandes, Walter (2009). 'Development-induced displacement: Impact on tribals', in Ota, A.B. (ed.), *Development-Induced Displacement: Impact on Tribals*, Bhubaneswar: SCSTRTI.

Iyer, K. Gopal and Maharaja, R.N. (1982). 'Background of Jharkhand in Fourth World Dynamic: Jharkhand', in Nirmal Sengupta (ed.), *Fourth World Dynamics, Jharkhand*, New Delhi: Authors Guild Publications.

Padel, Felix and Das, Samarendra (2008). 'Orissa's Highland Clearances: The Reality Gap in R&R', *Social Change*, 38(4): 576–608.

Prasad, Sushama Sahay (1955). *Tribal Woman Labourers: Aspects of Economic and Physical Exploitation*, New Delhi: Gyan Publishing House.

Rao, Nitya (2005). 'Questioning Women's Solidarity: The Case of Land Rights, Santal Parganas, Jharkhand, India', *The Journal of Development Studies*, 41(3), A Frank Cass Journal, Abingdon (UK).

Sharma, B.D. (2006). 'People's Revolt in Kalinga Nagar, in Search of Development with Equity, Toward a New Frame of "Community Sector" Industries', *Bharat Jana Andolan*, New Delhi: Sahyog.

CHAPTER 5

IN BETWEEN TRADITION AND MODERNITY: THE CASE OF TRIBAL WOMEN IN INDIA

Karma Oraon

The human population has two distinct form men and women as we call it gender difference, which is based on physical or biological characteristics. The historical perspective of women as we perceive to have its status in terms of attribution to women is lower than men in almost throughout of the human population baring a few community groups. For these conditions, in the human population, social, cultural, and ecological settings are responsible factors or elements, but gradually a majority of women also attended the position of the male notion of women unimportance. In some instances, the identity of women was suppressed by men in the perspective of traditionally accepted women and inheritance of what they had from ancestors. The only identity they have since the time is immemorial daughters, sisters and wives, and in other form, it is the status of women which determines the level of civilized society or even the country, whether it has developed or not.

There has been no doubt that the right of women over the dominant men folk out to be reduced to equal footing in terms of socio-economic and political matters. There are a number of legislations which are protective in nature but they are not adequate and effective. Nationwide debate on the issue is continuing.

After independence immediate task were initiated to women welfare and empowerment, but the diverse socio-cultural upbringing of India's population come on the way to rationalize the desired issue to be solved by the destitute and unbecoming conditions of the women folk of the societies of India.

Today, the desired issue of the national seminar is tribal women; we must think over some of the matters related to the status of tribal women. It seems that the position of tribal women is largely based on these aspects such are patriarchal, matriarchal/matrilineal and polyandrous forms of society. The position of women seems to be even better in comparison to the other society even if the majority of tribal societies are enjoying patriarchal form of societies. A few tribal societies are matriarchal or matrilineal, such as Garo and Khasi of the North Eastern region and Toda, Chenchus and Tharu in the Northern and Southern regions of India. Some of the tribals', such as Oraon, Munda, Ho, Santhal and Kharia, position in the society is not bad. They enjoy the freedom of even choosing the husbands, and after marriage they enjoy ample opportunity to depart with husband. The studies regarding the status of women in various societies have been carried out by various anthropologists and sociologists, for example, Hutton among Sema Naga, Majumdar among Jhasis, Haiman Dorf among Tharus and Hunter among Garos. In their opinion, all tribals, whether they have patriarchal or matriarchal form of societies, as far as the status of women is concerned enjoy comparatively better than other non-tribal communities. Among polyandrous tribals of Jaunsar Bawar of Uttaranchal, the tribal women actively participate in entomic activities in significant way and their knowledge is also significant regarding the intellectual property of the society.

In most of the tribal communities of central India, there is a practice of bride price just reverse to that of dowry. Bride price is the token amount paid in lieu of service rendered by the parents till the women folk attend the age of marriage. Bride price shows the status of women more than of male folk.

In most of the tribal societies, the inherited property particularly the land is owned by male folk and not by women even if there are no male members in the family. The brother inherits the land property and not the sister. There have been series of debates on the issue in the tribal societies and sometimes in the apex courts also, but matters have been referred to the village council, where the decisions are taken as per the customary practices they have had from the ancestors. In the case of matriarchal societies, women folk inherit ancestral property of land.

The discrimination still persists, in terms of wages in economic activities. The tribal women in the traditional form of wage determination for their labour in most of the societies get lower than that of men. Sometimes the wages of women are just half of what men get. Even if in the daily labour in the mega cities and elsewhere, the wages are not equal. Males are in advantage. Males are considered physically stronger than that of women. In rural areas, the tribal women share 27.74 per cent whereas non-tribal women share 11.64 per cent in the economic activities traditionally owned by their respective societies. The education among the tribal women has the significant position as the total literates in India are about 900 lakhs where the tribal women are 580 lakhs in comparison with tribal male folk, but average literacy rate is no higher than 25 per cent.

Women empowerment and participation in decision-making processes in tribal society needs to be discussed here. Although the majority of tribal communities enjoy the patriarchal form of social condition, the condition of women is not very deplorable, even if they are traditionally not allowed to participate in the matter of decision-making process in the village council. In the matter of social and cultural offences, only on the occasion of witness or to place their position before verdict, they (women) are/were allowed to attend village council. The 73 amendment of Panchayati Raj Institution, where one-third of the seats are reserved for women, has the significant role to play in the traditional practices. Lack of adequate education, employment, social assistance and political awareness are with them, even if they are availing the opportunity of legislative supports provided to them by the state. There is a major contradiction in-between the traditional feature of self-governance and legislative support system of governance in the tribal societies. Under the Fifth Schedule (Ref. Article 244) of the Constitution in the scheduled area, special provisions have been made—the Panchayats (Extension to Scheduled Areas) (PESA) Act of 1996 for empowering tribals as well as women in the light of self-governance. Here also one-third of the seats are reserved for women in some state. There have been other legislative mechanisms of empowerment for women such as reservation in jobs where a significant percentage of women are getting jobs at all levels in the government and other sectors.

Tribal women or non-tribal women have to face many challenges; even if for their protection and security, dozens of legislations have been enacted, faithful compliance is still to be insured by the so-called civil society and the law enforcing agencies.

In the tribal-dominated provinces, there have been a series of murders of women in the name of witch (dyne). The honour and prestige of women are at stake at the instance of black magic or superstitions still prevailing in tribal societies. In some cases, we find these killings are for the land ownership among the clan members (gotras). Women are subjected to practising witchcraft for harming her siblings or clan members (gotras). The gotras feel that the ancestral property particularly the land would be owned by her, although it is not possible as per the customary law but intolerances develop in the case of her long living age or marriage at her father's house and living with her husband in the father's house. The gotras feel that they (women) may capture the ancestral property, i.e., the land. Hence, it may be concluded that the social status of tribal women is at the cross roads. In certain fields, their status is better but in many realms of life their conditions are pitiable. Hence, there is need to not only pass different acts and laws and introduce development schemes but also to implement these schemes in an honest manner.

CHAPTER 6

CONTEMPORARY STATUS OF TRIBAL WOMEN: A CRITIQUE TO LENSKI'S 'STATUS INCONSISTENCY'

M.C. Behera

THE ISSUE

This paper is a preliminary enquiry on the topic of 'status inconsistency' with reference to the emerging status of tribal women when their communities are passing through transition. The issue is addressed with reference to achieved status in the formal system and ascribed role performance in traditions. It tries to examine if 'status inconsistency' as an analytical tool of social behaviour would benefit us to understand the behaviour pattern of tribal women with both achieved and ascribed status in the changing context.

Approaches to study the status of women particularly in India have followed two broad approaches – synchronic and diachronic – studying the status from both contemporary and historical perspectives. In both the approaches, the issue of status is addressed either with reference to a cultural group (e.g. status of Bonda women) or to two or more of such categories (say, status of Birhor, Ho, Khasi and Adi women) in a comparative perspective. Often their status has also been compared with women of Hindu society.

Cultural variables like religion, traditional body politics, inheritance and marriage used to be the analytical concepts of examining the status in a gender perspective. After tribal communities got exposed to forces of modernization, the status is examined with reference to development variables such as education, occupation, political and religious participation and ownership rights. These variables are also applied to macro understanding of status of tribal women. Their participation in democratic system or achievement of higher literacy rate is considered to be a marker of tribal women's higher status. Nevertheless, cultural variables are remarkably significant in terms of their influence on status in contemporary studies.

No doubt, contemporary tribal women have achieved in the fields of education, political participation, economic position, etc. which are not confined to their respective communities. The status they have achieved has a regional or national or international dimension beyond the community boundary and in the fields which are not parts of their respective cultures. They have achieved something which other members of their group have not, and which has raised them at par the status of women from non-tribal counterparts. But the achieved status may or may not fall within the status-domain of respective cultures which these women belong to. In that case, the study of their status with reference to culture only will ignore achieved status. On the other hand, the study of achieved status will most likely ignore the ascribed cultural status. In either of the cases, the status of tribal women in contemporary society will be only a partial understanding of the whole issue.

The paper is based on interviews and observations of eight tribal women of Arunachal Pradesh. The researcher has been interacting with them on various issues for the last 18 years. Out of these eight women, four have been interviewed to triangulate the observations of the researcher on their role performance in both formal (Western model of development and culture) and informal (cultural) systems. The other four are very close to the searcher as students and colleagues working in different educational and research institutes of the state. The researcher often has had the opportunity of interacting with them, sharing their experiences, besides observing their role performance in their respective cultures. The researcher has not mentioned the names of the respondents to maintain consistency in presentation in spite of the fact that a few of them had agreed to mention their name. Further, the four cases of women in educational and research institutes have been grouped under one case from the point of view of research ethics.

THE CONTEXT

The first case is about a woman who is a woman activist and had held the position of Chairperson in State Woman Commission and President and Secretary of Arunachal Pradesh Women Welfare Society. The second case is about a woman of former Indian Administrative Service (IAS), a poet and a Padma Shree awardee. The third case is of an IAS officer in state bureaucracy. The fourth case is of a Non-Governmental Organization (NGO) activist, an entrepreneur and also a Padma Shree awardee. The fifth case is about four academicians and researchers having similar experience in some contexts.

The First Case: The first case is about the woman who is a state figure. She has held important positions like the Chairperson of State Woman Commission and President and Secretary of Arunachal Pradesh Women Welfare Society and has represented the women cause abroad and influenced the policy decision of the state government. She was heading the National Forum of Forest People and Forest Workers, which got renamed as All India Union of Forest Working People on June 5, 2013, in Puri, Odisha. In addition to this, she also held the position of Chairperson in the contemporary organization of her own tribe. She travels across the country and is a role model of women across the tribal communities in the state.

Despite all these achievements, her status in patriarchy remains uncompromising. The patriarch value system was intolerant to her holding the tribe level organization. 'How the community can be in the hands of a lady?' was the undercurrent feeling of patriarchy. The lady happens to be a reformer. Born in 1962, she got married at the age of 17 before Class-X result was out. However, with an understanding husband and support from in-laws, she pursued her study and completed Masters in English; her company to her husband on different occasions or her pursuance of higher education after marriage did not go normal with patriarch mind set of the tradition. She is aware of the comments, 'shadowing her husband', which she revealed during the interview. As she belonged to an elite family as a daughter, perhaps she did not get confrontation, though her actions were not approved of. As a person, she has attended traditional *Keba* (traditional village council), but women participation in *Keba*, for which she has been advocating, is still tabooed. It is not always patriarch, but female mind set moulded in it also do not appreciate her non-traditional role in the community. For orthodoxy, she is a 'cultural outsider' but she considers herself 'an interface between cultural insider and outsider'.

The traditional houses in this region are built on raised platforms with ladders to going up and coming down. The tradition of her community does not prescribe the use of same *koba* (ladder) by both male and female. Naturally, there is one *koba* for male members and the other for female members of the household. Although the tradition is dying out in many areas, it still survives in many others. As a person, she has used the *koba* (ladder) the males use. But that has not stopped the practice and she is tolerated because she is, to orthodoxy, a cultural outsider and the behaviour is tolerated as a one-time mistake which would not be repeated as she lives in Itanagar, the capital town of the state and beyond the cultural boundary of the community. That is why she is not popular among the orthodox persons. She has not still participated in *Lura* (the community fencing for Mithuns-*bos frontalis*) and the accompanying feast which is a privilege in male domain. She has kept herself away from bamboo basketry as the tradition considers women participation as an indication of short life for men. Obviously, her stand as 'interface' holds. She organizes *Mopin* (a community festival) in the capital complex but does not attend such ritualistic performances in villages which are tabooed for women. Her status is a dichotomous reality – one in the community and the other outside of it; one among the people of non-traditional outlook in her community and the other among 'tradition holders' in it.

The Second Case: The second woman represented here has national stature. She qualified IAS in 1979, but preferred to be a freelance journalist and worked as BBC Stringer for a quite long time. She also worked as correspondent in *Sentinel*, *Telegraph* and *Hindustan Times*. She is a writer, a poet and has been awarded Padma Shree in 2011. She travels across the country and participates in different forums in different capacities. Presently, she is a member of Arunachal Pradesh Public Service Commission (APPSC) since August 20, 2011. But her traditional status as far as her role in traditional body politics, participation in festivals and in decision-making process in customary affairs has not changed.

As a writer, she presents the universality of her Adi culture – the human feelings of love and hatred, the aesthetic sense of appreciation to beauty which has universal appeal – in her writings. This has given her a status in her community, a recognition above other community members and thus, as she feels, 'acceptable as a community person' despite the fact that she is not a practitioner of culture with other members of the community. She feels herself a 'cultural insider' because she considers herself 'traditional in outlook', but like many writers she also questions herself. 'Do I represent my culture while writing?' She is conscious of her traditional role, and whenever an opportunity comes she keeps herself away from participating in Tapu dance and traditional *Kebang* (traditional village council), entering into *Moshup* (roughly can be translated and boys' dormitory) and even from events where other women do participate, for she is unaware of the nitty-gritty of ritualistic nuances which are expected from participants who observe. No doubt, she gets jocular teases, 'she does not know', from female members of her community.

The Third Case: She is an IAS officer and is working in the state. As she married to a non-Arunachalee, she is considered an outsider to the traditions of the tribe.

Being the only biological child from her parents, she has encountered her status as a female child when her parents adopted a boy child who would inherit ancestral property. She attributes low status of women to the tradition, and quotes *Niid* (prayers) in which there is no mention of women. Although born to the culture, she feels more of a 'cultural outsider' and that is what her community people think her of. As a matter of fact, most of the community elders and other traditional people did not attend her marriage ceremony. She remarks that her professional status has not changed her 'cultural status' as a female. She is prohibited from attending rituals like Ropi *yullo* and *Pih/pwkhe/pe-ee* (the ritual performed after killing a tiger) and places tabooed for women.

The Fourth Case: She has also been awarded Padma Shree because of her service to the cause of humanity. She runs school for orphans, creates employment opportunities by undertaking different production activities and holds posts in different state- and national-level committees. In terms of role performance, she is not a decision maker in traditional affairs of the tribe as per the custom. Nevertheless, she acts as member in various contemporary community-level organizations to organize festivals and meetings to address to emerging issues. However, she is prohibited to tabooed spheres in her culture despite her active role in preservation efforts of the community. She is a conformist to her cultural role and at the same time having modern outlook in conformity with her achieved status in formal system.

The Fifth Case: They are academicians and researchers and work in educational institutions and research departments of the state government. During the field study for Ph.D. assignments, all of them have had the experience of being considered cultural outsider in their respective communities. When one of the respondents touched the items customarily tabooed for women, she was tolerated because she was not well-versed with the custom. On the other hand, they were ridiculed of ignorance of the culture to which they are born. Interestingly, the respondents in the villages of their respective tribes were suspected to be the agents of the government deputed to collect information so that tax can be levied. This has been the experience with many insider researchers and field workers who try to seek information. Surprisingly, the community feeling of 'we' is divided between villagers and urban dwellers, and there has emerged a sense of suspicion at some levels of relations. When one of the respondents could not become a mother after 10 years of marriage, the clan members of her husband tried for his remarriage as she did not qualify the status of a woman as the custom demands. The four women respondents were found to be conformist to their cultural role and have been trying to maintain a balance between ascribed and achieved roles.

THE TEXT

In all these cases, the women are pride for the tribe, but outsiders to the culture as they are not the practitioners. They are important for the community when situated with other communities. The woman with high status in formal system is often a representation from the community, but not of the community as her new role performance does not conform to status role what other women in the community perform as per the culture-prescribed behaviour pattern. The tradition has two visible spheres. One pertains to the traditional role of women and its violation is tabooed and the other, beyond the tabooed sphere, has greater scope of interaction. From this sphere of interaction, the status so acquired does not penetrate into the tabooed sphere. The changing status role therefore has two distinct domains.

It is found that three of the cases have purchased land in the capital town of the state. They have the ownership rights, but this land does not belong to the community. In tribal community though individual ownership exists, it has a community context. The land cannot be sold to members other than the community and the women do not have the ownership rights till date. This is also evident during the field study. In order to avail of the Indira Awaas Yojana (IAY) scheme, the land was registered in the name of the woman beneficiary. This ownership has contextual and notional meaning from community point of view, though legally it is not so. The woman cannot transfer the land in any way to any members even within the community (Basar, 2011).

The status of tribal woman does not remain tribe-specific with change in education and occupation, though she may occupy a different status in the family. In terms of changing role performance, women of a tribe do not remain as a category, but as individuals; and when the women with changing status are viewed as a category, it does not remain tribe-specific. These women are members of the community but not with a status that could affect decision making and participation in traditional and tabooed spheres.

The emerging status of tribal women has significance beyond the tribe, but not within the traditions of the tribe. Within the tribe, the woman plays her specific role in conformity with the customs.

LENSKI AT PERSPECTIVE

Let us discuss the differentiated status perception of an individual in two social settings – formal and informal – following Lenski (op.cit.). In this discussion, 'status inconsistency' is used as a conceptual category without going into the explanation of behaviour pattern and the social action related to it. Moreover, the 'status' is examined in a formal system, following Lenski: the system characterized by vertical stratification, in which balance between investments (e.g., education) versus rewards (e.g., income) is at the heart of understanding and explaining apparent status inconsistency (Geschwender, 1967). Lenski's example of status inconsistency of a teacher with low income/poverty has social meaning in such societies where economic and social aspects of status go together. Both dimensions – social and economic – of the status are elements of the same cognitive domain of perception in the society. Thus, the concept of 'status' examined in the formal context has been compared with the informal system (the tradition-bound tribal culture) which is non-vertical, in which investments and rewards have different connotations.

Status inconsistency is an analytical tool to understand the situation in a society in two contexts. In transitional societies, however, there are distinct cognitive divisions. Tribal societies in contemporary period are examples as these societies are in the process of change through development interventions and at the same time adhering to a cognitive universe – their respective cultural identity. Needless to say, transitional section of people of the community perceives social and economic status as two sides of the same coin. But in traditional domain, social status is important, and distinct from the economic status, which in fact has little or no value in the cognitive universe of the people.

In addition to transitional traditions, there is a dominant society, though ambiguous, transcending cultural boundaries of different communities at a higher level with boundary penetrating potentialities, and all other communities strive to achieve those levels which characterize the dominant society. Indian society with its measures of development like industrialization, urbanization, globalization and indicators like growth in aggregate terms could be an example of such category of a society: formal institutions and vertical and horizontal stratifications being considered its characteristics.

Status of a person, his/her role performance and social expectations may not have the same consideration in the first category of societies as these are held in the second category. The status of a teacher and its comparison in formal system as Lenski (1954, 1956, 1967) makes us to understand that the concept of status inconsistency does not have any comparable standing in informal systems characterized by tribal communities. The concept of 'teacher' has a different connotation and the expectations do not go with money/material standards in tribal traditions. Rather the expectations are more on achievements through role performance. The status of a hunter in a tribal community is not judged in terms of how much he acquires, but from how many successful hunting expeditions he has to his credit. The study on status of a person therefore has to be approached not thorough the context but across the contexts. There exists inconsistency, but two different contexts may not be comparable.

Persons with distinct status in a formal system have their own understanding of it in the informal system to which they belong. The person could be indifferent or try to force upon the status to reform what he/she considers unnecessary in the informal system or may conform to her ascribed status role. The perceived status in the formal system either as a reformer or as a conformist could be explained through looking glass self theory (Cooley,1902), for the reformist looks through the teachings of formal system which consider cultural practices to change, while the conformists look through what people expect him/her to do as a cultural person. Such status differentiation has cross-cultural implication rather than having a culture-specific explanation and so does not go with the concept of Lenski's status inconsistency. Moreover, there is another point of departure while answering the question: Whether people who are studied as status inconsistent actually feel so and behave the way Lenski has outlined? In our findings, the social action and behaviour pattern do not come in conflict as the achievers conform to the behaviour pattern (both achieved role and ascribed role) expected from them. Although the context is different, it supports the logic of Blocker and Riedesel (1978) that there is no correlation between 'objective' and 'subjective' status inconsistency. Lenski's tool of analysis is not adequate to explain the status inconsistency in transitional tribal cultures, which in fact differentiate between the ascribed and achieved status positions. The differentiations and different levels of social realities propose a multiple status complex to study the behaviour pattern, and this proposition of course needs further investigation.

REFERENCES

Basar, J. (2011). 'A Study of Indigenous Knowledge System in Development Policies and Programmes with Special Reference to Resource Management by the Galo of Arunachal Pradesh', Unpublished Ph.D. thesis. Itanagar: Arunachal Institute of Tribal Studies, Rajiv Gandhi University.

Blocker, T.J. and Riedesel, P.L. (1978). 'The Nonconsequences of Objective and Subjective Status Inconsistency: Requiem of a Moribund Concept', *The Sociological Quarterly* (Spring), 19(2): 332–339.

Cooley, C.H. (1902). *Human Nature and Social Order*. New York: Charles Scribner's Sons.

Geschwender, J. (1967). 'Continuities in the Study of Status Consistency and Cognitive Dissonance', *Social Forces*, 46: 160–171.

Lenski, G. (1954). 'Status Crystallization: A Non-Vertical Dimension of Social Status', *American Sociological Review*, 19 (August): 405–412.

Lenski, G. (1956). 'Social Participation and Status Crystallization', *American Sociological Review*, 21 (August): 458–464.

Lenski, G. (1967). 'Status Inconsistency and the Vote: A Four-Nation Test', *American Sociological Review*, 32 (May): 298–301.

CHAPTER 7

STATUS OF HEALTH AND HEALING PRACTICES PREVALENT AMONG TRIBAL WOMEN: AN ANALYSIS

Madhu Nagla

In India, the health behaviour and health status of the tribal groups are greatly determined by the varying health practices, use of indigenous herbal drugs, taboos and superstitions. Apart from this, these tribal groups are also constrained by the various environmental and climatic factors (Basu, 1996: 207–220).

In general, health is a function, not only of medical care, but also of the overall integrated development of social, cultural, economic, educational and political. Each of these aspects has a deep influence on health which in turn influences all these aspects. Hence, it is not possible to raise the health status and quality of life of people unless such efforts are integrated with the wider one to bring about the overall transformation of a society. Good health and good society go together. This is possible only when supportive services such as nutrition and improvements in the environment and in education reach a higher level.

The common beliefs, customs and practices connected with health and disease have been found to be intimately related to the treatment of disease. It is necessary to take a holistic view of all the cultural dimensions of the health of a community. In most of the tribal communities, there is wealth of folklore related to health. Documentation of this folklore available in different socio-cultural systems may be very rewarding and could provide the model for appropriate health and sanitary practices in a given ecosystem. Maternal and child care is an important aspect of health-seeking behaviour which is largely neglected among tribal population groups (Basu and Jindal, 1990).

PHYSICAL ENVIRONMENT

Disease and its cure system among the tribal communities cannot be properly understood in isolation. Rather, these are well connected with environment particularly the forest ecology. The traditional health care system and treatment are based on their deep observation and understanding of nature and environment. For example, forest is the rich source of medicinal plants.

HEREDITARY AND GENETIC DISORDER

The nutritional problems of different tribal communities are very sparse, and very little information on dietary habit and nutrition status are available due to lack of systematic and comprehensive research. Malnutrition is common and has greatly affected the general physique of the tribals. Maternal malnutrition, which is quite common among the tribal women, is also a serious health problem, especially for those who have frequent pregnancies. The nutritional status of pregnant women directly influences their reproductive performance and the birth weight of their children, a factor that is crucial to an infant's chances of survival. Chitrey (1976) studied the dietary status and health of the tribals of Bihar and Maharashtra and observed deficiency of their diets in calorie as well as protein and essential amino acids (Chitrey, 1976: 101). Apart from this, Mahapatra and Das observed a high incidence of malnutrition in Sundergarh District of Orissa (Mahapatra and Das, 1990). Moreover, food and dietary habits of tribes are also linked with their certain norms and tradition. For instance, the Saora of Orissa regards drinking milk as taboo. Besides, under the influence of the caste society, some communities have turned vegetarian like Tana Bhagat of Bihar and Gonds of Chattisgarh region of undivided Madhya Pradesh (Singh, 1996).

In addition, there are specific diseases which are quite rampant among tribal population. In his reports for 1960–1961 and 1979–1981, the commissioner for scheduled castes and scheduled tribes provided the various incidences of specific diseases among tribals within some states:

Madhya Pradesh – yaws, malaria, tuberculosis, leprosy

Maharashtra – tuberculosis, skin ailment and malnutrition

Orissa – malaria, filaria, yaws and leprosy

Rajasthan – related with digestive system and skin, tuberculosis, high incidence of venereal diseases

Uttar Pradesh – venereal diseases, goitre and leprosy

Tripura – yaws, tuberculosis, leprosy, and venereal disease and skin diseases

These above-mentioned diseases which are perpetually found among tribal community is contradictory to the general impression that tribals are free from any maladies due to their proximity with nature and breathing pure air (Singh, 1996). There are some tribes which are even worst of the other tribes in terms of their health indicators. For example, the various primitive tribal groups like Jarwa, the Sentineulese, the Onge, the Great Andamanese, the Juang, etc. suffer from any ailments, although we have little knowledge about their health status in detail (Singh, 1996).

HEALTH DELIVERY SYSTEM IN TRIBAL AREAS

Health delivery system is also a major factor for determining the tribal health problem. There is no doubt that the health institutions in tribal areas are deficient. In fact, these institutions do not work in conformity with the local situation. The Primary Health Centres (PHCs) and sub-centres are often overburdened by 30,000 people at each centre instead of 20,000 people. Besides, there is also a pressing need to mitigate the cultural gulf between the health care personnel and tribal people, continuous supply of drugs and equipments, etc. (Singh, 1996).

Existing health machinery is designed in such a fashion that except for a few additional PHC and SU centres more or less similar pattern of health care delivery system exists for general as well as for tribal population in the country. In spite of the so-called expansion of the health facilities and government's efforts to improve health situation of the tribals, hardly any significant impact on the important health indices of the tribal people has been achieved.

As Basu in his various studies among the tribals of Bastar District, Madhya Pradesh, and Dudh Kharias of Sundergarh District, Orissa, explains that simple linear expansion of the existing health care delivery system is not an appropriate answer for improving health and family welfare status of the tribal population; location of health facilities should be as per local needs depending on geographical and population consideration, resources, manpower and availability; constraints and bottlenecks of the existing health and family welfare delivery system should be identified, specifying clearly the infrastructures required, strategies to be developed which are in consonance with the felt needs of the local tribal population; and health functionaries manning the different health care institutions should be exposed to socio-cultural background of different tribal groups.

SOCIO-CULTURAL DIMENSION OF HEALTH

No culture is devoid of influence of its own beliefs and practices over health and system of medicine in order to treat diseases, even though it does not conform to the standard set by modern rational system of health. So, every culture works in a systematic fashion in its treatment of diseases. This treatment of disease varies from group to group. If a health policy meant for rural destitute is to be formulated, it is quite pertinent to study these traditional practices and their outcomes for the modern health. Among others it would be interesting to analyse how the opposite approaches, i.e., traditional and modern system of health care, interact in the process of healing a disease in a particular society (Chaudhuri, 1992). But, very little studies have been done on the interaction between traditional and modern health care practices. As the empirical work on health, disease and the nature of treatment are very sparse and limited, there is a dearth of substantial empirical research in this field. The various areas that demand an immediate need for various sociological studies like in the area of their belief system are related with health and diseases. In the tribal context, medicine men, health, food habits and environment, medicine and other health indicators like fertility, mortality, etc. are also important.

In general, people working in the field of health and diseases in India have been reporting that very often people do not utilize the medical facilities available to them. This is particularly conspicuous in rural areas, more so in the case of tribes and other backward communities. In this regard Chaudhuri (1994) raises some basic questions like why is that even though modern medical health facilities are available, quite often those are not utilized? Unless and until reasons for the failure or non-acceptance of these programmes are known, any development programme cannot be successful. It is due to the fact that the success of health programmes depends much on the modification of human behaviour. These are the aspects that should be studied by social scientists. But this is not done adequately in India (Chaudhuri, 1994). Moreover, health demands special attention particularly in the context of tribes for two obvious reasons: firstly, due to their backwardness and isolated habitat, which makes modern health facility almost inaccessible to these terrains. Secondly, they constitute a very high growth rate but in a very random manner. This is very much evident in the total population of various tribal communities from only 18 in the case of Andaman to 40 lakhs among the Gonds. For the obvious reason, this demands careful attention and study of the socio-cultural habits and health practices. Moreover, the lower rate of fertility can also be linked with high mortality due to inefficient health practices. Therefore, apart from studying socio-cultural dimension of the health, it is equally pertinent to examine the degree of acceptance of modern health facilities (Chaudhuri, 1992).

HEALTH AMONG TRIBAL WOMEN

In general, women's health is mediated by a number of factors such as women's lack of power, lower status in family and society, discrimination, lack of knowledge, biased cultural practices based on patriarchy and lack of safe and empathetic services. All these factors find manifestation in women's early marriage and early child-bearing age, multiple and short-spaced pregnancies making them very vulnerable to get physical and mental strain. Although gender discrimination is said to be relatively unknown among tribals, girls tend to receive less attention than their brothers which has serious implication on their health and nutritional status. The nutritional biasness leads to some of the rampant incidence of diseases like stunted growth and chronic anaemia which are associated with pregnancy, child birth and other gynaecological problems. In addition, other factors like cultural and traditional practices, which are often antithetical to women, also aggravate their nutritional deficiency particularly during pregnancy (Ali, 1995).

So gender discrimination makes women more vulnerable to various diseases and associated morbidity and mortality. From socio-cultural and economic perspectives, women in India find themselves in subordinate positions to men. They are socially, culturally and economically dependent on men. Women are largely excluded from making decisions, have limited access to and control over resources, restricted in their mobility and are often under threat of violence from male relatives (Jejeebhoy and Sathar, 2001).

There have been a number of studies on the status of women relating to their socio-cultural problems, economic rights, participation in management, and access to employment, food, health, etc., but these issues have not been properly focused in relation to the tribal women. There are only a few studies on the status of tribal women in India (Singh, Vyas and Mann, 1988; Chauhan, 1990).

Talking in terms of tribal women as opposed to her non-tribal counterpart, a peculiar contradiction is noted by various scholars. There is a general perception that tribal women enjoy traditional equality with the males (Mohanty, 1995). Although there is no doubt that the tribal women enjoy a greater economic independence and freedom of movement than the non-tribal counterpart, it is not correct to regard this significant indicator of their superior social status (Nongbri, 2003). If we scrutinize tribal women's status, then it shows that gender inequality is not very new to the tribal societies too. In fact, it is mainly disguised by rampant incidence of poverty which often compels men and women to cooperate in joint economic activities (Nongbri, 2003). If we analyse these phenomena sociologically, then it shows that the tribal customary laws which include people's beliefs, customs, social mores, rites, etc. are not always conducive to the interest of women. In fact, most of the customary or personal laws mainly relating to the property and marriage are highly oppressive to women. Nongbri (2003) notes

> ....although women shoulder heavy economic responsibilities, commensurate with men, the tribal customary laws like those of non-tribal societies deny them equal rights to property. The system of inheritance amongst most tribes is invariably in favour of men. In general, women are entitled only to maintenance right an expenses for marriage while men inherit land and all other movable and immovable properties. Even in societies that follow the matrilineal principle of descent and inheritance, where the women is the focal point of household organization, when it comes to the allocation of rights over land, a sharp distinction is maintained between 'ownership' and 'control'. While ownership of land is transmitted through women, control invariably lies with men. This is true among particularly all the matrilineal groups in north east India such as the Khasis, Jaintia, Garo, Lalung and Koch. Similarly, in the patrilineal system, where women have access to land, they mostly enjoy usufructory rights only while proprietary and managerial rights with men. Indeed, in the majority of cases, women's rights to land are contingent on a variety of factors such as subject to their remaining unmarried, have no brothers are widowed or marry a prescribed kin.

The study of tribal women becomes important because the problems of tribal women differ from one area to another, owing to variation in their geographical location, historical background and the process of social changes (Chauhan, 1990). Therefore, there is a need for a proper understanding of their problem specific to time and space, so that more streamlined programmes and approaches could be devised for positive outcomes. Moreover, there is a greater need for undertaking region-specific study on the status and role of tribal women, which alone can throw up data that will make planning for their welfare more meaningful and effective (Singh, Vyas and Mann, 1988).

A tribal woman occupies an important place in the sonic–economic structure in her society. The Dhebar Commission Report (1961) mentions that the tribal woman is not a beast of burden, she is found to be exercising a relatively free and firm hand in all aspects of her social life unlike women in non-tribal societies (Dhebar, 1961). The tribal women in general and in comparison with caste enjoy more freedom in various walks of life. Traditional and customary tribal norms are comparatively more liberal to women. The status of tribal women in matrilineal societies has been observed to be somewhat better than that of women in a patrilineal society, e.g., their legal status is much higher than that of their counterparts in patrilineal society and they have a significant role in tribal economy. However, after a comparative analysis of the various indicators (like political organization, religious, ritual practices, etc.) among the different tribes in India, it has been observed that the status of tribal women has gone from good to worse as a result of the impact of social change which has affected the social structure of tribal society (Chauhan, 1990).

HEALTH AND LITERACY

Literacy is universally recognized as a powerful instrument of social change. The level of literacy is undoubtedly one of the most important indicators of social, cultural and health development among the tribal communities. Literacy is important for the young girl; it had correlations with the survival of her children. Infant mortality is found to decrease significantly when the mother is educated up to the primary level and above. Majority of Indian tribes have been exposed to literacy only recently. By and large their response to programmes of literacy and formal education vary significantly between tribes and regions. These responses depended on their socio-cultural, economic and demographic characteristics and on the magnitude and direction of the forces of modernization, such as urbanization and industrialization.

The census recognizes an individual as literate if one could both read and write with understanding in any of the languages. According to the 2001 Census data, the literacy rate among the general population aged 7 years and above was found to be 64.84 per cent (75.26 per cent for males and 5367 per cent for females). Literacy among the tribals was found to be very low, i.e., 47.10 per cent and especially among the tribal females (34.76 per cent) (Census of India, 2001). Most of the literates among the scheduled tribes were literates only up to the primary level. Within the country, the levels of literacy among the tribals vary widely.

FERTILITY AND MORTALITY

Limited studies are available on infant mortality among the tribal population. Basu and Jindal (1990) made an in-depth study of a primitive tribal group, i.e., Kuttiya and Kondhs of Tudibandha block of Phulbani District in Orissa. The average age at menarche among Kuttiyas was found to be 14.5 years. It was observed that the average number of pregnancies per mother was 5.09 and 3.89, respectively, among mothers of completed and incomplete reproductive life cycles. Infant mortality was found to be very high, i.e., 62.11/1,000 (National Family Health Survey (NFHS)-3). The fertility record of Kuttiya Kondh mothers in various age groups indicated a total fertility of 5.0 estimated from the average fertility of the women in the age group 45–49 (Basu and Jindal, 1990).

Basu and Kshatriya (1989) studied the fertility and mortality trends among the Didh Kharia of Sundergarh District in Orissa. They reported that the estimated total fertility, crude birth rate, crude death rate and infant mortality rate were 5.39, 38.5, 11.80 and 102.4, respectively. All these demographic indicators showed higher values than the Indian national population level. In an another study, Basu and Kshatriya (1989) reported the fertility and mortality estimates on the basis of demographic analysis of genealogical data collected from 792 households of the four tribal populations, namely, Muria, Maria, Bhattras and Halba from Bastar District of undivided Madhya Pradesh. The results of the study indicated that total fertility rates (TFR) were 5.64, 6.00, 5.95 and 5.89, respectively, for the four groups which were higher than the state rural non-tribal population and Indian national population and was in accordance with high fertility levels among the tribal. The study groups showed higher mortality among males than females. A very high rate of infant mortality was observed among males Bhattras (148.56) followed by Murias (123.25), whereas Marias (85.44) and Halbas (92.78) from the same area displayed lower infant mortality rate.

Sociologically speaking high fertility and mortality owe immensely to the women's social situation in a given family structure where motherhood has been designated as a high social value, that is, having children gives women status and respect. So women are proud of their child-bearing capacity. Apart from this, children are also valued for the help and care they may provide for the family, by working even at an early age. Children when grow up provide security to their old parents.

Moreover, the high rate of fertility and mortality are also due to low level of education and income, lack of knowledge of family planning methods, importance of small size, poor medical facilities and lack of proper drinking water (Pandey, 1990)

NUTRITIONAL DEFICIENCY AMONG MOTHERS

The nutritional problems of different tribal communities located at various stages of development were full of obscurities and very little scientific information on dietary habits and nutrition status was available due to lack of systematic and comprehensive research investigations. Malnutrition was common and greatly affected the ability to resist infection which led to chronic illness and in the post-weaning period led to permanent brain impairment.

Good nutrition is an essential requirement throughout life and is particularly vital to women in terms of their health and work. Nutritional anaemia was a major problem for women in India and more so in rural and tribal belt. In developing countries, it was estimated that at least half of the non-pregnant and two-thirds of the pregnant women were anaemic (UN Report, 1984). Moreover, in the case of tribal women, the situation is very severe as 64.9 per cent of the tribal women are anaemic in comparison to 51.8 per cent (NHDR, 2001). Moreover, the situation is very grim in some of the states like Bihar (82.1 per cent), West Bengal (80.6 per cent), Orissa (74.7 per cent) and Madhya Pradesh (70.30 per cent) which show very high anaemic incidence among tribal women. The situation was particularly serious in view of the fact that both rural and tribal women have a heavy work load and anaemia has profound effect on their psychological and physical health. Anaemia lowered resistance to fatigue, affected working capacity under conditions of stress and increased susceptibility to other diseases. Maternal malnutrition which is quite common among the tribal women is also a serious health problem, especially for those having many pregnancies too closely spaced, and reflects the complex socio-economic factors that affect their overall situation.

MATERNAL MORTALITY

Childbearing imposed additional health needs and problems on women, physically, psychologically and socially. The complications of pregnancy and of childbirth and of illegally induced abortions in areas where environmental and health conditions were adverse resulted in large number of female deaths (UN Report, 1984). In India, the maternal mortality has increased from 424 maternal deaths per 100,000 live births to 540 maternal deaths per 100,000 live births (NFHS-II, 1998–1999). Poor nutritional status along with its concomitant problems of poor body weight, poor weight gain during pregnancy and low haemoglobin levels was one of the primary underlying causes of maternal mortality in India. More maternal deaths occurred in India in one week than in all of Europe in one year; generally malnourishment and poor medical facilities that cause unfavourable social conditions were the major underlying causes for high maternal mortality in India. Nutritional anaemia, as a serious problem in pregnancy, affected 50 per cent of the women of childbearing age in South East Asia (Shiva, 1992). The situation was all the more aggravated among women in the tribal belt of India because of the prevailing magic-religious and socio-cultural practices.

Maternal mortality was reported to be high among various tribal groups but no exact data could be collected. The main causes of maternal mortality were found to be unhygienic and primitive practices for parturition. For example, it was observed that among the Kuttiya Kondhs the delivery was conducted by the mother herself in half squatting position holding a rope tied from the roof of the hut (Basu, 1990). This helped her in applying pressure to deliver the child. In complicated labour, obviously it might lead to maternal as well as child mortality. Similar crude birth practices were found to exist in other tribal groups like the Kharias, Gonds, Santhals, etc.

In general, the high maternal mortality rate is prevalent mainly due to the poor socio-economic condition of the tribal community, which makes women vulnerable to the health risks associated with bearing children in quick succession. Pregnancy and breastfeeding make big nutritional demands that the tribal women are hardly able to fulfil. Undernourished women are more likely to have spontaneous abortion, still births or babies with low birth weights (below 2.5 kg) whose chances of survival are thereby reduced.

The poor access to health facilities meant that most deliveries are continuing to take place at home under unhygienic condition attended by relatives or traditional birth attendants (TBAs). But culturally, birthing is considered unclean or polluting process; TBAs are not only accorded low social status, but also lack in proper training. So, they are unable to perform many of the tasks expected of them by modern medical standards.

SEXUALLY TRANSMITTED DISEASES

Infections of the female genital tract were numerous and widespread. They constituted a large part of morbidity among women, contributing to a continuous and physically draining fatigue. These infections were closely related to inappropriate care or poor hygiene in connection with child birth, abortion or menstruation. They included the Sexually Transmitted Diseases (STDs) which were most prevalent in the tribal areas. These infections were often untreated as they were difficult to diagnose and would even lead to infertility. Venereal Disease Research Laboratory (VDRL) test, a very sensitive test to diagnose if a person is suffering from syphilis or not, was found to be positive in 17.12 per cent cases (relative in dilution of 1.8 or more) of polyandrous Jaunsaris of Chakrata, Dehradun. Out of 17 per cent, 9.92 per cent were found among the Santhals of Mayurbhanj District, Orissa; 8.90 per cent cases (relatively in dilution of 1.8 or more) of VDRL were observed, out of which 4.99 per cent were females and 3.91 per cent were males.

The prevalence of STD was also reported to be high in the polyandrous Toda tribal group of Nilgiri hills. While conducting a morbidity study among the Kondh tribe of Phulbani District, Orissa, Swain et al. (1990) found syphilis (10 per cent) in Desia Kondhs (reactive in dilution 1.8 or more), whereas it was not diagnosed among the primitive Kuttiya Kondh tribal group. The presence of STD was also reported in Andamanese tribal groups of Madhya Pradesh, Rajasthan and Mysore.

The rampant incidence of STD is mainly determined by socio-cultural and economical reasons than by individual behaviour. As women are valued for marrying and remaining married, bearing children, caring for their families, placing men's and children interests above their own and deferring to men's authority, they have little say in the decisions regarding sex and reproductive health, e.g., whether or not to have children or whether to breastfeed or bottle-feed a child. Moreover, for young women, societal norms increase the risk of infections. As they are not expected to learn about sex and others decide when and whom a woman will marry, reproductive health services, preventive or curative. are often inaccessible to young people. Child marriages and female circumcision are still common practices that increase the risk of STDs.

Finally, due to the unavailability and lack of comprehensive studies, there have been many constraints at work while analysing the empirical health scenario of the tribes in India. Nevertheless, we can safely conclude that the health indicators of tribes, in general, and women, in particular, are pointing towards an alarming situation. Although sex ratio among tribes is not as alarming as the national average, situations regarding MMR, nutritional intake, morbidity and literacy are very dismal. As per the available data on tribal women, the incidence of anaemia is also highest.

WOMEN AND THEIR TREATMENT SYSTEM

Important aspects of the Santhals' system of cure are related to the belief of witchcrafts and sorcery. For the Santhals, witchcraft possesses serious threat to life and well-being. Witches undermine the security of people through invisible attacks. In fact, a witch is not only considered as an enemy of the entire society but also as a criminal, murderer, robber, etc. (Archer, 1979). Some scholars attributed the rampant occurrence of witchcraft and human sacrifice to the lack of modern medical facilities. For instance, Nityanand Das (1979) claims that these practices are mainly prevalent due to lack of modern medical facilities, because mining and industrial areas have adequate medical facilities they witness low levels of witchcraft practices. Other sees witchcraft as an outcome of religious isolation or ritual exclusion of women in the Santhal society (Culshaw, 2004). An important consequence of witchcraft practice which is quite oppressive to the Santhal women is the witch hunt. Witches, which are invariably women, are killed either by ticking their neck with axe or by strangulation through rope or cloth. Rout (1979) gives a succinct account of various incidence of witch hunt in Mayurbhanj where a man killed his step mother on the suspicion that she had eaten his sons. In another incident, an old woman of Kunjakacha in Bisoi Police Station was suspected to be a man-eating witch. In another case, a young widow Sita Benea of Pitijahari Village in Bisoi Police Station was suspected to be a witch and was murdered by 'Hira Naek' and Singa Naek'. In fact, all these witch hunts are said to be well supported by the entire society, and therefore, after killing a witch not only the murderer, but also the people living in that area are supposed to feel safe and secured.

For the purpose of cure and diagnosis of the sufferings from these bad forces, two types of healers are present in the Santhal society. One is *Ojha* and another in the *Sakha*. Both enjoy considerable prestige in the society for their proficiency in detecting witches and curing diseases and other related ailments. However, there is a basic difference between these two figures in terms of their working domain. An Ojha is sought mainly to cure the sufferings at personal level, but Sakha is approached when the problem is at societal or entire village level, i.e., when the natural catastrophe affects the village and inflicts the existence of people. There is no restriction for pursuing these two professions of Ojha and Sakha. Anyone can become an Ojha or Sakha by undergoing certain rites and rituals (Rout, 1979). The Ojha and Sakha work as an agent to safeguard the society from evil forces of the witches by diagnosing diseases and sickness. They are held responsible to cure those diseases caused by witchcraft by means of divination and prescribe the various preventive measures to curtail this. They are also believed to have power towards off malevolent spirits, evil-eyes and safeguard peoples' health and happiness. Not only the Santhals believe in witchcraft and the power of supernatural forces in determining health and well-being, but also other tribes in the state share similar belief. The Asur and Sauria-Paharia tribes have their own tradition of etiology concerning health disorder. According to them, illness is any sort of disorder in the body which makes a person incapable of performing normal activities. As far as healing processes are concerned, it has been noticed that what is spiritually caused must be treated spiritually through the agency of magico-religious specialists. Traditional healer's help is sought for treating various kinds of diseases. They provide herbal medicines as well. But the main method is to drive away the disease by magical enchantment and other magico-religious treatments, which include sacrifice of fowls and propitiation of the particular disease-causing deity. Thus, the knowledge of medicinal value of herbs is an essential feature of the traditional healer (Elwin, 2002). Another tribe, Baiga is completely unaware of the notion of natural infection or contagion. For them, disease has nothing to do with dirt, contaminated water or food. Rather it is always with the acts of witches or evil spirits. However, the Baiga have developed a fairly elaborate theory of venereal disease. In addition, although the Baiga do understand the link between disease and its natural causes, a new awareness appears to be emerging, as when they say that fever is caused by drinking a lot of water when you are cold (Elwin, 2002). In most of the cases, causes of diseases are traceable to some supernatural agency like the *bhoot*, *churelin* and *saksa*. In addition to this, Baiga life is heavily influenced by the ideas of witchcraft. Although many diseases and disasters are believed to be caused by the hostility of unseen forces, the majority of evils are attributed to witchcraft. When illness strikes a family a magician called *Gunia* is required to carry out the diagnosis. After diagnosing the nature and cause of disease, the Gunia proceeds to initiate various remedies to cure. These remedies include offering, breaking the power of witches, the use of mantra, etc. (Elwin, 2002).

CONCLUSION

In general, health is a function not only of medical care, but also of the overall integrated development of social, cultural, economic, educational and political. To understand the health of any community, it is necessary to unfold the heath practices and behaviours of that community. Women's health is mediated by lack of power, lower status, discrimination, lack of knowledge, illiteracy, biased cultural practices based on patriarchy a lack of safe and empathetic services. The status of tribal women has gone down from good to worse as a result of social change and this in turn affected their health. Female literacy is also quite lower as compared to males and as compared to overall female literacy rate of general population which translated into less understanding of healthy life. Malnutrition is common among tribal women and affects the ability to resist infection. Anaemia is quite common among tribal women, which also results into high maternal mortality rate. Infections of the female genital tract were numerous and widespread and form a large proportion of morbidity. Further, the treatment process among tribal women is based on belief pattern of witchcraft and sorcery.

REFERENCES

Ali, A. (1995). 'Health and nutritional status of women in Orissa and their empowerment', in Bhupinder Singh and Neeti Mohanty (eds.), *Tribal Health in India,* New Delhi: Inter India Publications.

Archer, W.G. (1979). 'The Santhal', in J. Troisi (ed.), *The Santhals: Readings in Tribal Life,* Vol. I, New Delhi: Indian Social Institute.

Basu, S. (1996). 'Health and socio-cultural correlatives in tribal communities', in R.S. Mann (ed.), *Tribes in India: Ongoing Challenges,* New Delhi: M.D. Publications, pp. 207–220.

Basu, S. and G. Kshatriya (1989). 'Fertility and Mortality in Tribal Population of Bastar District, Madhya Pradesh in India', *Biology and Society,* 6: 100–112.

Basu, S.K. and A. Jindal (1990). 'Genetic and socio-cultural determinants of tribal health: A primitive Kuttiya tribal groups of Phulbani District, Orissa', ICSSR Final Report, NIHFW.

Census of India (2001). Government of India, New Delhi.

Chaudhuri, B. (1992). 'Cultural dimensions of health: A study of West Bengal villages', in Budhadeb Chaudhuri (ed.), *Religion, Ritual and Festivals,* New Delhi: Inter India Publications.

Chaudhuri, B. (1994). 'Social and environmental dimensions of tribal health', in Salil Basu (ed.), *Tribal Health in India*, New Delhi: Manak Publications.

Chauhan, A. (1990). *Tribal Women and Social Change in India*, Etawah: AC Brothers.

Chitrey, D. (1976). 'The Concept of Essential Amino Acid in Human Nutrition: A Need for Reassessment', *Indian Journal of Nutrition, Dietal*, 13: 101.

Culshaw, W.J, (2004). *The Tribal Heritage: A Study of Santhals*, New Delhi: Gyan Publishing House.

Das, N. (1979). 'A brief note on the practice of witchcraft among the Santhals of Mayurbhanj', in J. Troisi (ed.), *The Santhals: Readings in Tribal Life*, Vol. I, New Delhi: Indian Social Institute.

Dhebar, U.N. (1961). *Report of Schedule Areas and Scheduled Tribes Commission*, New Delhi: Government of India.

Elwin, V. (2002). *The Baiga*, New Delhi: Gyan Publishing House.

Jejeebhoy, S.J. and Z.A. Sathar (2001). 'Women's Autonomy in India and Pakistan: The Influence of Region and Religion', *Population Development Review*, 27: 687–712.

Mahapatra, L.K. and J. Das (1990). 'Nutritional ecosystem of Orissa tribal', in B. Chaudhuri (ed.), *Cultural and Environmental Dimension on Health*, New Delhi: Inter India Publication.

Mohanty, N. (1995). 'Area of concern in tribal women's health', in Bhupinder Singh and Neeti Mohanti (eds.), *Tribal Health in India*, New Delhi: Inter India Publications.

National Family Health Survey (NFHS)-II (1998–1999). Mumbai: International Institute of Population Sciences and ORC Macro.

Nongbri, T. (2003). *Development, Ethnicity and Gender: Selected Essays on Tribes in India*, Jaipur: Rawat Publications.

Pandey, A.K. (1990). 'Ecology and Tribal Demography: A Comparative Study of Idu and Digaru Mishmis of Arunachal Pradesh', Ph.D. thesis, Delhi University, Delhi.

Rout, S.P. (1979). 'The Santhals', in J. Troisi (ed.), *The Santhals: Readings in Tribal Life*, Vol. I, New Delhi: Indian Social Institute.

Shiva, M. (1992). 'Women and health: State of India's health', in Alok Mukhopadhyaya (ed.), *State of India's Health*, New Delhi: Voluntary Health Association of India.

Singh, B. (1996). 'Factors influencing health of tribal population groups', in Salil Basu (ed.), *Tribal Health in India*, New Delhi: Manak Publication, pp. 40–56.

Singh, J.P, N.N. Vyas and R.S. Mann (1988). *Tribal Women and Development*, Jaipur: Rawat Publications.

UN Report (1984). *Health Status of Women, Improving Concepts and Methods of Statistics and Indicators on the Situation of Women, Studies in Methods*. Series F.No.33.

CHAPTER 8

REPRODUCTIVE HEALTH STATUS OF BHIL WOMEN IN AN URBAN SETTING

Rahul Banerjee and Subhadra Khaperde

A sixteen-years-old unmarried Bhil tribal girl from a slum in Indore city in Madhya Pradesh was recently taken to a quack doctor for an abortion when she was five months pregnant. The quack gave her some potion to drink and also pressed her lower abdomen with his hands continuously and aborted the foetus. Later on after coming home she began bleeding profusely and had to be rushed to a government hospital where the doctors removed her uterus and saved her. This horrendous incident on analysis brings out the following serious obstacles that prevent poor urban tribal women from successfully addressing their reproductive health problems:

1. A taboo on discussing reproductive health problems unless matters go out of control.
2. A taboo on discussing sexuality issues with adolescents leading to unwanted pregnancies among unmarried girls.
3. The lack of access to good and certified reproductive health treatment.

It would be profitable to review the historical development of the women's health sector in India to gain an understanding of the structural reasons that have given rise to this alarming situation in Indore.

CAUSE OF REPRODUCTIVE HEALTH PROBLEMS

Current thinking among feminists broadly defines the discipline of reproductive and sexual health as the social and clinical study of those problems and diseases that arise from the social asymmetries influencing human sexuality and reproduction. Specifically, a reproductive health approach has been defined as that which 'enables women, including adolescents, everywhere to regulate their own fertility safely and effectively by conceiving when they desire, terminating unwanted pregnancies and carrying wanted pregnancies to term; to remain free of disease, disability or death associated with reproduction or sexuality and to bear and raise healthy children' (Germain and Ordway, 1989). In reality, however, this ideal state of affairs does not prevail anywhere in the world, and especially in India most women have to suffer from serious reproductive and sexual health problems. Feminist sociology has pinpointed the dominance of men in society as the prime reason for this and termed this phenomenon as *patriarchy* (Lerner, 1986). Analysing all the main institutions of society like the family, marriage, kinship groups, media, religious hierarchies and the state, they have shown that all these play a role in maintaining the overall patriarchal structure of society. Over thousands of years, this structure has become so well entrenched that to most people, including women, it seems quite natural instead of being the social construct that it is.

As a result traditionally women have had to work more, they have been denied the right to inheritance of property, they have had to assume total responsibility for house work and the care of children and the elderly and this work is not counted as of being of any economic value, they have had to go underfed and have been subjected to domestic and external violence of the worst kind. As a consequence of this secondary status, women have to bear more babies to ensure that there are male progeny who will inherit the property and provide security in old age. Along with this there is social control over the sexuality of women so that men can be assured that the children born to their wives are truly theirs and so ensure the purity of their descent. Naturally, all this affects the overall health of women and especially their reproductive and sexual health. Since there is a taboo on the discussion of these issues, women have to suffer their troubles in silence and this leads to mental problems. Thus there is a deafening culture of silence surrounding women's reproductive and sexual health problems (Dixon-Mueller and Wasserheit, 1991). The biggest irony is that the menstrual cycle which is an integral part of the reproductive process is considered in the prevailing patriarchal system to be the cause of various negative things and has been given a dirty connotation in India. This affects the ability of women to maintain personal hygiene and results in their being afflicted by various diseases of the reproductive tract.

Over the years, a substantial number of Bhil tribal people from the neighbouring districts of Alirajpur, Jhabua, Dhar, Barwani, Khargone, Khandwa and Dewas have come and settled down in the slums of Indore in search of livelihoods. The condition of the tribal women in these slums is very bad due to a lack of toilet facilities and privacy and the prevalence of insanitary living conditions. This paper will briefly explore the history of women's health in India and then describe the reproductive health situation of tribal women in slums in Indore in detail before proposing ways in which it can be improved.

HISTORY OF WOMEN'S HEALTH IN INDIA

Analysing the history of health policy in India, Prakash has shown how patriarchal social structures have resulted in the marginalization of women in the health system in this country (Prakash, 1984). Right from the time in the late nineteenth century, when for the first time women's health problems were addressed the concentration has been on the provision of maternal health services like safe delivery practices. Even though as a consequence of the efforts of Pandita Ramabai and Lady Dufferin pregnant women began to get access to institutional health services, the general reproductive health and associated psychological health problems of women remained unaddressed. Thus, continuously ante-natal and post-natal care has been provided and the problems of the reproductive tract and sexuality have been neglected. Health policies have been silent about the negative effects of patriarchy on the physical and mental health of women. Thus it is no surprise that the sex ratio which was 972 females to 1,000 males in 1911 had declined to 914 by 2011. Matters have been compounded by the use of pre-natal diagnostic techniques to abort female foetuses and this is done mostly by higher income groups, indicating that patriarchy is prevalent throughout society irrespective of various divisions (Mari Bhat and Francis Zavier, 2007).

The report submitted by the Health Survey Committee headed by Sir John Bhore in 1946 did stress that the whole gamut of health problems of women should be addressed instead of just concentrating on safe motherhood, but there was no specific mention of the problems or reproductive health and sexuality and the ways in which these could be solved. Immediately after independence, the economists engaged in the preparation of the First Five Year Plan did not consider the work put in by women inside the home to be of a productive nature and so made no allocation for the overall health of women and concentrated only on providing for safe motherhood. The stress on maternal health over the first half of the twentieth century did produce a number of female doctors and nurses who were also abreast of the latest developments in reproductive health, but only the women of rich households had access to the benefits of this knowledge and the vast majority of poor women in this country remained without access to quality reproductive health services.

Government policies for women largely centred around putting most of the responsibility for family planning onto them. Completely ignoring the ground reality that in the patriarchal social structure which prevails in India, there is a preference for male children which forces women to bear more children and so the thrust of the programme should be towards mitigating patriarchy the government family planning programme concentrated on doing sterilizations of women given the reluctance of men to get sterilized irrationally fearing a loss of their sexual powers. Thus in addition to the suffering from poor reproductive health, women had to shoulder the burden of family planning also. All kinds of dubious experiments involving injectables were carried out during this campaign (FWH, 1995).

Consequently, when a joint study group of the Indian Council of Medical Research and the Indian Council of Social Science Research conducted a review of women's health in 1980, it found that the main reasons behind high maternal mortality rates and the decline of the sex ratio were the malnutrition and poor reproductive health of most women. The group also averred that this had happened because the government had looked at women only as prospective mothers, neglecting their exploitation within and outside the home in a highly patriarchal social setting. However, despite this scathing report there was no improvement in the health policies with regard to women. This despite the fact that the government had endorsed the declaration of the First World Women's Conference organized by the United Nations in Mexico in 1975 which exhorted both governments and the people at large to 'recognize the health needs of women of all ages and situations, those with children, girls who were yet to reach child bearing age and women who had passed the child bearing age range and also those living singly or as couples, give women the right to choose the number of children they wish to have and also the spacing between them and prevent any such discrimination and violence that is against the welfare of women, that prevents them from taking active part in the social, economic and political development of their societies and that violates their human rights' (Whitaker, 1975).

SEARCH FOR A SOLUTION

The first effective steps towards improving the status of women's reproductive health in India were taken by Non-Governmental Organizations (NGOs) in the 1980s. The pioneer in this respect is the NGO SEARCH in Gadhchiroli District of Maharashtra. In the course of their work among the Gond indigenous people, they found that all women were not reporting their gynaecological problems properly. So they decided to conduct a detailed study which has now become a landmark in this field (Bang, 1989). The study revealed that 55 per cent of the women surveyed admitted to some gynaecological problem or other, but when they were tested clinically this proportion rose to 92 per cent. The most disturbing finding was that only 8 per cent of these women had come to the NGO for treatment of their problems, indicating a tremendous level of reticence to confront their serious reproductive health problems. Many other studies later have confirmed these disturbing findings (Jeejeebhoy, 1997).

The decade of the 1990s saw a concerted effort by feminists all over the world to improve this sorry state of affairs. The basis of this campaign was the establishment of the reproductive and sexual rights of women (Correa and Petchesky, 1994). According to this view, there are four aspects of reproductive and sexual rights:

1. *Bodily Integrity* – All women have the right to protect their bodies and have control over them. Thus women cannot be deprived of their sexual and productive abilities by men or the state and they cannot be made to use these abilities according to the latter's whims and fancies.
2. *Personhood* – Women will take their own decisions regarding reproduction and sexual behaviour and nobody can interfere in this.
3. *Equality* – Women are equal to men in all respects and so the gender division of labour under which women have been given the work of exclusively tending the children and the elderly and also doing housework has to be abolished and men should also take up these responsibilities. Apart from this, women's health issues should be better addressed on par with those of men.
4. *Diversity* – The differences arising from difference in values, culture, religion, class, nationality and the like should be respected.

The International Conference on Population and Development organized by the United Nations in Cairo in 1994 and the World Women's Conference in Beijing in 1995 finally led to the adoption of this feminist viewpoint and an appeal was made to all governments to tailor their women's health programmes to meet these parameters. In consonance with this, the Government of India made a revolutionary change in its population policies and replaced the sterilization target-oriented family planning programme with a more comprehensive reproductive and overall health programme in which the participation of women was made mandatory (DoFW, 1996).

This new programme charted out a major role for NGOs assuming that the government machinery was incapable of ensuring the participation of women. As a result, throughout India a number of NGOs became active in this field and adopted the reproductive and sexual rights approach to women's health. One such is the Stree Hitkarini in Mumbai, working among poor slum women. In order to assess the extent of the reproductive health problems of the women in its area of work before embarking on a programme of amelioration, this NGO conducted a reproductive health survey among 750 slum women. This study too revealed that 73 per cent of the women suffered from some reproductive health problem or other and did not seek any remedy for them (Parikh et al., 1996).

However, since NGOs have only a limited reach, they have not been able to make much of an impact on a national scale, and so even after a decade and a half of the adoption of the new reproductive health approach, the status of women has not improved much because in practice the government health system continues to neglect women's health needs. The National Family Health Survey III has confirmed this (IIPS, 2007). Given in Table 1 are data for selected characteristics from NFHS III for the whole of India and they are quite disappointing.

Table 1 Selected Reproductive Health Characteristics of Indian Women

Characteristic	Female	Male
Adults with BMI indicating acute under nutrition (%)	33.0	28.0
Adults with anaemia (%)	56.2	24.3
Mothers with complete ante-natal care (%)	50.7	
Mothers with complete post-natal care (%)	36.4	
Institutional deliveries (%)	40.7	
Women 20–24 yrs married before 18 years of age (%)	44.5	
Women15–19 yrs who were pregnant/had child (%)	16.0	
Women who have suffered domestic violence (%)	37.2	
Total fertility rate (%)	2.7	

Source: National Family Health Survey III conducted by International Institute of Population Sciences, Mumbai.

A comparative study of the data from the first, second and third National Family Health Surveys has come up with an extremely disturbing finding (Shrinivasan et al., 2007). Even though the spending on family planning by the Government of India after the initiation of the new reproductive health approach in 1996 in the years 1998–2004 has been double than that in the earlier period from 1992 to 1998, the improvement rate in the case of many characteristics given in Table 1 has been less during the later period. This clearly means that not enough is being done to tackle the deleterious effects of patriarchy which is at the root of most of the reproductive and sexual health problems faced by women.

SITUATION IN INDORE

The tribal women living in slums in Indore have largely remained outside the purview of qualified medical help and have had to rely mostly on quacks as borne out by the story of the girl related in the beginning. Thus it has been left to NGOs to deliver what little service they can to them. The most important of such efforts was the five-year project undertaken by the Urban Health Resource Centre, New Delhi, with funding from United States Agency for International Development (USAID) in collaboration with five local NGOs of Indore (Agarwal and Bhanot, 2004). The main thrust of this programme named the Environmental Health Programme was on involving the community to accessing the government's reproductive and child health services and by doing so improving the health of women and children so as to reduce the infant, child and maternal mortality rates. Eighty-seven Community-Based Organizations (CBOs) were formed in the slums peopled mostly by tribals and dalits and these were then grouped together to form nine lead CBOs. Apart from creating health awareness among the people, the NGOs also hold monthly health camps in which doctors did checkups and provided medicines to the women. However, this programme too following the general trend in India provided only help for maternal and child health and skirted the larger issue of reproductive and sexual health and patriarchy. Indeed, the programme had initially begun with interventions only in child health and took up maternal health also because it found that this was imperative if child health was to be improved (Agarwal et al., 2005).

Another NGO, Family Planning Association of India, also provides reproductive health services to poor urban women. However, this organization too has not done any work on the issues of reproductive and sexual health of women and the larger issue of patriarchy which gives rise to problems in this area. There are a number of other NGOs that work on the livelihood aspects of slum dwellers and their rights as citizens to proper housing, civic amenities and other benefits. One such NGO, Deenbandhu Samajik Sansthan, did an extensive study of the vulnerability of the slum dwellers in Indore in 1997–1998 (George et al., 1998). This study found that 63 per cent of the population of Indore live in slums and 50 per cent of these slum dwellers live in houses of less than 35 sq. metre area. Seventy-eight per cent of these people have only kuccha housing and 70 per cent have no ration cards. Forty-three per cent of the households do not have access to any toilets either individual or community and have to defecate in the open. Eighty-eight per cent of the households depend on public taps for their water supply. None of the women surveyed at that time had any access to government health services and relied wholly on quacks.

Thus, it is clear that the status of reproductive and sexual health and rights of poor tribal women in Indore is very poor. Consequently, there is an

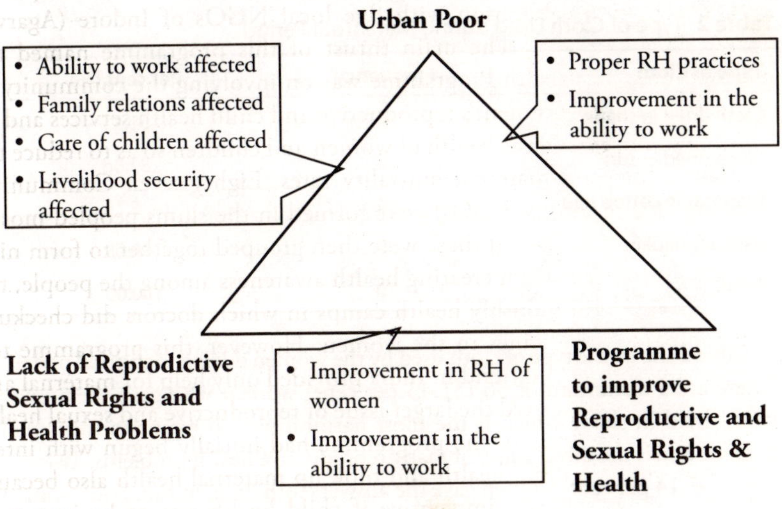

Figure 1. Reproductive Health and Rights Framework.

urgent need for introducing a participatory reproductive and sexual rights and health programme for urban poor women as depicted in the framework in Figure 1. This framework focuses on the reproductive and sexual rights and health problems of urban poor women and shows how their lack affects them. A programme to improve this situation will impact positively on health, social and economic status. Given the inability of the government health system to initiate such a process, there is a need for a larger number of NGOs to step into this dark and neglected area as it is directly related to the well-being of half of the nation's population.

PROGRAMME OF ACTION FOR INDORE

A pilot programme was started along these lines within the Urban Health Resource Centre (UHRC) project with one NGO, Bharatiya Gramin Mahila Sangh, and its female para health workers in the slums of Bajrangnagar, Martandnagar and Jeetnagar. The para health workers were first given a basic training so as to make them aware of the patriarchal social relations that contribute to reproductive health problems and also to make them capable of taking the women into confidence regarding their problems. A survey was conducted in the slums and the crucial data related to gynaecological health are presented in the following paragraphs.

Table 2 Type of Cloth Used during Menstrual Period

Type of Cloth	Frequency	Per cent (%)
Cloth dried in shade	36	51.43
Cloth dried in sun	23	32.86
Disposable cotton pad	4	5.71
Sanitary napkin	7	10.00
Total	70	100.00

Table 2 shows the type of cloth used by the women during menstrual period. There are a maximum of 36 (51.43 per cent) women who gave the answer cloth dried in shade which is the most harmful way to maintain menstrual hygiene and is the direct cause of many reproductive health problems. Twenty-three (37.14 per cent) women gave the answer cloth dried in sun. Four women (5.71 per cent) gave the answer that they use disposable cotton pad. Seven women (10 per cent) gave the answer that they use sanitary napkins.

Table 3 Reason for Using Type of Cloth during Menstrual Hygiene

Reason	Frequency	Per cent (%)
Healthy way	23	32.86
Force of circumstance	18	25.71
Custom	15	21.43
Space available to dry in sun	8	11.43
Affordable	6	8.56
Total	70	100.00

Table 3 shows the reason for use of type of cloth during menstrual period by women. The maximum of 23 women (32.86 per cent) said that it is a healthy practice. Eighteen women (25.71 per cent) said that the situation forces them to use the type they have used. Fifteen women (21.43 per cent) said that they are following the established custom. Eight women (11.43 per cent) said that there is space available to dry cloth in the sun. Six women or 8.56 per cent said that they can afford sanitary napkins. Thus, it is clear that there is a serious lack of awareness among the women regarding the ill effects of using the same cloth dried in the shade during menstruation and they are also constrained by lack of space and patriarchal customs.

Table 4 shows the prevalence of reproductive health problems among women. The most prevalent problem is that of waist pain reported by 24 women (24.24 per cent) of all reported problems. This is followed by haziness of sight by 16 women (16.16 per cent) of all reported problems. Lower abdomen pain was reported by 12 women (12.12 per cent) of all problems. A total of 26 women (26.26 per cent) of all problems were regarding menstruation. The average morbidity of the sample is Number of Disease Sufferers/Number of Respondents = 1.41. The number of women who did not report any problems is 27. Thus, the average morbidity of the disease-prone women is 2.3.

Table 5 shows the reason for Reproductive Health Problem (RHP) of women. Seventeen (24.29 per cent) women said physical weakness is the cause of RHP. Two (2.86 per cent) women said delivery at home is the cause of RHP. Four (5.71 per cent) women said lack of resources is the cause of RHP. The maximum of 23 (32.86 per cent) women said all of the above causes are responsible for RHP. Twenty-four women (34.29 per cent) did not respond.

Table 4 Type of Reproductive Health Problems

Problems	Frequency	Per cent (%)
Hazy sight	16	16.16
Dizziness	1	1.01
Waist pain	24	24.24
Lower abdomen pain	12	12.12
White discharge	5	5.05
Itching in vagina	1	1.01
Burning in urination	2	2.02
Uncontrolled urination	7	7.07
Continuous cough	3	3.03
Prolapse of uterus	2	2.02
Less menstruation	7	7.07
Irregular menstruation	7	7.07
Excessive menstruation	5	5.05
Pain during menstruation	7	7.07

Table 5 Reasons for Reproductive Health Problems

Reason	Frequency	Per cent (%)
Physical weakness	17	24.29
Delivery at home	2	2.86
Lack of resources	4	5.71
All of the above	23	32.86
Not responded	24	34.29
Total	70	100.00

Table 6 Awareness about Reproductive Health Care

	Frequency	Per cent (%)
Yes	15	21
No	55	79
Total	70	100

Table 6 shows the level of awareness about reproductive health care of the women. Fifteen (21 per cent) women said Yes as the answer for awareness about reproductive health care and 55 (79 per cent) women No as the answer for this. There is thus a critical lack of awareness among the women about reproductive health care.

Table 7 Techniques of Reproductive Health Care

Techniques	Frequency	Per cent (%)
Good and adequate food	1	1.43
Immediate treatment of problem	2	2.86
Not to be tense	6	8.57
Maintain personal hygiene	1	1.43
All the above	25	35.71
Not responded	35	50.00
Total	70	100.00

Table 7 shows the knowledge of techniques of reproductive health of women. One (1.43 per cent) woman who answered that good and adequate food is necessary for reproductive health care of women. Two (2.86 per cent) women said that immediate treatment of the problem is necessary for reproductive health care of women. Six (8.57 per cent) women said that not to be tense is necessary for reproductive health care of every woman. One (1.43 per cent) woman said that maintaining personal hygiene is necessary for reproductive health care of women. The maximum of 25 (35.71 per cent) women said that all the above techniques of reproductive health care are necessary. Thirty-five women or 50 per cent did not respond. This is once again indicative of a lack of awareness among the women.

Table 8 Knowledge of Government Health Services for Women

	Frequency	Per cent (%)
Yes	22	31.43
No	48	68.57
Total	70	100.00

Table 8 shows the knowledge of government health services among the women. There are 22 (34.29 per cent) women who said Yes regarding the knowledge of government health services for women. The maximum of 48 (65.71 per cent) women said No.

Table 9 shows whether the government health staff attend to the respondents when they visit the hospital. Fifteen (21.43 per cent) women said Yes, while the maximum of 55 (78. 57 per cent) women said No.

Table 9 Whether Government Health Staff Attend When Respondents Visit Hospitals

	Frequency	Per cent (%)
Yes	15	21.43
No	55	78.57
Total	70	100.00

Table 10 Whether Free Medicines and Tests Availed by Respondents from Hospitals

	Frequency	Per cent (%)
Yes	12	17.14
No	58	82.86
Total	70	100.00

Table 10 shows whether free medicines and tests are provided by government hospitals when respondents visit them. Twelve (17.14 per cent) women said they have got free medicines and tests when they visited government hospitals for their problems. The maximum of 58 (82.86 per cent) women said No for this.

All the women were then motivated to attend the camps for clinical checkups by the doctors, regardless of whether they reported having problems or not. Forty-one women agreed to be examined clinically. Special arrangements were made to ensure privacy in the camps so that the women felt comfortable about being examined. Medicines were prescribed and given to the women who were diagnosed with problems, and the para health workers did follow-up rounds to ensure that the women were indeed taking the medicines. The results were very encouraging as all 41 women reported improvement in their condition and agreed to attend repeat camps over three months. Thus, the intervention was very successful and both the para health workers and the women felt that for the first time they had gone through a liberating experience. Unfortunately, the UHRC project wound up just after this and so these camps could not be conducted further in Indore, even though they continue in the villages.

These camps are very easy to organize and require only about Rs. 30,000 per camp. Some organizational support is required which can easily be accessed from an NGO. The crucial input is that of the para health worker who has to prepare the women for the camps and then carry out follow-up and monitoring to ensure that they are taking the medicines. There is a cost involved in training and coordinating the para health workers which is high in the initial phases, but when more slums are included this cost will be less as it will be shared among all the slums. The important thing is to ensure continuity of the camps so that the programme gains some credibility, sustainability and impact over time and a replicable model is established. The NGO Dhas Gramin Vikas Kendra is currently implementing this programme in a pilot phase. Once a replicable model is developed, it can be disseminated widely.

REFERENCES

Agarwal, S. and A. Bhanot (2004). *Participatory Community Health Enquiry and Planning in Urban Slums*, New Delhi: Urban Health Resource Centre.

Agarwal, S., A. Bhanot, S. Kumar, S. Rao, P. Jha, M. Gupta and K. Shrivastava (2005). *Partnerships for Improving Health in Vulnerable Slums of Indore*, New Delhi: Urban Health Resource Centre.

Bang, R. (1989). '*High Prevalence of Gynaecological Diseases in Rural Indian Women*', *Lancet*, 337: 85–88.

Correa, S. and R. Petchesky (1994). 'Reproductive and sexual rights: A feminist perspective', in G. Sen, A. Germain and L. Chen (eds.), *Population Policies Reconsidered: Health, Empowerment and Rights,* Cambridge, MA: Harvard University Press.

Dixon-Mueller, R. and J. Wasserheit (1991). *The Culture of Silence: Reproductive Tract Infections among Women in the Third World*, New York: IWHC.

DoFW (1996). *Manual on Decentralised Participatory Planning in Family Welfare*, New Delhi: Department of Family Welfare, Government of India.

FWH (1995). 'Contraceptives: Our choices, their choices', in M. Karkal (ed.), *Our Lives Our Health*, New Delhi: CUIWWWC.

George, R., B. Rajeev and T. Sarwal (1998). *Poverty and Vulnerability in Indore*, New Delhi: Oxfam India Trust.

Germain, A. and J. Ordway (1989). *Population Control and Women's Health: Balancing the Scales*, New York: IWHC.

IIPS (2007). *National Family Health Survey III*, Mumbai: International Institute of Population Sciences.

Jeejeebhoy, S. (1997). 'Addressing Women's Reproductive Health Needs: Priorities for the Family Welfare Programme', *Economic and Political Weekly*, Vol. 32, No. 9 & 10.

Lerner, G. (1986). *The Creation of Patriarchy: Women and History*, New York: Oxford University Press.

Mari Bhat, P.N. and A.J. Francis Zavier (2007). 'Factors Influencing the Use of Prenatal Diagnostic Techniques and the Sex Ratio at Birth in India', *EPW*, Vol. 42, No. 24.

Parikh, I., V. Taskar, N. Dharap and V. Mulgaonkar (1996). *Gynaecological Morbidity among Women in a Bombay Slum*, Mumbai: Stri Hitkarini.

Prakash, P. (1984). 'Who controls the health of women: Health policies and the medical profession', in A. Bhaiyya and K. Bhasin (eds.), *Aspects of Women's Development*, New Delhi: FAO.

Shrinivasan, K., C. Shekhar and P. Arokiaswamy (2007). 'Reviewing Reproductive and Child Health Programme in India', *EPW*, Vol. 42, No. 27 & 28.

Whitaker, J.S. (1975). 'Women of the World: Report from Mexico City', *Foreign Affairs*, 54: 173–181.

CHAPTER 9

ELEMENTARY EDUCATION OF TRIBAL GIRLS: A SITUATIONAL ANALYSIS OF SELECTED DISTRICTS IN ODISHA

R.K. Mohanty

A woman is the full circle. Within her is the power to create, nurture and transform.

Diane Mariechild (1989)

INTRODUCTION

Tribe refers to the endogenous primordial solidarities living in close proximity to forest territories united by ties of descent from a common ancestor, community of customs and traditions, adherence to the same culture and language distinctly of their own. Accordingly, the terms like *adivasi*, *vanvasi*, *janjati* and even scheduled tribes (STs) are not found without criticisms (see Xaxa, 1999: 3589–3596). The tribes constitute the most disadvantaged section of India's population from ecological, economic and cultural points of view. Ecologically, the tribes are isolated in selected geographical area. Economically, their life and living are tied with forest and shifting cultivation. Culturally, the tribes enjoy a unique style of life characterized by a distinct language and heritage distant from modern mainstream culture. They are the bulk of the matrix of India's poverty. From the historical point of view, they have been subjected to the worst type of exploitation and social injustice. Such disadvantages are reflected in the status of their girl children affecting most specifically the educational prospects of the latter. The UNESCO survey identifies common features across the 18 countries studied, that 'the children denied schooling come from rural areas, from urban slums, and from minorities and marginal groups who are either geographically and economically isolated, culturally isolated or both. In some countries, girls can be included as one of the categories' (Ranaweera, 1989: 13).

A child is human species below 18 years of age that is in need of care of and protection because of tender age and inexperienced personality. *Webster's Dictionary* defines a girl as any female human from birth through childhood and adolescence to attainment of adulthood when she becomes a woman. The term may also be used to mean a woman in becoming. The hardest challenge to take in life is being a girl child and more so a tribal one. Discrimination, differences, dominance, disadvantage, drudgery and discrepancy are six most vitamin D deficiencies under social pathology that hamper the journey of every female from womb to tomb. Starting from her presence into her mother's womb to infancy, childhood and finally to adulthood and age, she is under the stranglehold of notorious traditions and stereotypical myths. Social disadvantage outweighs natural biological advantage of being a girl. Education plays a particularly important role as a foundation for girls' development towards adult life. It should be an intrinsic part of any strategy to address the gender-based discrimination against women and girls that remains prevalent in many societies.

This paper attempts a situational analysis of elementary education of tribal girl children in Odisha based on reports available through Child Tracking System (CTS) adopted by the District Primary Education Programme (DPEP) in the state duly triangulated through Census data, Odisha Human Development Report of 2004 and other official statistics published from time to time including the secondary literature on the subject. Reliance is placed primarily on the available literature (books, papers published in journals, documents) and research reports including the publications of various organizations. Official data include the census data of 2001, including those of 2011 were available, and the data of Odisha Primary Education Authority (OPEPA) under District Information System for Education (DISE) 2010–2011 made available through CTS. CTS is a comprehensive database of both in-school, dropout and out-of-school children in the relevant age groups. The CTS, generally an online web-enabled system, helps create a database that would track every child in a given province/district through household survey, gathering information (on educational status and other key variables) about children between 6 and 14 years age group corresponding to the basic education cycle under Sarva Siksha Abhiyan (SSA). For the purpose of comparison, situational status of ST children has been compared with that of total general category children in the selected districts of the State of Odisha. For the purpose of analysis, it has been decided to include nine tribal districts, namely, Mayurbhanj, Keonjhar, Sundargarh, Kandhamal, Kalahandi, Koraput, Malkangiri, Nawarangpur and Rayagada.

The rationale behind choosing these districts is the following: (1) The tribals of Odisha mostly inhabit the hilly regions of these districts, mainly in close proximity to forests comprising nearly more than 45 per cent of population in these districts and 60 per cent of the tribal population of the state. (2) These are the districts in which almost all of the Primitive Tribal Groups (PTGs) live for centuries, being far away from the mainstream in their relatively isolated, inaccessible, less fertile and less agriculturally productive regions of forests, hills and mountains. (3) These districts have lowest female literacy, greater gender disparity and dismal retention with high dropout rate.

Accordingly, the ambitions of this paper are principally analytically descriptive. Thus the paper divides itself into five inter-related sections. The first section sets the stage by discussing the problems relating to the objective of this study, methodological frame work adopted and the rationale thereof. The second section deals with the overall tribal scenario in the state. The third section looks at the gender dimension of education of tribal children followed by the analysis of the elementary education of tribal girl child in the selected districts through the parameters listed *supra* in the fourth section. The concluding section ends up with summarizing the analytical stakes and the actionable strengths of the issue at hand.

TRIBAL SCENARIO IN THE STATE OF ODISHA

As per 2001 Census, the ST population of the State of Odisha constitutes 22.1 per cent of the total population of the state and 9.7 per cent of the total tribal population of the country. Out of 62 STs, Khond is the most populous tribe with a population of 1,395,643 constituting 17.1 per cent of the total ST population. Gond is the second largest tribe with a population of 782,104. (Gond has 9.6 per cent share in the total ST population.) Six other tribes, namely, Santal, Kolha, Munda, Saora, Shabar and Bhottada, along with Khond and Gond constitute 64.2 per cent of the total ST population of the state. Bhumij, Bhuiya, Oraon, Paroja and Kisan have a population ranging from 248,144 to 321,592. Together, they form 18.1 per cent. Five STs, namely, Bhumia, Binjhal, Koya, Gaddava and Didayi having population in the range of 103,537 to 196,846 constitute 9 per cent of the total ST population. Remaining 44 tribes along with the generic tribes constitute the residual 8.8 per cent of the total ST population of the state. Five tribes, namely, Chenchu, Mankidi, Desua Bhumij, Ghara and Tharua, are very small groups having negligible less than 500 population (Census of India, 2010: 207).

Odisha houses 13 PTGs, but only eight STs are declared as PTGs by the Government of India. Those tribes are Juang, Bondo Poraja, Lodha, Didayi, Mankidia, Birhor, Kharia and Soura. The Registrar General and Census Commissioner of India are not publishing the figures and data (Nayak, 2010: 203) of remaining five tribal ethnic groups, namely, Kutia Khond, Dongria Khond, Lanjia Saura, Chuktia and Paudi Bhuyan. So far, development concerned with these tribal groups are as marginalized as the other eight and continue to be techno-economically backward; therefore, their demographic information deserve inclusion as primitive tribes. Table 1 gives details of tribes available in the selected districts included in this study.

Table 1 Tribes of Odisha in the Selected Districts

District	Tribes
Mayurbhanj	Santal, Kharia, Kolh, Lodha, Bathudi, Bhumija, Ho, Munda, Saunti
Keonjhar	Bhuinya, Juang, Bathudi, Gond, Kolha, Munda, Santals, Sabar, Saunti
Sundargarh	Bhuinya, Oraon, Gond, Kisan, Kharia, Munda
Kandhamal	Kondh, Gond
Kalahandi	Kondh, Bhotoda, Gond, Paraja, Sabar
Undivided Koraput	Diadyi, Koya, Kondh, Saura, Paraja, Bond, Gadaba, Bhotada, Bhumia, Gond, Omanatya

Several macro indicators of tribal development relating to education, health, employment, income and work participation point towards an adverse status of STs vis-à-vis the general population. The STs comprise a decisive segment of the poverty struck population in the State of Odisha. Development of STs has been given priority in successive Five Years Plans, and of late, huge public expenditure programmes have been directed to achieve the objectives of tribal development in Odisha. However, the outcomes of the administrative intent and legislative programme are not properly realized. The status of any social group is determined by economy – poverty, health-nutrition and literacy-education. The persistence problems of tribals in Odisha can be seen from the following Human Development Index (HDI) Report (Table 2).

The eight districts of Kalahandi, Bolangir and Koraput (KBK) region, comprising the district of Kalahandi, Nuapada, Bolangir, Sonepur, Koraput, Malkangiri, Nawarangpur and Rayagada, are considered as one

Table 2 Indicators of Human Development Index in Selected Districts of Odisha

District	% STs to Total Population	Literacy Rate	Health Index	Income Index	Literacy Index	Education Index	HDI Value	HDI Rank
Malkangiri	57.43	30.53	0.122	0.497	0.313	0.491	0.370	30
Mayurbhanj	56.60	51.91	0.782	0.489	0.524	0.647	0.639	9
Nawarangpur	55.03	33.93	0.340	0.453	0.343	0.516	0.571	26
Kandhamal	51.96	52.68	0.006	0.516	0.530	0.645	0.389	29
Rayagada	55.76	36.15	0.250	0.547	0.356	0.531	0.443	25
Sundargarh	50.19	64.86	0.692	0.618	0.652	0.740	0.683	4
Koraput	49.62	35.72	0.218	0.539	0.362	0.535	0.431	27
Keonjhar	44.50	59.64	0.340	0.547	0.598	0.704	0.530	24
Kalahandi	28.65	45.94	0.763	0.471	0.462	0.585	0.606	11

Source: Orissa Human Development Report; 2004 Compiled.

of the poorest regions not only in the state but also in the country, with about 71.40 per cent of families living below poverty line. As estimated in Odisha Human Development Report 2004, the women with any anaemia are 74.7 per cent among tribal women, which is significantly higher than that of general population (54.4 per cent) and STs (66.3 per cent). There are overwhelmingly illiterates among the tribes. When education is considered to be the heart of all development, it is evident that education scenario among STs is in a very bad shape. It is imperative to know about the gender dimension of child population scenario both for general population and for the ST community in the selected districts.

Table 3 depicts the percentage of 6–14 years ST children in comparison to total children. It is visible from Table 3 that, in Nawarangpur, Rayagada, Sundargarh and Mayurbhanj districts, the percentage of ST children to overall children is almost near to or higher than 60. However, the overall scenario of the total nine districts (54.46 per cent) is much higher than the state average of 26.80 per cent.

In terms of gender, Koraput District clearly gives a different picture, with boys being 52.42 per cent and girls being only 25.39 per cent to the overall children. This leaves scope for a lot of empirical curiosity. Among all other districts, only Mayurbhanj District shows a visible variation between boys and girls (boys being 61.7 per cent and girls being 65.52 per cent). However, it is also interesting to note that Kandhamal, Malkangiri, Nawarangpur and

Table 3 Child Population of Overall and ST Community in Selected Districts

District	6–14 yrs Overall			6–14 yrs ST			% ST to Overall		
	Boys	Girls	Total	Boys	Girls	Total	Boys	Girls	Total
Kalahandi	142,093	131,938	274,031	45,403	41,382	86,785	**31.95**	**31.36**	**31.67**
Kandhamal	76,853	73,404	150,257	43,842	42,182	86,024	**57.05**	**57.47**	**57.25**
Keonjhar	164,781	153,795	318,576	84,243	77,545	161,788	**51.12**	**50.42**	**50.78**
Koraput	115,653	109,179	224,832	60,626	27,721	88,347	**52.42**	**25.39**	**39.29**
Malkangiri	51,654	48,365	100,019	30,233	28,443	58,676	**58.53**	**58.81**	**58.66**
Mayurbhanj	204,454	193,226	397,680	126,279	126,611	252,890	**61.76**	**65.52**	**63.59**
Nawarangpur	108,760	103,451	212,211	64,206	61,946	126,152	**59.03**	**59.88**	**59.45**
Rayagada	81,181	72,051	153,232	48,086	43,143	91,229	**59.23**	**59.88**	**59.54**
Sundargarh	115,882	115,563	231,445	86,500	84,723	171,223	**74.64**	**73.31**	**73.98**
Nine districts total	**1,061,311**	**1,000,972**	**2,062,283**	**589,418**	**533,696**	**1,123,114**	**55.54**	**53.32**	**54.46**
State total	**3,331,116**	**3,157,757**	**6,488,873**	**906,846**	**832,079**	**1,738,925**	**27.22**	**26.35**	**26.80**
% to state total	**31.86**	**31.70**	**31.78**	**65.00**	**64.14**	**64.59**			

Rayagada districts have more percentage of girls in comparison to boys. These selected districts account for a total 65 per cent of the total ST students of the state (boys being 65 per cent and girls 64.14 per cent) and clearly describes the ST-dominated situations in the districts. The figure also indicates that the gender parity among the ST children in this age group pertaining to Kalahandi, Koraput, Keonjhar and Sundargarh districts is not in favour of the girls.

GENDER DIMENSION OF EDUCATION OF TRIBAL CHILDREN

Education plays a particularly important role as a foundation for girls' development towards adult life. Girls are less likely to access school, to remain in school or to achieve in education. Education helps men and women claim their rights and realize their potential in the economic, political and social arenas. It is also the single most powerful way to lift people out of poverty. Everybody has the right to education, which has been recognized since the Universal Declaration of Human Rights (UDHR) in 1948. As a minimum, the states must ensure that basic education is available, accessible, acceptable and adaptable for all. The right of girls to education is one of the most critical of all rights – because education plays an important role in enabling girls and women to secure other rights. The right to free and compulsory primary education, without discrimination and of good quality, has been reaffirmed in all major international human rights conventions. Both the Cairo and Beijing conferences affirmed this. Gender inequality in education is extreme. The Convention on the Rights of the Child and the Convention on the Elimination of All Forms of Discrimination against Women establish it as a basic human right. Millennium Development Goal 2 mandates that Universal Primary Education (UPE) be achieved by 2015 and in this respect; major components thus include 'Early Childhood Care Education', Universalization of Elementary Education (UEE), reduction in school dropout rate and promoting SSA.

At the time of adoption of the Constitution in 1950, the aim was to achieve the goal of Universalization of Elementary Education by 1960. Elementary education implies eight years of free and compulsory schooling for all ensured by the government that begins from the age of 6 to 14. This includes education at both Primary (P) and Upper Primary (UP) levels. The National Policy on Education (1987 and 1992) recommended strengthening of Early Childhood Care and Education (ECCE) programme as an essential component of human development and UEE. In 1993, the Supreme Court of India declared education up to 14 years of age to be a fundamental right of children in India.

DPEP was launched in the state in the year 1996–1997. In order to improve the literacy rate in the state, SSA has been implemented in all 30 districts with three objectives, i.e., universal enrolment, retention and quality of education. SSA is Government of India's flagship programme for achievement of UEE in a time-bound manner, as mandated by 86th Amendment to the Constitution of India, making free and compulsory education to the children of 6–14 years age group as a fundamental right. Similarly, for reduction of the gender gap and greater participation of girls in education, two special schemes, the National Programme for Education of Girls at Elementary Level (NPEGEL) launched in the state in 2003 and Kasturba Gandhi Balika Vidyalaya (KGBV) launched in the state in 2005, have been implemented in educationally backward blocks of the state.

There are substantial social, regional and gender gaps in literacy. Statistics on the situation of the girl child in tribal India do not make for comfort. Gender gap refers to the percentage share of girls to total enrolment at both primary and upper primary levels of education. Recognizing the Census 2001, the overall literacy rate of tribals is 37.37 per cent. This is significantly lower than that of the general population (63.08 per cent) and is even lower than the literacy rate of 55.53 per cent among the scheduled castes. The literacy rate of tribal male is 51.48 per cent, which is much lower than the state average of 75.35 per cent. The female literacy rate of 23.37 per cent is also lowest of all social groups in terms of literacy (Acharya, 2007: 95). When education is considered to be the heart of all development, it is evident that education scenario among STs is in a very bad shape. The ST female literacy has increased from a very low level of 4.76 per cent in 1981 to 23.23 per cent in 2001, which is significantly lower than SC and general female literacy (Mohanty, 2010; 2012). Although the ST male literacy has increased from 23.27 per cent in 1981 to 51.48 per cent in 2001, there is still a big gap between that and the general male literacy. Table 4 shows the gender gap in literacy in selected districts of Odisha.

Five districts out of a total nine districts exhibit greater gender gap more than that of not only the state average but also the average of nine districts. The situation in Kandhamal and Kalahandi shows a very dismal picture as can be seen in Table 4.

Table 4 Gender Gap in Literacy in Selected Districts of Odisha

District	Gender Gap in Literacy
Kandhamal	33.9
Kalahandi	33.4
Rayagada	23.6
Koraput	22.9
Nawarangpur	26.4
Mayurbhanj	27.9
Malkangiri	19.2
Keonjhar	25.8
Sundargarh	21.5
Average of nine districts	**23.13**
All Odisha	**24.08**

Source: Odisha Economic Survey 2010–2011, p. 283 (Compiled).

SITUATIONAL ANALYSIS OF ELEMENTARY EDUCATION OF TRIBAL GIRLS

This section now attempts a situational analysis of elementary education of tribal girls with specific reference to nine selected districts of Odisha. The parameters chosen for such analysis include (1) the number of Primary and Upper Primary (UP) schools established, (2) schools with percentage of ST children enrolment, (3) Gross Enrolment Ratio (GER) and Net Enrolment Ratio (NER), (4) out-of-school children, (5) dropout rate, (6) retention and transition rate and (7) Pupil–Teacher Ratio (PTR).

Number of Primary and Upper Primary (UP) Schools Established

Availability of schooling facilities is measured by a set of indicators concerning to access. As per norms, a habitation is entitled to have a primary school if it has a total population of 300 and more and has no school within a distance of one kilometre (Table 5). For upper primary schools, the corresponding norm is a total population of 500 and more and a distance of three kilometres. However, the norm is often relaxed in case of hilly and tribal dominated areas, difficult terrains and border districts. A distance of one and three kilometres is treated as the maximum walking distance to which a child is expected to travel from his residence to school. The states have their own norms according to which they provide schooling facilities.

Microplanning and school mapping-related activities play an important role in making provision for schools and also deciding a location for where a school is to be opened.

As per the DISE 2010–2011, there are 36,642 primary and 20,597 UP schools comprising a total of 57,239 schools as the state-level total. Compared to primary schools, the number of UP schools is abysmally lesser not only at the state level but also in the nine selected tribal districts. There are 20,927 schools in the nine selected tribal districts out of which 14,278 are primary and 6,649 are UP schools. Schools of Mass Education Department represent nearly double the number of schools that have been established by all others including SC and ST Department of Government of Odisha. Mayurbhanj has the highest number of 3,882 schools followed by Sundargarh (2,769), Kalahandi (2,418) and Keonjhar (2,404). Malkangiri has the least number of (1,270) such schools. Kandhamal, Nawarangpur and Rayagada have a number of such schools little less than 2000. Looking at the geographic size of the selected districts, the number of schools appears to be adequate. Despite all the impressive achievements, there are still a few habitations that may not have access to primary and UP schooling facilities within the specified norms. Establishment of number of schools is not the real issue for achieving the goal of UEE, especially in tribal areas. The real issue is enrolment, retention, transition and the dropout rate including the availability of gender beneficial facilities.

Schools with Quantum of ST Enrolment

With a natural disposition towards the local dialect, a tribal child is generally unfamiliar with the state language. As a child's first exposure to education, there is debate around the language used for instruction and communication. Tribal children have limited contact with the state language and tend to speak in their own local dialect. Government schools, where the tribal girls are largely educated, use the state language for teaching and communication, which is most often not familiar to a tribal child at the primary and UP levels. They are thus unable to fully comprehend classroom teaching and activities, read in the state language or understand the texts properly. Gradually introducing the state language can boost enrolment enhancing the linguistic capital as well as improve the child's potential in mainstream education systems. The use of the tribal language in the initial years helps development of a sense of comfort for the tribal girl child. It must be the first language and taught as a means of acquiring knowledge of tribal culture, ethnicity, literature and arts. The child is required to be exposed to

Table 5 Number of Primary (P) and Upper Primary (UP) Schools in Tribal Districts

District	Edu. Dept.		SC/ST Dept.		Aided		Others*		Total		TOTAL
	P	UP	P	UP	P	UP	P	UP	P	UP	
Kalahandi	1,579	650	13	12	2	21	89	52	1,683	735	2,418
Kandhamal	1,251	532	22	81	0	2	12	17	1,285	632	1,917
Keonjhar	1,582	715	37	20	4	96	74	65	1,697	896	2,593
Koraput	1,592	610	79	42	22	5	36	18	1,729	675	2,404
Malkangiri	851	304	12	40	2	4	47	10	912	358	1,270
Mayurbhanj	2,440	1,185	10	98	6	41	39	63	2,495	1,387	3,882
Nawarangpur	1,190	483	7	49	8	4	46	18	1,251	554	1,805
Rayagada	1,238	434	73	31	0	2	67	24	1,378	491	1,869
Sundargarh	1,531	776	66	26	151	51	100	68	1,848	921	2,769
Nine districts	**13,254**	**5,689**	**319**	**399**	**195**	**226**	**510**	**335**	**14,278**	**6,649**	**20,927**
Total	**33,941**	**16,915**	**616**	**674**	**285**	**1,459**	**1,800**	**1,549**	**36,642**	**20,597**	**57,239**

Source: DISE 2010–2011. *Others include schools by local body, unaided, unrecognized and missionaries.

the state language steadily, which is imperative for integration into mainstream schools and society. Table 6 represents the schools with percentage ST enrolment in the State of Odisha in relation to the impact of language used for instruction and communication.

Table 6 Schools with % ST Enrolment in the State of Odisha

100% ST enrolment	5,151	**7.84**	Monolingual
99–90% ST enrolment	3,281	**4.99**	Monolingual
89–80% ST enrolment	2,810	**4.28**	Monolingual at home and bilingual school
79–70% ST enrolment	2,873	**4.37**	Monolingual at home and bilingual school
69–60% ST enrolment	2,801	**4.26**	Monolingual at home and bilingual school
59–50% ST enrolment	2,834	**4.31**	Monolingual at home and bilingual school
Below 50% ST enrolment	45,962	**69.94**	Monolingual at home and bilingual school
Total no. of schools	65,712*	**100**	* includes 8,473 high schools

Table 6 shows that only 8 per cent schools are there with 100 per cent enrolment of ST children and 5 per cent schools with 90–99 per cent enrolment of ST children in the State of Odisha. There are 70 per cent schools where the ST children enrolment is less than 50 per cent, apparently for the compulsive use of state language as the medium of instruction. However, the schools where there are 90–100 per cent of ST communities are monolingual by nature, whereas the rest of the schools are monolingual at home and bilingual at school. The data show that the language used for teaching in the schools is also a prime factor for enrolment of ST children. It is evident that the numbers of bilingual schools are more in the state. The figure indicates that there is a need of more number of monolingual schools in the state, particularly in these tribal-dominated districts to enhance the ST children enrolment. The fact seems to be that the children can relate and internalize the education better in their own language and can be attracted to schools. It may thus be required to open more schools imparting education in the languages of the ST children. The teaching materials and books should be in the local tribal languages, and thus the linguistic imposition may prove out to be detrimental to the realization of goal of UEE.

Considering the language issue faced by the tribal children in the tribal areas and with the aim to boost enrolment, the State Tribal Advisory Committee (STAC) in the year 2006 decided to adopt 10 tribal languages as the mother tongue-based multilingual medium of instruction in 10 tribal districts. These 10 tribal languages are Santali, Soura, Koya, Kuvi, Kishan, Oram, Munda, Juanga and Bonda (OPEPA, 2010–2011).

Out-of-School Children

The definition of 'out-of-school' encompass a wide range of realities and refer to children who (1) do not have access to a school in their community, (2) do not enrol despite the availability of a school, (3) enrol but do not attend school or (4) drop out of the education system. Literature indicate that income, poverty, poor health and nutrition, disability, gender, ethnicity, child labour, migration, geographical disadvantages, cultural factors, linguistic barrier and situations of fragility and conflict contribute to limiting access to school and excluding children from a proper education. Reaching out-of-school children cannot be done by simply constructing more schools, distributing more books or training new teachers. School systems should be strengthened with a special focus on reaching the out-of-school children.

Table 7 describes the percentage of ST children in comparison to children of the general category across gender. It shows that the Kandhamal, Koraput, Malkangiri, Nawarangpur and Sundargarh districts have more than 60 per cent out-of-school ST girl children in comparison to overall children there. The gap may be due to factors of accessibility, household level discrimination to let them to utilize the time in studying, unavailability of facilities at schools like toilets and water, involvement in household work, earning money to supplement family income in the face of poverty, insecure environment or language followed for imparting education and so on. It is thus crucial to understand the situation in these districts and take necessary plan to bridge the gaps. Kalahandi and Keonjhar reflect a better picture with less than 30 per cent, although Keonjhar represents more out-of-school girl children compared to their male counterparts. Further on an average, there are more out-of-school ST girls in relation to the boys both at district average and percentage to the state total. This leaves a serious question mark on UEE in the tribal districts of the state.

GER and NER at Primary and Upper Primary Level

The enrolment ratio is considered as an ideal indicator for assessing the situation and success of education for all Education For All (EFA) programme. The Gross Enrolment Ratio (GER) is derived by the number of

Table 7 Out-of-School Children among Overall and ST Community in Selected Districts

District	6–14 yrs Overall			6–14 yrs ST			% ST to Overall		
	Boys	Girls	Total	Boys	Girls	Total	Boys	Girls	Total
Kalahandi	2,712	2,443	5,155	756	681	1,437	**27.88**	**27.88**	**27.88**
Kandhamal	751	810	1,561	544	534	1,078	**72.44**	**65.93**	**69.06**
Keonjhar	5,950	4,785	10,735	1,574	1,305	2,879	**26.45**	**27.27**	**26.82**
Koraput	2,354	2,554	4,908	1,363	1,582	2,945	**57.90**	**61.94**	**60.00**
Malkangiri	1,336	1,183	2,519	1,033	882	1,915	**77.32**	**74.56**	**76.02**
Mayurbhanj	8,563	7,788	16,351	3,200	3,291	6,491	**37.37**	**42.26**	**39.70**
Nawarangpur	1,059	997	2,056	646	600	1,246	**61.00**	**60.18**	**60.60**
Rayagada	3,860	4,330	8,190	2,157	2,417	4,574	**55.88**	**55.82**	**55.85**
Sundargarh	1,968	1,655	3,623	1,414	1,164	2,578	**71.85**	**70.33**	**71.16**
Nine districts total	**28,553**	**26,545**	**55,098**	**12,687**	**12,456**	**25,143**	**44.43**	**46.92**	**45.63**
State total	**37,070**	**34,978**	**72,048**	**15,118**	**14,882**	**30,000**	**40.78**	**42.55**	**41.64**
% to state totala	**77.02**	**75.89**	**76.47**	**83.92**	**83.70**	**83.81**			

Table 8 GER and NER at Primary and Upper Primary Level in Selected Districts

District	GER (P)		GER (UP)		NER (P)		NER (UP)	
	All	ST	All	ST	All	ST	All	ST
Kalahandi	100.73	101.93	95.98	80.75	82.21	85.05	66.08	99.10
Kandhamal	93.84	97.40	124.74	120.13	91.56	93.46	90.20	87.88
Keonjhar	92.45	94.02	104.69	108.53	84.70	89.50	80.89	82.53
Koraput	105.52	132.58	84.26	104.81	96.37	95.46	78.53	77.62
Malkangiri	106.41	113.73	118.97	111.40	98.17	97.72	94.31	90.83
Mayurbhanj	110.10	100.35	94.05	121.95	94.70	96.46	70.84	97.90
Nawarangpur	102.34	102.71	98.86	97.06	94.06	90.23	78.67	70.37
Rayagada	103.21	116.62	96.03	64.16	95.64	95.67	91.38	93.18
Sundargarh	113.79	99.99	136.02	102.18	98.75	98.71	97.60	97.98
All nine districts	**103.15**	**106.59**	**105.96**	**101.22**	**92.91**	**93.58**	**83.17**	**88.60**
State total	**99.60**	**101.84**	**105.45**	**98.83**	**91.83**	**92.76**	**83.84**	**85.87**

students enrolled in educational sector of elementary level of education by the population of school age children of this level. An elementary formula used to calculate the GER is that the geographical unit divides the number of individuals who are actually enrolled in schools by the number of children who are of the corresponding school enrolment age. Gross Elementary School Enrolment Ratio considers children usually between the age of 6 and 14. Net Enrolment Ratio (NER) in elementary education is the number of children of official school age, who are enrolled as a percentage of the total children of the official school age population. The purpose of NER is to show the extent of participation in a given level of education of children belonging to the official age group corresponding to the given level of education. This is a very important indicator in measuring rates of access to education, when considering gender inequality issues, as well as regional or rural/urban inequalities. Table 8 leaves a glimpse of GER and NER of tribal children at primary (P) and upper primary (UP) level in selected districts. Due to non-availability of data, it is not possible to show the gender differences as such.

The available data show that Koraput has the highest GER in the primary level for the ST children, which interprets that the enrolment is not being done at the right ages. In Kandhamal and Keonjhar districts, the ST GER is below 100 thus there seems to be serious issues attached to enrolment of children. In all the other districts and the state as a whole, the ST GER is much above 100 which shows that children are not getting enrolled at right ages. In case of overall GER, the figures are better than that of ST. Districts, namely, Nawarangpur, Rayagada and even Koraput, show better GERs. It is also reflected during the analysis that the average of nine districts for GER stands at 103.15 percent for overall children and for the ST it stands at 106.6 per cent.

Similarly at the upper primary level also the GER for ST children is very poor for Rayagada and Kalahandi districts. Koraput has the lowest overall GER and Sundargarh has the highest. Kandhamal has high GER in both overall as well as among the ST children. The analysis also reflects that the average of these nine districts for GER at upper primary level stands at 106 per cent for overall children and 101 per cent for the ST children. GER beyond 100 per cent may indicate that the situation has improved significantly but the same is not adequate to attain the status of universal enrolment if overage and underage children are taken out from enrolment. However, it may be noted that as we approach UPE, the percentage of overage and underage children as well as the enrolment ratio (gross) will decline. The erratic trend in GER is because of the projected population used in computing ratio. Otherwise, a consistent trend is noticed in absolute enrolment both at the primary and upper primary levels of education.

The figures show that the NER for both ST children and overall children in primary level is best in the district of Sundargarh and it is lowest in case of Kalahandi (ST, 85.05; overall, 82.21). Keonjhar is another district which has a significantly low NER. However, the NER of ST children is relatively better than the overall children NER in Mayurbhanj, Keonjhar, Kandhamal and Kalahandi districts. In rest of the districts, the NER of ST children is either at par with overall NER or lower than it. The low NER may be a cause of lack of awareness, priority to education for the children and accessibility issues. The NER at primary level may be improved by improving the coordination between the Integrated Child Development Scheme (ICDS) centres and the primary schools and improving the awareness level of the community. The analysis for the NER for primary level reflects that the overall average for the nine districts is 92.91 per cent and for ST is 93.58 per cent.

Again, it is seen that the NER at upper primary level is even worse than the primary level. The state average and all of the districts except for Sundargarh has lower NERs at upper primary than the respective NERs at primary level. It is interesting to see that the NERs at upper primary level in case of ST children of Kalahandi and Mayurbhanj districts are significantly better than the overall NER; in fact in Kalahandi, it is the best among the selected districts and even much better than the state average. There is a significant drop in NERs in both the categories in Nawarangpur and Koraput districts compared to the NERs in primary. The drops in NERs at the upper primary level is to be seen as a serious issue as it may have factors attached like transition rates, dropouts after primary, accessibility of schools, facilities of toilets (separate for girls) and water, proportion of female teachers, quality of education, medium of instruction and the household-level constraints. The analysis also reflects that the overall data for NER for upper primary level stands at 83.17 per cent for the overall children, whereas for the ST it is 88.60 per cent.

Dropout Rate

Dropping out rate refers to annual incidence proportion of students quitting school before they complete the course or avoiding further continuance in educational attainment. Leaving school early is the outcome of a long process of disengagement from the school; dropout is preceded by indicators of withdrawal (e.g., poor attendance) or unsuccessful school experiences (e.g., academic or behavioural difficulties) that often begin in elementary school. Overt indicators of disengagement are generally accompanied by feelings of alienation, poor sense of belonging and a general dislike of school. Dropout statistics can be used to monitor the success of schools and identify students needing special attention. In addition, statistics would provide an overall indication of the success of the educational system. To make these assessments, however, data must be collected according to the same definitions, using the same procedures and over the same period of time.

The data (Table 9) show that the dropout rate at primary level is higher than the state average in Malkangiri and also the dropouts of girls are highest in this district followed by Kandhamal. The dropout rates are low in Keonjhar and Rayagada districts, even for the girls. It is important to reduce the dropout rates at the primary level through efforts in improving the GER and NER, attaching the community with the management and monitoring of the school, improving the infrastructure and facilities at school, improving awareness in the community and enhancing the interest and attraction towards the school by inducing child-friendly and quality education components.

There are higher rates of dropouts among the ST children compared to the overall dropout rates, which can be seen from the data presented. The state average is higher; the three districts, namely, Malkangiri, Kalahandi and Mayurbhanj, also show dropout rates abysmally higher than the state average. Interestingly in most of the districts, the ST girls' dropout rates are comparatively higher than the boys. It is important to thus have

Table 9 Dropout Rate at Primary Level in Selected Districts

District	All Community			ST		
	Boys	Girls	Total	Boys	Girls	Total
Kalahandi	1.20	1.98	1.59	3.70	9.05	4.25
Kandhamal	3.38	2.82	3.11	1.99	2.20	2.09
Keonjhar	0.48	0.15	0.32	3.75	2.94	3.36
Koraput	0.78	1.30	1.04	4.26	4.56	4.41
Malkangiri	2.43	4.03	3.22	4.06	6.44	5.23
Mayurbhanj	2.66	2.63	2.64	4.61	9.16	4.77
Nawarangpur	1.52	1.64	1.58	2.61	3.23	2.92
Rayagada	0.30	0.34	0.43	1.44	3.39	2.37
Sundargarh	2.18	1.93	2.08	2.54	2.03	2.29
All nine districts	**1.66**	**1.87**	**1.78**	**3.22**	**4.78**	**3.52**
State total	**2.35**	**2.86**	**2.60**	**4.12**	**5.35**	**4.85**

special arrangements and facilities for the ST children in the schools like education in their language and teaching materials in their languages by which they can relate their education with their environment and culture.

The average of nine districts in terms of the dropout rates is 1.78 per cent, whereas the girl's dropout is slightly higher than the boys (girls being 1.87 per cent and boys being 1.66 per cent). Similarly for the STs, the average is 3.52 per cent, with boys being 3.22 per cent and girls being 4.78 per cent. This reinforces that the dropout rate among ST boys and girls are much higher than the general communities.

The figures clearly show that there is a sharp increase in the dropout rates as we move to higher levels (Table 10). In Koraput, the dropout level is as high as about 20 per cent for girls and 15 per cent for boys. Four out of the nine selected districts show higher dropout rates than the state average. It is interesting to see that except for Koraput and Kalahandi the dropout rates of girls are below the dropout rates of boys in other districts.

It is also evident that the dropout rates in the ST community in upper primary are less compared to overall rates of dropouts. Kalahandi, Koraput and Rayagada are the districts which have higher dropout rates, more than the state average. Koraput, Rayagada and Kandhamal also have the dropouts more for the girl child, whereas in the other districts the dropout rates are more for ST boys.

Table 10 Dropout Rate at Upper Primary Level in Selected Districts

District	All Community			ST		
	Boys	Girls	Total	Boys	Girls	Total
Kalahandi	6.06	9.45	7.57	7.50	7.04	6.99
Kandhamal	10.03	6.20	8.33	1.47	4.59	5.16
Keonjhar	4.91	1.77	3.45	9.12	4.96	5.95
Koraput	15.20	19.29	16.98	7.57	9.67	8.85
Malkangiri	16.69	11.65	14.53	1.98	2.40	1.74
Mayurbhanj	10.71	5.71	8.35	8.44	5.40	6.78
Nawarangpur	14.56	11.10	13.02	6.61	4.08	5.26
Rayagada	11.40	7.31	9.56	8.32	11.88	8.55
Sundargarh	4.26	0.14	2.22	6.49	5.80	6.16
All nine districts	**10.42**	**8.07**	**9.33**	**6.39**	**6.20**	**6.16**
State total	**7.15**	**7.31**	**7.23**	**7.18**	**6.96**	**7.85**

The overall average of the nine districts stands at 9.33 per cent for all communities in comparison to ST dropout rate of 6.16 per cent, which is lower. Similar to the primary level, the upper primary level also reflects a clear gender variation in dropout rates. The overall average dropout rate for boys is 10.42 per cent in comparison 8.07 per cent for girls, whereas for the ST community the dropout rate for the boys stands at 6.39 per cent and at 6.20 per cent for girls. This leads to an interesting finding that in ST community the dropout rate is more for the girls at primary level whereas for the overall community the dropout rate of boys is higher than the girls at upper primary level.

Retention Rate and Transition Rate of Girls

Retention rate refers to the proportion of enrolment in any school year that continues to be in school the following year. A high retention rate suggests that a school is supportive and enjoyable and that the workload is manageable. Transition rate is the percentage of pupils who pass from one level of education and move on to the next higher level like from primary to upper primary level. The situations pertaining to retention rate and transition rate of tribal girls from primary to upper primary in the selected districts of Odisha are presented below.

The retention rate in case of girls in the selected districts is poor in almost all the districts. The state average retention rates are 82.32 per cent and 80.77 per cent from primary to upper primary, respectively. In Kalahandi, Kandhamal, Keonjhar, Mayurbhanj and Sundargarh districts, the retention rates of girls at upper primary level is better than in primary level. In Koraput, Malkangiri and Rayagada, the retention rates are better compared to the upper primary level. Retention rates of girls in primary level are lowest in the Keonjhar district, while in upper primary it is Malkangiri district. The low retention rates add on to the dropout rates, hence the reasons mentioned earlier need immediate attention to improve the retention rates at both levels. Special analysis of the situation in case of Malkangiri is needed to be done to find out details and to take corrective measures.

The data reflect that the retention rate for the nine districts is 70.58 per cent at the primary level and 73.9 per cent at the upper primary level, in comparison to 82.32 per cent of state average for primary level and 80.77 per cent for upper primary level. Table 11 shows that only 85.7 per cent of the girl children are going to class VI from class V. The situation is worst in Malkangiri (58.1 per cent) and only two of the selected districts, Kandhamal and Keonjhar, have transition rates more than the state average. In the districts with lower transition rates, it is important to find out the reasons for dropouts and also to improve the education with quality components and child-friendly teaching mechanisms. Similarly, Table 11 reflects that the transition rate from primary to upper primary for the nine districts is 78.78 per cent in comparison to 85.73 per cent of state average, which needs a special attention.

It may also be noted that despite the policy of no detention up to the class V, a large number of tribal girl children used to repeat a class. The ideal number of years a student should take to become a primary graduate is five years. The data suggest that not a single school in tribal pockets is exactly taking five years to produce all its primary graduates, and further precarious is the situation of girl child. The inefficiency in the system is due to possible reasons that the 11–14 year children are out of system, or there may also be dropped out children or they are still in the primary classes. So far as the computation of transition rate is concerned, the procedure followed is that first the repeaters are taken out from enrolment in the first grade (V/VI) of upper primary cycle which is then divided by the terminal grade of previous cycle (IV/V), that is primary level (Mehta, 1999).

Therefore, upper primary level of education cannot be expanded in isolation. An inefficient primary system would send fewer children to upper primary level. Thus, the availability of graduates along with transition from

Table 11 Retention Rate and Transition* Rate of Girls from Primary to Upper Primary

District	Retention Rate		Transition Rate
	Primary	Upper Primary	Primary to Upper Primary
Kalahandi	65.58	79.64	80.30
Kandhamal	66.43	78.48	88.50
Keonjhar	66.31	80.94	88.61
Koraput	76.33	62.89	73.19
Malkangiri	73.66	43.56	58.10
Mayurbhanj	66.32	89.90	82.78
Nawarangpur	73.81	73.07	74.55
Rayagada	72.38	67.14	78.24
Sundargarh	74.40	89.52	84.77
All nine districts	**70.58**	**73.90**	**78.78**
State total	**82.32**	**80.77**	**85.73**

Source: DISE, 2010–2011: *From Class V of 2009–2010 to Class VI of 2010–2011.

primary to upper primary level would decide the future expansion of upper primary level. The demand is more likely to be in the educationally disadvantaged areas where primary education has not been fully expanded. Further expansion of primary education in these areas and high transition from primary to upper primary level will generate more intensive demand for upper primary education to expand. Although significant progress has been made in the provision of education for all girls, the task seems to be not yet complete. Provisions of post-primary education to girls in rural areas continue to thrust on gender-sensitive and gender-inclusive curriculum, etc., which are the major issues that are yet to be tackled with regards to education of tribal girls.

Pupil–Teacher Ratio in Selected Districts

Pupil–Teacher Ratio (PTR) can be calculated as gross and net units. Gross PTR is the proportion of the number of authorized positions for imparting teaching at a certain level in a given year to the enrolment at the same level in the same year. Net PTR is the proportion of the number of teachers actually teaching at a certain level in a given year to the enrolment at the same level in the same year. Unfortunately, the data on net PTR are not available.

Table 12 depicts the PTR in the selected districts and the state average in primary and upper primary sections.

Table 12 Pupil Teacher Ratio in Selected Districts 2010–2011

District	Primary	Upper Primary
Kalahandi	33.88	27.61
Kandhamal	26.83	17.50
Keonjhar	39.38	24.89
Koraput	33.38	18.27
Malkangiri	33.28	17.49
Mayurbhanj	33.97	20.35
Nawarangpur	41.33	23.30
Rayagada	25.60	17.00
Sundargarh	26.18	28.50
All nine districts	**32.65**	**21.66**
State total	**31.73**	**26.55**

Source: DISE, 2010–2011.

The state PTR seems to be quite favourable as in primary it is 31.73 and 26.55 in upper primary level. All the selected districts have encouraging PTR in upper primary level while in the primary level it is little more in case of most of the districts, highest being in Nawarangpur (41.33). It was also found that the average of nine districts at the primary level is 32.65 per cent and for the upper primary level it is 21.66 per cent. Interestingly, while at the primary level the average of nine districts (32.65 per cent) is little higher than the state average of 31.73 per cent, at the upper primary level it is much lower (21.66 per cent) than state average, i.e., 26.55 per cent.

PTR at the upper primary level has been abysmally lower than that at the primary levels. Teachers are generally appointed for the elementary level and then they are deployed either in primary or upper primary schools. The number of teachers in primary schools suggests that teachers are involved in multi-grade teaching, but the same is not true in case of upper primary teachers. In this context, it is also necessary to know the ratio of male/female teachers for better appreciation of the situation. Table 13 shows data ratio of male/female teachers.

The number of male and female teachers in primary schools is shown in Table 13. The state average shows that of the total teachers only 39.5 per cent are females. Seven out of the nine selected tribal-dominated districts

Table 13 Number of Male/Female Teachers of All Government Schools in Selected Districts.

District	Primary			Upper Primary			Total
	Total	Female	Male	Total	Female	Male	
Kalahandi	5,083	1,237	3,846	1,197	196	1,001	6,280
Kandhamal	3,594	1,107	2,487	1,278	412	866	4,872
Keonjhar	4,767	1,581	3,186	1,562	360	1,202	6,329
Koraput	4,892	1,735	3,157	1,309	440	869	6,201
Malkangiri	2,310	581	1,729	775	207	568	3,085
Mayurbhanj	7,459	3,277	4,182	3,373	1,173	2,200	10,832
Nawarangpur	3,600	929	2,671	1,346	366	980	4,946
Rayagada	4,054	933	3,121	1,319	329	990	5,373
Sundargarh	5,908	3,081	2,827	2,181	923	1,258	8,089
Nine districts total	**41,667**	**14,461**	**27,206**	**14,340**	**4,406**	**9,934**	**56,007**
State total	**116,481**	**46,029**	**70,452**	**42,697**	**14,018**	**28,679**	**159,178**
% to state total	**35.77**	**31.42**	**38.62**	**33.59**	**31.43**	**34.64**	**35.19**

Source: DISE, 2010–2011.

have female teachers' percentage lower than the state average. Rayagada, Kalahandi, Malkangiri and Nawarangpur have about only 25 per cent female teachers. Mayurbhanj and Sundargarh are the only two districts which have female teachers' percentage above the state average, with Sundargarh having the highest percentage of 52.1. This situation indicates that there is a dearth of female teachers in all the districts, which may be due to unavailability of enough female teachers, vacancies, accessibility of the schools, means of communication, security and safety factors and un-uniform deployment of the female teachers in a few specific districts. All these factors need immediate attention to improve the teacher's deployment status in the schools. A recent problem arising in tribal districts is that aspiring teachers from outside the districts are not allowed to enter into the district which proves to be detrimental to the availability of quality teachers. The analysis shows that at the primary level, the nine districts contribute to 35.77 per cent of the state average, out of which the male percentage is 38.62 and the female being 31.42.

Looking at the availability status of the female teachers at the upper primary level, the situation is even worse compared to the primary level. The state average is only 32.8 per cent, and Sundargarh with 42.3 per cent female teachers is the best district on this indicator. Kalahandi with a mere 16.4 per cent female teachers is at the bottom along with Keonjhar, Rayagada and Malkangiri districts which have female teachers' percentage below 25. The situation becomes more serious as in upper primary it is expected to have more female teachers because the girls are of higher age in this section and parents become more concerned of their child's safety and security. This reason may be a vital factor in certain areas for dropouts of girls and leading to early marriage and further to early motherhood. The data also reflect that at the upper primary level the nine districts contribute to 33.59 per cent of the state total, out of which the male percentage is 34.64 and the female being 31.43. The overall percentage of male/female teachers of all government schools in selected districts to the state total is 35.19.

SUMMARY AND WAY OUT

Down from National Policy for Education (1986) to SSA, importance has been laid on the education of tribal children. One of the key objectives of SSA was to bridge the social category gaps at primary stage of education by 2007 and at upper primary stage by 2010. Looking at the poor literacy rate among ST population, in particular the female literacy, the enrolled children are most likely to be the first-generation learners of their respective family. In such circumstances, mere enrolment is not enough, unless it is followed by retention and type of education being imparted causes of substantive material and cognitive development of children.

ST children have poor ability to concept acquisition and comprehension. Large-scale failure of tribal children, in general, and their girl children, in particular, has been due to learning difficulties and poor intellectual abilities. The display of poor performance of tribal children is mainly due to economic deprivation, malnutrition and low parental education and lack of early childhood care and proper environment as well as the factors of inadequate schools in the communities, poor motivation of teacher and lack of administrative responsibility. The disadvantage suffered by tribal girl children is quite evident from the above analysis of this paper. A large number of tribal girl children still remain out-of-school. The estimates of enrolments and attendance give reasonably sound reasons to believe that stipulated targets may not be achieved in the near future, but universalization of tribal girls' education continues to remain not very satisfactory.

Again, without attaining the status of universal primary enrolment, the goal of universal elementary education cannot be achieved. Further expansion of primary education in these areas and high transition from primary to upper primary level will generate more intensive demand for upper primary education to expand. A lot more efforts are required to adequately create, utilize and make available alternative facilities in all unserved habitations and areas where out-of-school children concentrate. A few schools still do not have school buildings and other teaching-learning facilities. The number of teachers and PTR over time has improved significantly, but still there are schools that do not have adequate number of teachers and instructional rooms. The number of female teachers over time improved significantly, but still their number is far less than their male counterparts.

The enrolment at the primary and upper primary levels of education over time improved significantly, but still more girls are out-of-school than their boy counterparts. The enrolment ratio at the upper primary level is much lower than at the primary level. A large number of children continue to dropout from the system before completion of an education cycle, which severely affects the efficiency of the elementary education system. The children are taking more years to become primary graduates than ideally required. The unfinished task in terms of unenrolled and out-of-school children is a challenging one. Rigorous efforts are needed to bring and retain them under the umbrella of education system. The community, in this direction, can play a vital role in bringing and retaining unenrolled children to schools. Microplanning exercises in this regard and development of village education plans shall be useful.

There is enough evidence that investment in the girl child results in making a better, healthier, happier and more creative family, community and society (Nayar, 2011: 20). When families, schools, neighbourhoods and communities take this as the agenda for action, it is likely to result in a great contribution for the present and future generations of the nation. To make girls' care and protection a reality for every girl in every place requires not only our resources and policies, but also our voices and actions. But more than that love, respect and support for girls must be the reality of all our homes, schools and communities. By educating a boy we can educate a person, but by educating a girl we can educate a generation.

REFERENCES

Acharya, P.K. (2007). *State of Children in Orissa*, Cuttack: Committee for Legal Aid to Poor (CLAP).

Census of India (2001). *Individual SC/ST Odisha Census Data Products in (CD)*, Bhubaneswar: Directorate of Census Operations, Odisha, Govt. of India.

Census of India (2010). 'Odisha Data Highlights: The Scheduled Tribes – 2001', *Odisha Review* (Census Special), LXVII(5): 206–210.

Census of India (2011). *Provisional Population Total*, Bhubaneswar: Directorate of Census Operations, Odisha, Govt. of India.

Govt. of Odisha (2004). *Odisha Human Development Report*, Bhubaneswar.

Govt. of Odisha (2012). *Annual Report and Audited Accounts*, Bhubaneswar: Odisha Primary Education Authority.

Govt. of Odisha (2012). *Economic Survey 2011–12*, Bhubaneswar: Department of Planning and Co-ordination.

Govt. of Odisha (2012). *Odisha Sarva Siksha Abhiyan Achievements*, Bhubaneswar: Odisha Primary Education Authority, http://www.opepa.in/website/Achievement.aspx.

Mehta, A.C. (1999). 'Status of Education for All in India in the Light of Sixth All India Educational Survey Data', Occasional Paper No. 27, NIEUPA, New Delhi.

Mohanty, R.K. (2010). 'Tribal Identity in Indian National Secular Perspective: Contributions from Orissa's Indigenous Traditions', *The Eastern Anthropologist*, 63(3–4): 309–318.

Nayak, A.N. (2010). 'Primitive Tribal Groups of Odisha: An Evaluation of Census Data', *Odisha Review* (Census Special), LXVII(5): 202–205.

Nayar, U.S. (2011). 'Gender Equity and Girl Child in India', *Journal of Psychosocial Research*, 6(1): 11–21.

.anaweera, A.M. (1989). *Non-conventional Approaches to Education at the Primary Level* (edited), Hamburg: UNESCO Institute for Education.

Xaxa, V. (1999). 'Tribes as Indigenous People', *EPW*, 34(51): 3589–3595.

CHAPTER 10

PROBLEMS OF DISTRESS MIGRATION OF TRIBAL WOMEN IN KBK DISTRICTS OF ORISSA: AN ANALYSIS

S.N. Tripathy

According to the 2001 Census, scheduled tribes (STs or Adivasis) are 84.3 million in number, or 8.2 per cent of the country's population. Almost 9 out of 10 Adivasis depend on agriculture for their livelihood, this is more than any other social section. The states of Madhya Pradesh, Chhattisgarh, Maharashtra, Orissa, Jharkhand and Gujarat have more than half of the total tribal population in India.

There have been a number of studies on the tribes, their culture and the impact of acculturation on the tribal society in India. There have also been studies on the status of women relating to their socio-cultural problems, their economic rights, their participation in management, their access to employment, food, health, etc. But there have been very few studies relating to the status of tribal women in India. A tribal woman occupies an important place in the socio-economic structure of her society. The well-being of the tribal community, as that of any other community, depends importantly on the status of their women.

OBJECTIVES OF THE STUDY

1. To present a macro-dimension of issues relating to tribal women; and
2. To assess the impact of migration on tribal women's security in the context of work, food and health, in order to provide policy implications of the study.

STUDIES ON TRIBAL WOMEN IN INDIA

The tribal women constitute half of the tribal population, like any other communities. The status of tribal women is an important indicator of the well-being of the tribal community. The popular image and perception of the tribal women is that of being better off than their non-tribal counterparts. There is no child marriage, no stigma on widowhood, existence of bride price indicating high social status of the tribal woman. She enjoys the right to decide about her marriage, divorce and remarriage. Because she earns, thus she enjoys economic independence.

However, there are many facts which also indicate low status for the tribal woman. For example, in most of the tribal society woman does not have property rights. She obtains lower wage than male counterpart for same job. In certain tribes, only the males can participate in ancestor worship. The Toda and Kota women are provided to cross the threshold of a temple. The Santal women cannot attend communal worship.

There have been a number of studies on tribes, their culture and impact of acculturation on the tribal society. There are only a few studies on the status of tribal women in India (Singh, Vyas and Mann, 1988; Chauhan, 1990). According to the study of Chauhan (1990), the problems of tribal women differ from a one area to another area owing to their geographical location, historical background and the process of social change.

The Dhebar Commission Report (1961) has mentioned that the tribal women are not a beast of burden. She is found to be exercising a relatively free and firm hand in all aspects related to her social life unlike in non-tribal societies.

HEALTH STATUS OF TRIBAL WOMEN

Health is an important function not only of medical care, but also of the overall integrated development of socio-cultural, economic, educational, social and political base and superstructures of the society. Each of these aspects has a deeper influence on health which influences all these aspects. Thus, in order to improve the health status and quality of life of people such efforts are required to be integrated with the wider effort to bring about the overall transformation of a society. The achievement of good health and good society is only possible when supportive services such as nutrition, environment and education reach a sufficiently high level.

Environment, specially the forest ecology has a strong contribution on health and treatment of tribal groups. Different parts of a plant are used by the tribal groups for the treatment of diseases as well as for population control. The mode of utilization of available natural resources often determines the long-term impact on health.

SEX RATIO OF TRIBES

Sex ratio (females per thousand males) measures the balance between males and females in human population. Large imbalances in this aspect affect the social, economic and community life in many ways. The status of socio-culture, maternal and child health care programmes are reflected by a higher or lower sex ratio. Table 1 presents the profile of sex ratio of the tribal and general women for different years.

Table 1 Sex Ratio of Tribal and General Female

Category	Year				
	1961	1971	1981	1991	2001
Sex ratio (ST)	987	982	983	972	970
Sex ratio (Non-ST)	941	930	935	927	924

Source: Census of India.

There appears more even distribution of males and females among the ST than the general population. The result reflects that the females in the tribal society are not at all neglected. However, it should be noted that the tribal sex ratio shows a definite decline in 1971, 1981, 1991 and 2001 censuses as compared to the 1961 Census (987), although in each year the sex ratio for the non-ST population is much lower.

The sex ratio of the STs varied widely within the country. According to 1991 Census, among the states, Orissa had the highest sex ratio (1002) and Uttar Pradesh had the lowest sex ratio (914). In case of Union Territories, it was highest in Dadra and Nagar Haveli (1022) and lowest in Daman and Diu (931). However, the violence in the form of female foeticide and infanticide suffered by women of other castes and communities is not present among tribes.

EMPLOYMENT STATUS OF TRIBAL WOMEN

Almost 90 per cent of the tribal population is engaged in agriculture. The other major economic activities of the tribal population are linked with the collection of food, which includes hunting and fishing, pastoral, handicrafts, trade and commerce and industrial labour.

Tribal population is rarely engaged in only one particular occupation. We can analyse the employment status of tribal women in terms of their work participation in agriculture, forests, non-agricultural activities and impact of development programmes. Table 2 presents the work participation rates for general and ST males and females for different years.

Table 2 Female Work Participation Rates

Class	Year									
	1961		1971		1981		1991		2001	
	Male	Female	Male	Female	Male	Female	Male	Female	Male	Female
General	53.35	10.54	52.60	12.10	51.60	14.00	51.00	16.00	50.94	16.00
ST	56.45	17.91	55.00	20.80	56.70	28.20	53.70	30.30	54.46	31.50

Source: Census of India.

The work participation rates among tribal females are higher than that of general female. From Table 2, it follows that the work participation rate among tribal women although has been increasing overtime, it is still lower than that of tribal males. However, our analysis reflects that the work participation rate of tribal women is higher than that of general female. As in the general population, the tribal population also shows higher work participation rate for males rather than females.

Besides, women play a dominant role in food production in some farming systems, such as the tribal system of shifting cultivation. In the states of Maharashtra, Madhya Pradesh, Bihar, Orissa and Andhra Pradesh (and the north-eastern hill states) – home for most of the Indian tribes – the subsistence economy is entirely dependent on the forest. Shifting cultivation, known as a female farming system, persists in these areas. Further, it has become increasingly clear that tribal women are aware of the importance of maintaining the ecological balance; that much more than men they see the damage done by the degradation and destruction of forests. This is partly because they are the first to face difficulties in finding food, fuel, fodder, water and other household essentials.

The status of any social group is determined importantly by its levels of health, nutrition, literacy–education, employment and income. We have attempted to analyse the status of tribal women of India in terms of health, education and employment. Tribal women in India have specific problems, some of these are built-in problems of these tribal communities and some are imposed upon them.

WOMEN AND FORESTS

Minor forest produce forms a major source of income in many tribal communities, especially those having less than five acres of land. Women and children are almost exclusively involved in collection of minor forest produce, its storage, processing and marketing (B. Singh, 1993; Roy Burman, 1988).

Increased government control of forests has distributed tribal economy adversely affecting tribals lives, particularly that of women. Appointing of agents from outside for collecting forest produce has not only affected their livelihood, but has also made the work of women more difficult. Collection of fuelwood has become more difficult since it is less accessible and more time-consuming. The result has been less income combined with less fuelwood available for themselves and lesser nutrition. It also leaves them little time for earning wages. Government control over forests has also reduced hunting to a ritual (Singh and Rajyalakshmi, 1993).

TRIBES, ABJECT POVERTY AND ABYSMALLY LOW LEVEL OF LIVING

There are sixty two types of tribes in the state of Orissa. Indeed, Orissa, the poorest state in eastern India, has nearly 23 per cent of the total population as tribes, whose position is probably the worst in the entire country.

A small land base, low agricultural productivity and low incomes have led to rising indebtedness, trapping tribes into a vicious circle of exploitation. The life of the tribes is increasingly vulnerable due to a persistent lack of assured entitlements to their resource base and basic necessity of life. Land alienation has deprived them of their land; forest legislation has turned them into encroachers on land they have always used; and they have also been excessively affected by displacement due to mining operations, irrigation projects, wildlife sanctuaries, etc. In the words of the draft National Tribal Policy (NTP), 'Land is the most important source of livelihood for STs. However, and in spite of state enactments to prevent alienation of tribal land, wrongful alienation of tribal land is the single most important cause of pauperization of tribes....' Further, they are prevented from exercising their traditional rights over the forests, even as the forests have been opened up to all sorts of plunder and destruction by the process of so-called development. Suggesting that the 'deep sense of exclusion and alienation' among tribes was responsible for unrest in certain tribal areas, the NTP states candidly, 'A situation is thus developing where the STs view the state as their exploiter and enemy, and the preachers of violent actions as their protector and friend. Tribal people tend to support these violent movements as they feel that it would help them get their rights, protect them from exploitation and redress their grievances.'

VULNERABILITY OF TRIBES AND FACTORS CONTRIBUTING TO THEIR DISTRESS MIGRATION

Orissa, in eastern India, on the Bay of Bengal is the poorest state in India, with 46 per cent of people living below the poverty line in 1999–2000, as against 26 per cent for the entire country. Total literacy rate of Orissa is 63.8 per cent, while the female literacy rate is at 50.5 per cent. Proportion of male workers to male population and female workers to female population are 52.5 per cent and 24.7 per cent, respectively. The total women workforce in Orissa is at 31.1 per cent. The Infant Mortality Rate (IMR) stands at 75 per 1,000 live births. Maternal Mortality Rate (MMR), i.e., the number of maternal deaths per 100,000 live births, is at 738. Orissa ranks 11th in the Human Development Indicators (HDI) and the state is prone to both natural and man-made disasters. Since 1965, it has experienced floods for 17 years, droughts for 19 years and cyclone for 7 years (Economic Survey 2006–2007; Government of Orissa, Orissa Human Development Report, 2004)

In the light of the afore-said illustrations, we will focus on the problem of tribal women migration in KBK[1] districts of Orissa. There is a deep linkage between migration and poverty especially of survival migration where women are found at the bottom of the pyramidal structure of poverty. Migration is one of the strategies of households to improve livelihoods by way of remittances and use of human capital (knowledge, health, skills, labour, etc.), which reduces risk and vulnerability and increases assets may be human, physical, social and environmental (Ellis, 2003). In case of distress, migration of male members inter alia results in increase in female-headed households; feminization of poverty; impact on reproduction and population growth in sending areas; no formal entitlements to land or ownership; dependent on irregular and insufficient remittances; loss of social and other support networks; not enough labour to work the land; and limited political participation. The elderly are likely to be more dependent on family and 'community' networks which may decline through the out-migration of others. Increased dependence on government services and social welfare mechanisms; loss of young people and subsequent decline in the agricultural sector, consequences of an ageing population; social security systems are undermined (Tripathy, 2005)

REVIEW OF LITERATURE

Recent evidence shows that internal migration in India is a complex phenomenon that is produced by agro-ecological, social, economic, political and historical factors (Laxman, 2004; Deshingkar and Start, 2003; Rogaly et al., 2001). However, the combination of determinants, patterns and impacts of migration vary not only between source locations but also between households within a location. Internal labour movement in India is generally looked at from five broad perspectives: (1) *spatial and temporal dimensions*: rural-rural, rural-urban, urban-urban, temporary or seasonal and long-term or permanent; (2) *nature of work*: agricultural and non-agricultural; (3) *skill level*: unskilled, semi-skilled and skilled; (4) *socio-economic composition*: caste, class, ethnicity, gender, etc.; and (5) *returns from migration*: a low-return or survival mechanism and a high return livelihood strategy.

A few scholars like Breman (1985), who had continuously done micro-level studies all over Gujarat over several decades, have noted that there exists a growth in labour circulation. Some other micro-level studies spread over different parts of India also pointed out an increase in labour mobility when all forms of locational mobility are taken into account (Dreze, 1997; Krishnaiah, 1997).

Srivastava (1999) argued that rural to rural migration within India in the recent decades may be specifically seen to be a result of uneven capitalist penetration of agriculture leading to peaking of labour demands in certain seasons and resulting in the rise of mechanisms which source cheap labour over long distances.

Sahu and Rath (2010) in their study attempted to unravel the impact of forest protection committees under Joint Forest Management (JFM) on stress migration in four forest divisions of Orissa. In order to undertake this study, field investigations have been carried out in 12 villages of four forest divisions of the state. The findings of the study established that the improvement in forest cover under JFM has positive impact on the reduction of stress migration in the study area. The findings of the study have also established that the health of local labour market has improved a lot due to the proper and sustainable utilization of the common property resources through JFM.

Census data is destination-based and does not explain the deeper process of out-migration at the source areas. Although NSS provides data on out-migration, its coverage is critically restricted as it treats out-migrants as only those persons who have to stay outside the state during the last five years (Kundu and Gupta, 1996). There is a statistical difficulty in capturing short-duration migration. One reason for this is that the Indian statistical system is not really designed to capture short-term/seasonal/circular migration; as a result, policy makers may remain unaware of the sheer extent and likely increase in this phenomenon. Therefore, these secondary data sources are unable to capture the extent of short-duration and recent migrations that take place primarily for employment and other livelihood purposes (Chandrasekhar and Ghosh, 2007).

Kothari (2002) argues that certain groups are discriminated and disadvantaged based on social and cultural representations and limited access to economic opportunities and social services. Households that have less access to or control over resources are being excluded from resources at the origin are more likely to migrate. However, some poorer households may not afford to migrate because of the risk and cost of migration, which has been illustrated in the Table 3.

Table 3 Poverty-Related Capitals, Forms of Exclusion and Migration

Economic: Assets and Resources	Ownership of property and productive capital (land, cattle); savings	Exploitation, marginalization, deprivation and unequaldistribution of resources and assets	• Poor are less likely to migrate because they cannot afford, when they migrate the destinations may differ from the rich. • Rich households migrate more but the destinations may differ.
Human	Knowledge/skills: literacy/education Life stage: elderly and children Household size and structure	Disadvantage of certain groups through social/ cultural representations and limited access to opportunities and services	• Literates migrate. • Illiterates also migrate but the destinations may be different from literates. • Large family households tend to send migrants more.
Cultural and Identity	Identity: ethnicity, caste, class, gender and religion Cultural capital: knowledge/ skills and language	Elements of injustice; social patterns of representation, interpretation and communication; cultural-devaluation disadvantage; structural inequalities	• Excluded cultural groups are more prone to migrate. • Included groups also migrate but destinations may be different from excluded groups.

(Continued)

Table 3 Continued

Social	Networks, contacts, affiliations, (union, labour agencies, religious, etc.) Community-based organizations	Participation in social, community life, social isolation; rules and norms	• Those with social networks in receiving-areas and contacts with prospectiveemployers, contractors or middle-men, access to intermediaries and brokers migrate more. • Destinations may be different among migrants according to social networks based on migration history.
Geographical	Remote rural and urban, natural environment and region	Unequal distribution of resources and services	• Those from rural remote regions tend to migrate less. • People from advance regions tend to migrate less, but when migrate they prefer destinations that have more earnings.

Source: Adapted with some modifications from Kothari (2002), Tables 2 and 3, pp. 12–13.

Tripathy (2006) has examined the problems of tribal distress migration in the state of Orissa and is of the view that the insufficiency of income of the poverty-stricken tribes to cover the living expanses even on a subsistence level seems to be the basic underlying factor of their indebtedness leading to mass migration in search of employment as a coping strategy to mitigate the problem of unemployment. Moreover, due to deforestation, pressure on land, recurring drought, poverty and unemployment, the tribes of the study area migrate out of the districts and states along with their wives and children for a period of 6 months to eke out their livelihood (Tripathy and Das, 1997; Tripathy, 2006). It has been further observed by Tripathy that non-recognition of tribes over resources and restrictions on their use, alienation of tribes from the means of production, denial of due entitlement of labour, distressed payment of wages and misappropriation of funds have kept the tribal labour in the web of misery and starvation. In tribal-dominated states in India, the life support system of the local tribes has been snatched away by non-tribes and state institutions (Tripathy, 2000).

Despite a plethora of studies conducted pertaining to the issues of out-migration at macro as well as micro-level, studies relating to tribal women migration and more specifically in tribal concentrated KBK districts of Orissa are conspicuously extremely limited. As such, this study is first of its kind to study the problems of tribal women distress migration in KBK districts of Orissa.

KBK districts account for 19.72 per cent population over 30.59 per cent geographical area of the state and tribes constitute 38.72 per cent. Several socio-economic indicators highlight the backwardness of KBK region, which is one of the poorest regions in the country. The tribes in Orissa continued to remain socially, economically and educationally backward and are languishing at the bottom of the socio-economic ladder. The low level of income in KBK region, large-scale unemployment, underemployment and poverty ultimately distressed the migration of tribes. Further, there is little official recognition of the social dislocation caused by such short-term distress migration, and very rarely are there any interventions planned or implemented for families left behind. This has been especially a serious problem for families of migrant women with young children. There are issues of care of the young, the old and the sick. In addition, in poor households there are issues of daily survival of members left behind with uncertain remittance income. Such women migrant tribes fall prey to exploitative contractors and suffer bondage, social isolation and identity crisis (Tripathy, 1989). Their geographical isolation and improvised economy coupled with chronic poverty and illiteracy made them vulnerable, and they fail to withstand the forces and ultimately become the prey to all types of exploitation.

METHODOLOGY

Exploration of the motivations, compulsions and tribal women's experiences of internal migration; analysis of the direction of changes effecting in their personal and work lives; and identification of the new possibilities and tensions generated due to migration processes including its impact on family relations and economic structures are crucial to the study of tribal women migration. Bringing into focus the forms of labour migration by tribal women; highlighting the characteristics of the select sectors where tribal women migrant workers are concentrated and the issues and policies that affect them as workers and as women; identifying the issues where policy interventions are required to safeguard the rights as tribal women migrants; and bringing tribal women migrants within the ambit of 'inclusive growth' are of paramount significance.

Keeping these points in view, this study has been mainly confined to migrants of tribal-concentrated sample villages in which tribal women do accompany the male migrants of Kalahandi and Bolangir – the poverty-stricken, drought-ravaged, tribal-dominated districts of Orissa – where insecurity, food and livelihood options are conspicuously absent. These two districts have been purposively selected as these districts are the most backward districts in the country and known as KBK districts.

Keeping in view the constraints of time and cost, it was decided to collect field data from four blocks on the basis of random sampling method for the purpose of field study. Two blocks from each sample district have been randomly selected for the purpose of field study. First of all a list of the blocks falling in the selected districts has been prepared. From among the blocks, two blocks named Kesinga and Dharamgarh blocks in Kalahandi District and Belpara and Turekala blocks in Bolangir District have been selected on the basis of their tribal concentration, migration potentiality and accessibility.

It was found that usually the migrant households migrate to different place within the state and outside the state to work in the brick-kiln industries mostly in case of Bolangir District and in case of Kalahandi to Raipur, Bastar and other places of Madhya Pradesh during the month of November. After the list of tribal villages has been prepared, three villages in each block have been selected through random sampling method. Thus, a total of 12 villages have been covered under this study. It is revealed that due to unemployment and lack of purchasing power or income to maintain their livelihood these households mainly the tribes migrate for their survival as a coping strategy.

For the purpose of this study, even though there were both male and female migrants we have selected only the women migrants. Data were collected from the migrant households as already told particularly from the migrant women from the sample villages with the help of personal interview method through pre-tested schedules and questionnaire. The returned women migrant respondents in their native village were identified through village survey at different intervals during May–June 2012.

Table 4 presents a picture about the demographic and literacy position of KBK districts (Orissa). The table also reveals that there is high proportion of tribal population in these districts. Moreover, the rate of female literacy is much lower as compared to total literacy percentage.

Table 4 Demographic and Literacy Indicators in the KBK Districts: 2001

District	Popu-Density	Population Indicators					Literacy Rate	
		Total (000)	Female (%)	Rural (%)	ST* (%)	SC* (%)	Total (%)	Female (%)
1	2	3	4	5	6	7	8	9
Koraput	134	1,178	49.96	83.18	50.67	13.41	36.20	24.81
Malkangiri	83	480	49.91	92.79	58.36	19.96	31.26	21.28
Nawrangpur	192	1,018	49.81	94.18	55.27	15.09	34.26	21.02
Rayagada	116	823	50.71	85.98	56.04	14.28	35.61	24.31
Bolangir	203	1,336	49.56	88.45	22.06	15.39	54.91	39.27
Sonepur	231	541	49.13	92.59	22.11	9.50	64.07	47.28
Kalahandi	168	1,334	50.00	92.49	28.88	17.01	46.20	29.56
Nuapada	138	531	50.15	94.34	35.59	13.09	42.29	26.01
KBK Districts	**152**	**7,241**	**49.91**	**89.89**	**38.72**	**16.63**	**36.58**	**24.72**
Orissa	**236**	**36,707**	**49.29**	**85.03**	**22.21**	**16.20**	**63.61**	**50.97**

Note: Popu-density – population density (persons/sq.km). *As per 1991 Census.

Table 5 SC and ST Population of the Sample Blocks in the Study Area

Name of the District	Name of the Block	Percentage of SC Population	Percentage of ST Population
Kalahandi	1) Kesinga	15.9	23.5
	2) Dharamgada	16.7	17.4
Bolangir	1) Belpara	14.4	31.2
	2) Turekala	15.8	39.5

Source: Census of India (2001), District Statistical Handbook.

Table 5 depicts that among the sample blocks in the selected districts Dharamgada has the highest percentage of 16.7 per cent of SC population, followed by Kesinga (15.9) and Turekala (15.8). Similarly, Turekala block has also the distinction of highest percentage of ST population (39.5), followed by Belpara (31.2) and Kesinga (23.5).

Table 6 unfolds that among the sample villages in the selected blocks Titkela Village in Kesinga block has the highest percentage of 30.8 of SC population, followed by Patimal Village (29.1) in Turekala block. Similarly, Golmunda Village has also the distinction of highest percentage of ST population (46.3), followed by Juba (42.0) in Belpara block. It is found

Table 6 SC and ST Population and Sex Ratio of the Sample Villages in the Study Area

Name of the District	Name of the Block	Name of the Sample Villages	SC Population and Its Percentage to Total Population	ST Population and Its Percentage to Total Population	Sex Ratio (Females per 1000 Males)
Kalahandi	1) Kesinga	1) Tansir	330 (19.6)	184 (10.9)	972
		2) Titkela	318 (30.8)	143 (13.8)	975
		3) Godtola	12 (2.4)	91 (17.9)	1028
	2) Dharamgada	1) Golmunda	433 (9.7)	2,076 (46.3)	918
		2) Kadalimunda	301 (14.33)	73 (3.5)	942
		3) Dharamgada	19,912 (16.7)	20,728 (17.4)	982
Bolangir	1) Belpara	1) Bahabal	119 (14.4)	247 (29.9)	995
		2) Kapani	118 (9.8))	399 (28.6)	997
		3) Juba	220 (21.4)	433 (42.0)	1012
	2) Turekala	1) Barala	46 (8.0)	69 (11.1)	1032
		2) Kadalipali	29 (18.6)	56 (35.9)	1026
		3) Patimal	91 (29.1)	1 (0.3)	929

Source: Census of India (2001), District Statistical Handbook.

that the villages like Godtola, Juba, Barala and Kadalipali manifested more females per thousand of males. The Golmunda Village exhibited the lowest sex ratio (918) among the villages.

Table 7 presents the list of households from which sample households were selected for the study. As has been mentioned earlier, two blocks namely Kesinga and Dharmgarda were selected from Kalahandi district and similarly two blocks namely Belpara and Turekala were selected from Bolangir district for collection of sample data. From Kesinga and Dharmgada blocks there were 30 households and 75 households selected respectively for field study. Similarly, from Belpara and Turekala blocks there were 60 and 15 households selected respectively for field study. Thus, there were 180 sample tribal women migrant households from 12 villages, who were found to have adopted migration as a coping mechanism to earn their livelihoods outside their districts and states.

Table 7 Number of Tribal Women Migrant Households Surveyed from the List of Households

Name of the Block	Name of the Sample Villages	Sample Migrant Households
Kesinga	1) Tansir	15
	2) Titkela	10
	3) Godtola	5
Dharamgada	1) Golmunda	30
	2) Kadalimunda	5
	3) Dharamgada	40
Belpara	1) Bahabal	30
	2) Kapani	15
	3) Juba	15
Turekala	1) Barala	5
	2) Kadalipali	5
	3) Patimal	5
Total	12	180

Source: Field study.

EDUCATIONAL PROFILE OF THE TRIBAL WOMEN MIGRANTS

Education is a significant attribute and an asset to an individual. In this era, education is necessary to obtain gainful, productive and remunerative employment. Lower levels of education among the workers create vulnerability at two levels. It first denies access to 'good jobs' in the organized sector. Second, it confines the workers to mostly casual manual jobs which are in the unorganized sector only. Women workers in rural and backward tribal area are the worst victims of this double disadvantage. In the tribal-dominated backward regions of KBK districts, illiteracy coupled with extremely low level of education means that the workers remain stuck to the agricultural sector, which is having high incidence of seasonal cyclicality. Moreover, due to the non-availability of employment, low payment and landlessness of the tribes, the distress migrations continue unabated in these regions.

The high incidences of illiteracy deprive these migrants from the basic rights at the work site and high incidence of exploitation from the employers and contractors. The second generation of these migrants is also deprived of education since these people are moving population and parent's deprivation pass on to the next generation as well.

The education profile of the women migrants indicates that majority of them, 116 (64.44) out of 180 women migrants, belong to the illiterate class (Table 8). Out of 35.56 per cent who reported as literate only 46 migrant women (25.56 per cent) have lower primary level of education and the rest 18 migrant women (10 per cent) have up to primary level of education. This high incidence of illiteracy is a major lacuna of these seasonal tribal women migrant workers.

The reported 116 tribal women migrants were distributed in major unorganized economic activities like brick kiln (58 women, 55.77 per cent), road laying and earth work (24 women, 80 per cent), construction works, hotels/commercial establishments (8 women, 80 per cent), manual works and chips making (26 women, 72.22 per cent). It is deplorable that many of the legal provisions available for the migrant workers like the Minimum Wages Act, Equal Remuneration Act and the Inter-State Migrant Workers Act have been ineffective because of the lack of implementation as also the lack of awareness among the workers regarding the existence of the laws and their rights. Very small number of contractors has taken licenses and very few enterprises employing inter-state migrant workers have registered under the Act. The record of prosecutions and dispute settlement has been very weak. Migrant workers do not possess pass books, prescribed by law, which form the basic record of their identity and their transactions with the contractor and employers.

Several studies have revealed violation of all these acts. Further, migrant women workers are harassed by the police, postal department, owners of the establishments, owners of workers' dwellings, shopkeepers, labour

Table 8 Education Profile of Female Respondents

Activities	Education Profile of the Sample Migrant Women			
	Illiterates	**Up to Three Years of Schooling (Lower Primary)**	**More than 3 Years to Five Years of Schooling (Primary)**	**Total**
Brick kiln	58 (55.77)	30 (28.85)	16 (15.38)	104 (100)
Road laying, earth work	24 (80.00)	06 (20.00)	00	30 (100)
Construction works, hotels/ commercial establishments	08 (80.00)	02 (20.00)	00	10
Manual works and chips making	26 (72.22)	08 (22.22)	02 (5.56)	36 (100)
Total	116 (64.44)	46 (25.56)	18 (10.00)	180 (100)

Note: Figures in parentheses indicate percentages.

Source: Field study.

contractors and the railway police during their journey. Migrants contribute to growth by providing cheap and flexible labour, yet they remain without an identity and are unable to get access to government programmes and schemes related to health and education which are meant for the poor.

It is found from Table 9 that most of the women migrant households (37.77) are dependent on agriculture. In most of the households, there are no authentic records with regard to the possession of their land, size of holding, etc. The area of land holding by the migrant household is not only extremely limited but also barren, scattered and rain-fed, and as such the income and output from the agriculture is inadequate and thus no security of food to these households. The average monthly income in the place of origin is Rs. 432/- only, which is extremely meagre.

Table 10 reveals the nature of employment available to the women migrant households at the place of destination. It is evident that the migrant women are employed in a wide range of employments but mostly in brick-kiln industry (57.78 per cent) and road-laying (16.7 per cent) works. Scattered nature of work place and distressed and discriminatory wages are the reality of migrant workers leading to prolonged poverty. But they are compelled to pursue such migration process as a coping mechanism to fulfil their basic

Table 9 Occupation-wise Distribution of Migrant Tribal Women Households at the Place of Origin

Occupation	Migrant Women	%	Average per Women Worker Monthly Income
Agricultural work	68	37.77	300
Non-agricultural workers	23	12.77	450
Leaf-plate making	12	6.67	400
Bidi making	04	2.22	300
Date mattress	05	2.78	280
Rope making	03	1.67	300
Bamboo basket weaving	07	3.89	400
Hill broom collection	03	1.67	400
Collection of sabai grass	03	1.67	250
Wine production	10	5.56	600
Kendu leaf plucking	15	8.33	700
Preparation of stone-chips	27	15	650
Total	180	100.00	432

Source: Field study.

Table 10 Occupation-wise Distribution of Migrant Households at the Place of Destination

Different Occupation	No of Women Migrant Households	%	Average per Worker Monthly Income (in Rs.)
Brick-kiln industry	104	57.78	3,500
Road laying, earth work and other	30	16.67	3,600
Construction works, hotels/ commercial establishments	10	5.55	2,800
Manual works	16	8.89	3,000
Chips making	20	11.11	2,800
Total	180	100.00	3,356

Source: Field study.

requirements. However, in terms of availability of work and income at the place of destination is significantly higher. The average monthly income of the migrant women are considerably higher (Rs. 3,356) in the place of destination as compared to their place of origin.

Age profile of the women migrants is important from the demographic and economic point of view as it has an impact on labour productivity, fertility and human capability. From Table 10, out of 180 women migrants, 104 women were employed exclusively in brick-kiln industry, constituting 57.78 per cent – which is the major employer in the place of destination. We can observe that around 64 per cent of the female respondents belong to the age group of 18–45 engaged in brick-kiln industry. In the age group of 45+ to 60 years, there were 38 women constituting 36.53 per cent in brick-kiln industry.

There were 30 migrant women employed in road laying earth work, there were 20 women constituting 66.67 per cent out of the total number employed in this sector, who were in the age group of 18 to 45 years.

In the construction works, hotels/commercial establishments, which mainly involve hard manual work, 80 per cent of the women migrant

Table 11 Age Profile of Tribal Women Migrants

Activities	Age Group of Sample Women Migrants		
	18–30	**30+ to 45**	**45+ to 60**
Brick-kiln industry	14 (13.46)	52 (50.00)	38 (36.53)
Road laying, earth work	06 (20.00)	14 (46.67)	10 (33.33)
Construction works, hotels/commercial establishments	02 (20.00)	06 (60.00)	02 (20.00)
Chips making and manual work	06 (16.67)	18 (50.00)	12 (33.33)
Total	28 (15.56)	90 (50.00)	62 (34.44)

Note: Figures in parentheses indicate percentages.

Source: Field study.

workers were engaged in who belong to the age group of 18–45. There were 36 migrant women employed in chips making and manual work, out of which 24 women migrants constituting 66.67 per cent were in the age group of 18 to 45 years.

Table 12 Distribution of Women Migrant Households According to Their Sources of Debt

Sources of Debt	Women Migrant Households	%
Money lender	128	71.11
Regional rural bank	10	5.56
Commercial bank	4	2.22
Co-operatives	2	1.11
Self-help group	8	4.44
Friends, relatives	26	14.45
Others	2	1.11
Total	180	100.00

Source: Field study.

Despite vast expansion of the formal credit system in India, the dependence of rural poor on moneylenders continues in some areas particularly in tribal regions of the state. In our analysis, the moneylenders dominate the credit market as about 72 per cent of women migrant households are dependent on them (Table 12).

For various reasons, the credit flow to these sections of the population for meeting their credit requirements could not be institutionalized. This was due to the factors like inadequate supply of credit, demand–supply gap, improper identification of beneficiaries and unhealthy competition from informal credit agencies. Cumbersome and time-consuming banking procedure, failure to supply credit at the time of need and rigid collateral requirement are the major stumbling blocks causing poor access to formal credit institutions. The crop loss due to natural calamities and unproductive utilization of borrowed funds resulted in rising default rate and delayed loan payments. The credit market is not developed in the district which may cater to the needs of the poor tribes (Sarap, 1991; Swain, 2001; Tripathy, 2006). Indebtedness leads to bondage and a type of contractual labour agreement between the labour contractor and agents; bondage which in turn, reinforces exploitation and distressed payment of wages.

It is revealed that migration-based work and earnings are the major source of survival for the communities of this poverty stricken and low endowment regions of Bolangir and Kalahandi districts of Orissa. Although migration is an irreversible reality for the majority of those who depend on it, and indeed for many it is the single major outlet from rural poverty, it is an act fraught with immense hardship and other necessities of life. There are several reasons for this – skill levels are low, connections and networks are scarce, services are absent and above all, labour and remuneration practices in industries and markets that employ seasonal migrants tend to be callous and exploitative.

As has been observed, the most important reason for failure of economic development and removal of poverty in the tribal-dominated villages of sample villages of Kalahandi and Bolangir districts of Orissa is corruption, which is rampant causing 'leakages' in the amounts earmarked for rural employment-generating schemes.

It has also been observed that Public Distribution System (PDS) has not delivered essential commodities to meet the minimum food needs of the drought-hit villages of sample villages of Kalahandi and Bolangir districts of Orissa. A considerable amount of food grains and essential goods are supplied to the urban centre and sold directly to the businessmen by the dealers in a close nexus with the corrupt officials of the supply department. Thus, corruption has obstructed the noble objectives to deliver the essential food and other items to the rural poor. An inevitable sequel to the insensitivity and absurdity of the food security system is distress migration from the drought-hit villages of sample villages of Kalahandi and Bolangir districts to the urban areas. As a result of which there is a vicious circle of poverty, unemployment, indebtedness and migrations of tribes, both males and females, in the districts of Kalahandi and Bolangir.

Lack of employment and distressed condition of living compels the tribal women migrants to take advance from the contractors resulting in migration. Whatever paltry amount they save is insufficient to pay back the loan amount borrowed from the moneylenders, as the rate of interest is exorbitantly high. The cycle of poverty originates from the sordid reality of crop loss, unemployment, vulnerability to health hazards and, ultimately, indebtedness and chronic poverty. The vicious circle continues to be unabated for decades in the sample districts as the planned measures could not percolate benefits considerable in the rural regions of the districts.

SUGGESTIONS FOR POLICY IMPLICATION

It is apparent from the analysis that support to women's various livelihood strategies, including income-generating activities, ensures short-term safety nets.

Creation of necessary infrastructure like irrigation facilities will simulate private investments in agriculture. The focus on accelerated food grains production on a sustainable basis and free trade in grains would help create massive employment and reduce the incidence of poverty in rural areas. This will lead to faster economic growth and give purchasing power to the people.

In order to improve the status of tribal women, specific development programmes should be designed for each specific tribal group in such a way that it caters to their specific needs and problems by ensuring their personal involvement. The strategies that may be pursued for the welfare of the tribal women are as follows:

1. Formulation of realistic development plans for health, education and employment based on needs as felt by tribal women of the specific tribal group.
2. Need for promoting nutritional and health education among working, lactational and pregnant tribal women.
3. Development of poultry and fisheries are to be encouraged for enhancing employment programmes.

Studies have shown that there is a high percentage of population below the poverty line in forested areas, varying from 69.02 per cent in south Orissa to 44 per cent in Chhattisgarh, as against 37.2 per cent being the national average (Saxena, 1999). This clearly indicates that the local population is not being benefited by the revenue generated by forest as a natural resource.

Therefore, existing situation needs corrections through policy interventions, under which forests are used for the livelihood needs of the forest-dwelling and forest-dependent common people for their poverty alleviation. The first charge of forest products must be in favour of the neighbouring people. Sustainable management of forests and proper use of forest products can help in alleviating poverty of the forest dwellers. Low productivity is a result of unsustainable management and consequent degradation. The scope of generating employment potential from collection, value addition and sale of Non-Timber Forest Products (NTFPs) may be enhanced. The involvement of efficient, dedicated, honest administrators, stringent action on non-implementation of government schemes and dishonest officials, plugging the loop holes of corruption and leakages of fund will substantially mitigate the problems of distress migration, women migrants and their plight and exploitation.

ACKNOWLEDGEMENTS

The author expresses his thanks to the ICSSR, New Delhi, and acknowledges that the preliminary/primary data collected for the ICSSR-funded Research Project 'Problems of Rural-Urban Migration: A Study from Social Exclusion Perspectives' has been partially used in this research paper.

NOTE

1. KBK districts basically refer to the undivided districts such as Kalahandi, Bolangir and Koraput and newly organized eight districts of Orissa, namely, (1) Kalahandi, (2) Nuapara, (3) Bolangir, (4) Sonepur, (5) Koraput, (6) Nawarangpur, (7) Malkangiri and (8) Rayagada, which are among the most backward districts of India.

   Total population: 63,20,4.68 (19.96 per cent to total state population)

   ST population: 24,48;301 (38:73 per cent to total KBK population)

   SC population: 10,00,840 (15.83 per cent to total KBK population)

REFERENCES

Breman, J. (1985). *Of Peasants, Migrants and Paupers: Rural Labour Circulation and Capitalist Production in West India*, Oxford: Oxford University Press.

Chandrasekhar, C.P. and J. Ghosh (2007). 'Dealing with Short-Term Migration', *The Change*, Dec. 1993. 23(4): 3–18

Chauhan, A. (1990). *Tribal Women and Social Change in India*, Etawah: A.C. Brothers.

Deshingkar, P. and D. Start (2003). *Seasonal Migration for Livelihoods, Coping, Accumulation and Exclusion*, Working Paper No. 220, London: Overseas Development Institute

Dhebar, U.N. (1961). *Report of Scheduled Areas and Scheduled Tribes Commission*, New Delhi: Government of India.

Dreze, J. (1997). 'Palanpur 1957–93: Occupational change, land ownership and social inequality', in J. Berman, P. Kloos and A. Saith (eds.), *The Village in Asia Revisited*, Delhi: Oxford University Press.

Ellis, F. (2003). 'A Livelihoods Approach to Migration and Poverty Reduction', *The Hindu, Business Line*, September, 25

Kothari, U. (2002). 'Migration and Chronic Poverty', Chronic Poverty Research Centre, Working Paper No. 16, Institute for Development Policy and Management, Manchester: University of Manchester.

Krishnaiah, M. (1997), 'Rural Migration Labour Systems in Semi-Arid Areas: A Study of Two Villages in Andhra Pradesh', *The Indian Journal of Labour Economics*, 40(1).

Kundu, A. and S. Gupta (1996). 'Migration, Urbanisation and Regional Inequality', *Economic and Political Weekly*, 28 Dec., pp. 3391–3398.

Laxman Rao, S. (2004). *Rural Labour Migration in Andhra Pradesh, India: Towards Addressing New Policy Spaces*, Secunderabad: Foundation for Rural and Social Development.

Rogaly, B., J. Biswas, D. Coppard, A. Rafique, K. Rana and A. Sengupta (2001). 'Seasonal Migration, Social Change and Migrants' Rights: Lessons from West Bengal', *Economic and Political Weekly*, 8 Dec., pp. 4547–4559.

Roy Burman, B.K. (1988). 'Challenges of development and tribal women of India', in J.P Singh, N.N. Vyas and R.S. Mann (eds.), *Tribal Women and Development*, Udaipur: MLS Tribal Research and Training Institute, Tribal Area Development Department, Rajasthan.

Sahu, N.C. and B. Rath (2010). 'Impact of Joint Forest Management (JFM) on Environmental Stress Migration: Evidence from Orissa', *International Journal of Rural Management*, Vol. 6, April.

Sarap, K. (1991). *Interlinked Agrarian markets in Rural India*, New Delhi: Sage.

Saxena, N.C. (1999). 'World Bank and the Forestry Sector in India', in World Bank, 1999, *Alleviating Poverty through Participatory Forest Management: An Evaluation of India's Forest Development and World Bank Assistance*, Washington, DC: Operations Evaluation Department.

Singh, A.K. and C. Rajyalakshmi (1993). 'Status of Tribal Women in India', *Social Change*, 23(4): 3–18.

Singh, B. (1993). 'An Outline of Work to Be Taken Up on Tribal Women', Working Papers, NCW.

Srivastava, R. (1999). 'Rural Labour in Uttar Pradesh: Emerging Features of Subsistence, Condition and Resistance', *Journal of Peasant Studies*, 26 (2/3).

Swain, M. (2001). 'Rural Indebtedness and Usurious Interest Rates in Eastern India: Some Micro Evidence', *Journal of Social and Economic Development*, 3(1): 122–143.

Tripathy, S.N. (1989). *Bonded Labour in India*, New Delhi: Discovery Publishing House.

Tripathy, S.N and C.R. Das (1997). *Migrant Labour in India*, New Delhi: Discovery Publishing House.

Tripathy, S.N. (2005). *Female Headed Households in India*, New Delhi: Sonali Publication.

Tripathy, S.N. (2006). *Dynamics of Tribal Migration*, New Delhi: Sonali Publication.

Tripathy, S.N. (2000). *Glimpses on Tribal Development*, New Delhi: Discovery Publishing House.

CHAPTER 11

TRIBAL WOMEN AND HEALTH MODERNITY: STATUS AND SOLUTIONS

Neeta Tapan

INTRODUCTION

The Indian desire of *Sarve Santhu Niramayaha*, 'let all be free from disease, let all be healthy', is a seemingly difficult task for poor and oppressed populations. This powerful linkage between poverty and health has been characterized as bidirectional and synergistic (Das Gupta and Chen, 1996; Wagstaff, 2002). First, poverty exacerbates ill health. The poor have limited access to health inputs (e.g., nutritious foods, health services, non-toxic environment) and little capacity to convert (e.g., through education) the inputs they do have into health. Therefore, the poor have lower health productivity than non-poor, and consequently limited outputs. This is supported by global studies, which have shown that the poor suffer more from ill health (Gwatkins et al., 2000). Second, poor health may lead to impoverishment and downward mobility. Poor health restricts economic growth by reducing the availability of labour, limiting the productivity of workers, creating dependency on others and wasting resources (Abel-Smith, 1990). If a household member falls ill, it reduces their capacity to earn income, or perform necessary household tasks, thereby increasing economic vulnerability of the household (Wagstaff, 2001). Moreover, the burden of medical costs is higher for the poor, and in extreme cases, may push families who are just above the poverty line into destitution (Krishnan, 1999).

The Infant Mortality Rate in the poorest 20 per cent of the population is 2.5 times higher than that in the richest 20 per cent of the population. In other words, an infant born in a poor family is two and half times more likely to die in infancy than an infant in a better off family (National Family Health Survey (NFHS)-2). A child in the 'low standard of living' economic group is almost four times more likely to die in childhood than a child in the 'high standard of living' group. A person from the poorest quintile of the population, despite more health problems, is six times less likely to access hospitalization than a person from the richest quintile. This means that the poor are unable to afford and access hospitalization in a very large proportion of illness episodes, even when it is required.

The delivery of a mother from the poorest quintile of the population is over six times less likely to be attended by a medically trained person than the delivery of a well-off mother from the richest quintile of the population (NFHS-2).

However, besides the links between poverty and health, certain other equally important factors are being taken into consideration. As per the concept of 'HEALTH' being modified by the World Health Organization (WHO), the global agency on health and disease, health becomes a multi-factorial entity, which is the product of physical, mental and social status of an individual or a group in its existing set-up. More so, the economic status of an individual or community or region largely contributes towards the well-being of the people and thereby gives an indication to where lay the disease-causing factors. The economy of the sector leads to dictate the nutritional, occupational and behavioural pattern of an individual or community. Health is largely behavioural, profoundly social and has important emotional, cognitive and spiritual dimensions (WHO, 1992). This new approach to understanding and defining 'Health' lays down the importance of going beyond the well-established links between poverty and health status.

Thus, in assessing the interactions between different other parameters influencing health indicators, a society needs to identify the areas of vulnerability and their acute manifestations in highly vulnerable groups like the scheduled tribes (STs). A tribe consists of a group of people claiming a common ancestry, sharing a common culture and language. About a half of these indigenous people of the world, i.e., 84,326,240, are living in India as per the 2001 census, which constitute 8.2 per cent of the total population of India. There were about 698 communities or clans including 75 primitive communities who have been designated as 'primitive' based on pre-agricultural level of technology, low level of literacy, stagnant or diminishing population size, relative seclusion (isolation) from the mainstream population, economical and educational backwardness, extreme poverty, dwelling in remote inaccessible hilly terrains, maintenance of constant contact with the natural environment and being unaffected by the developmental process undergoing in India. Thus, tribes are socially weak and economically poor communities (Census, 2001). The percentage of tribals living below poverty line is 47.3 in rural and 33.3 in urban areas, which is higher than the corresponding national figures of 28.3 and 25.7, respectively (Planning Commission, 2008; NFHS-2). Although the Indian tribes are a heterogeneous group, most of them remain at the lowest stratum of the society. Around 91 per cent of the tribal population still lives in rural area as against 72 per cent for the whole nation. Although STs are accorded special status under the Fifth/Sixth Schedules of the Indian Constitution, their status on the whole, especially their health still remains unsatisfactory. Above all, tribal women face double disadvantage due to gender-specific reproductive health problems which are carried over automatically to the next generation.

PUBLIC HEALTH INFRASTRUCTURE

Health standards of a country reflect the social, economic, political and moral well-being of its ordinary citizen. Healthy living conditions and access to good quality health care for all citizens are not only basic human rights, but also essential prerequisites for social and economic development. Economic and social growth of a society or a country is directly dependent on the health of its constituents. The concept of human development already emphasizes the improvement of education and health standards besides the parameter of income.

There has been a definite growth in the overall health care resources and health-related manpower in the last decade. The ratio of hospital beds to population in rural areas is 15 times lower than that in urban areas. The ratio of doctors to population in rural areas is almost six times lower than that in the urban population (Health Information of India, 2000–2001). Per capita expenditure on public health is seven times lower in rural areas compared to government health spending for urban areas. Although the spending on health care is 6 per cent of gross domestic product (GDP), the state expenditure is only 0.9 per cent of the total spending. People using their own resources spend rest of it. Thus only 17 per cent of all health expenditure in the country is borne by the state and 83 per cent is borne by the people themselves. This makes the Indian public health system grossly inadequate. India ranks sixth in the world in the context of public health spending after Burundi, Myanmar, Pakistan, Sudan and Cambodia (WHO, 2003). As a result of this, the infrastructure of health system itself is becoming ineffective. In a recent survey, it was noticed that only 38 per cent of all Primary Health Centres (PHCs), the most vital units of India's public health infrastructure, have all the essential manpower and only 31 per cent have all the essential supplies (defined as 60 per cent of critical inputs), with only 3 per cent of PHCs having 80 per cent of all critical inputs.

The reduction on public health spending and the growing inequalities in health and health care are taking its toll on the marginalized and socially disadvantaged population like the tribal population. Non-availability of health staff in the health centres, poor quality of services, non-availability of essential drugs and equipments, lack of proper building facilities, difficult terrain and constraints of distance and time (one Auxiliary Nurse Mid-wife may typically be entrusted with 15–20 scattered villages), and lack of transport and communication facilities hinder the provision of health care. Poverty is the main cause for illness and early death among the tribals. However, lack of access to right foods (iron, protein and micronutrients such as iodine and vitamins) is the principle cause for the very high incidence of nutritional deficiency and diseases like anaemia, diarrhoea, night blindness, goitre, etc. These factors combined with lack of access to basic health care services are the main reasons for the unexceptionally adverse differentials with the more developed parts of the state and also with the general population. The maternal and child health indicators among tribals and others as recorded in the National Family Health Surveys (NFHS)-2 and 3 are shown in Table 1.

Table 1 shows the health indicators exhibit an improvement across the NFHS-2 and NFHS-3, which are not yet equated with the figures available for the non-tribal population.

Differences in the status of some other health indicators of the tribals and the general population can be highlighted as in Table 2.

The striking differences in the nutritional parameters among the tribal and non tribal women have serious consequences. A child born in the tribal belt is one and half times more likely to die before the fifth birthday than children of other groups. Female child is 1.5 times more likely to die before reaching her fifth birthday as compared to a male child (NFHS-2). The female to male ratios for children are rapidly declining, from 945 girls per 1000 boys in 1991, to just 927 girls per 1000 boys in 2001(Census 2001). Children below 3 years of age in STs and scheduled castes (SCs) are twice as likely to be malnourished than children in other groups. A tribal mother is over 12 times less likely to be delivered by a medically trained person (NFHS-2). A tribal woman is one and a half times more likely to suffer the consequences of chronic malnutrition as compared to women from other social categories.

Table 1 Maternal and Child Health Indicators among Tribal Women and Others (NFHS-2 & 3)

Indicator	Scheduled Tribes		Others
	NFHS-2	NFHS-3	NFHS-3
Median age at marriage	15.80	16.30	18.10
Awareness of legal age for marriage (%)	7.50	–	22.00
Age at consummation of marriage (in years)	16.60	17.00	18.50
Total fertility rate	3.06	3.12	2.68
Median age at first childbirth (in years)	18.80	19.10	20.60
Proportion of pregnancies with no antenatal checkups (%)	43.10	37.80	22.80
Proportion of pregnancies with no TT immunization (%)	25.80	36.90	16.40
Proportion of pregnancies receiving IFA tablets (%)	48.60	62.00	72.00
Home deliveries (%)	81.80	82.30	49.00
Family Planning (%)	39.10	42.70	51.40
Proportion of births of order more than two (%)	53.00	51.00	34.60
Infant mortality rate/1,000 LB	84.20	62.10	57.00
Neonatal mortality rate/1,000 LB	53.30	39.90	39.10
Under 5 mortality rate/1,000 LB	126.60	99.80	74.00
Completion of primary immunization (%)	26.00	31.30	53.80
No vaccination (%)	–	11.50	4.30

Table 2 Nutritional Parameters among Tribal Women and Non-Tribals (NFHS-3)

Parameter	Scheduled Tribes (%)	General Population (%)
Malnutrition in children	54.5	33.7
Anaemia in children	76.8	70.0
Anaemia in women	68.5	51.3
Underweight among women	46.6	29.4
Vitamin A deficiency among women	30.0	18.5

METHODOLOGY

Conceptual Framework

The unequal distribution of resources for health care is further complimented by inability of universal access to health care due to various access difficulties. Like in India, pre-existing inequality in the health care provisions is further enhanced by difficulties in accessing it. These access difficulties can be either due to

1. Geographical distance,
2. Socio-economic distance,
3. Gender distance, or
4. Attitudinal or mental distance.

Although the manifestations of some or all these types of distances are found in varying degrees among different sections of society, the vulnerable groups like the tribals face almost all of them and that too with greater intensity. Moreover, tribal women are even more disadvantaged as they face specific reproductive health problems, which in turn influence the health status of their children on certain levels. Although this gender disadvantage is universal, it is more pronounced in the tribal community. It can be laid down that rigidity in the attitude or mindset of this community can be a major hurdle in the process of overcoming all the other distances. The attitudinal blocks can even nullify the available public health resources. The behavioural aspect of health, as discussed by WHO, gains importance here. The tribal population is often associated with traditional methods of treatment and conservative approach towards health management. If mental distance from health care knowledge and resources can be reduced, then the inherent gender distance automatically gets addressed. On the other hand, the external factors like geographical distance and socio-economic distance are easier to handle as they require external treatment measures; whereas the mental blocks can be resolved only from within on an individual level. However, these problems can be addressed through Information, Education and Communication (IEC) measures on group level. Self-Help Groups in this case can be powerful tools of psychological change as they act as financial and social intermediaries.

SHG is generally an economically homogeneous group formed through a process of self-selection with membership ranging between 10 and 20. SHGs have well-defined rules and by-laws, hold regular meetings and maintain records, savings and credit discipline. They usually start by making voluntary thrift on a regular basis, internal lending through these pooled funds and then move on gradually to bank linkage, external credit leverage and income generation. Besides being potential tools of micro-credit delivery, the SHGs also work as social intermediaries resolving gender issues specifically as most of them are women SHGs by default. The members, especially women, not only gain financial literacy, but they also experience improvement in their status within the household, as they assume a new economic position in some way. The experience of moving out of their homes and participating in SHG functions also opens up new ideas and practices to women. Some SHG hold meetings on special topics of interest. New information can lead to changes in behaviours which are healthier and more empowering. In addition, women acquire new skills through various trainings which may not only lead to future income generation activities, but also increase their self-efficacy, which has been linked to improved health and well-being.

This paper thus tries to assess the health status modernity prevailing among the tribal women with respect to certain parameters selected from the secondary data of NFHS-3. At the same time, it uses certain primary data to reflect upon the impact of SHGs on tribal mindset. These primary data have been drawn from a larger study carried out in the Jhabua District of Madhya Pradesh. The sample included 75 SHGs covering two respondents from each group. Thus, structured schedules were administered on 150 respondents. The credit plus approach goes beyond the promotion of economic activities and facilitating IEC activities in the meetings of the SHGs. Field evidences provide contradictory views of both sides regarding the roles, effectiveness and success of the SHGs on the levels of all such tall claims.

TRIBAL HEALTH OF WOMEN: STATUS AND ATTITUDE

The health scenario of tribal community as a whole and women in particular projects peculiar traits. The health status of women and their attitude towards health care carries special importance as women are responsible for child bearing and rearing and the nutritional status of the family as well. However, women seem to be more distanced from the health care facilities as well as attitudinal modernity owing to the societal setup. Therefore, an analysis of selected data set of NFHS-3 has been done to assess the status of maternal and child health in the tribal community and their mindset.

Table 3 shows that the early motherhood is more prevalent among the STs as compared to the non-STs. Similarly, among all the tribal community forms the smallest percentage of category practising family planning. At the same time, the STs outdo their non-ST counterparts in exhibiting their preference for male child.

Table 3 Attitudes and Practices

Caste/Tribe	Early Motherhood	Family Planning	Son Preference
SC	19.8	69.5	25.4
ST	21.1	65.9	28.9
OBC	16.0	72.9	17.3

Source: NFHS-3.

Table 4 Exposure to Family Planning Messages

Caste/Tribe	Radio	TV	News Paper	Hoarding	None
SC	31.1	45.6	15.5	22.1	41.7
ST	21.3	25.4	9.2	14.9	61.0
OBC	33.8	48.0	20.0	26.6	39.5
Other	35.5	59.6	32.1	32.4	30.2

Source: NFHS-3.

The regular sources of IEC available besides social cohesion or interaction are the print and electronic sources of media and communication. The findings of NFHS-3 as shown in Table 4 reveal that the ST population is least exposed to all the sources of communication, which can disseminate family planning messages. On the other hand, they top in the category of no accessibility to any source.

Table 5 Early Childhood Mortality Rates

Caste/Tribe	NM[1]	PNM[2]	IM[3]	CM[4]	<5 Mort[5]
SC	46.3	20.1	66.4	23.2	88.1
ST	39.9	22.3	62.1	35.8	95.7
OBC	38.3	18.3	56.6	17.3	72.8
Other	34.5	14.5	48.9	10.8	59.2

[1]*Neonatal mortality.* The probability of dying in the first month of life.
[2]*Postneonatal mortality.* The probability of dying after the first month of life but before the first birthday.
[3]*Infant mortality (1q0).* The probability of dying before the first birthday.
[4]*Child mortality (4q1).* The probability of dying between the first and fifth birthdays.
[5]*Under-five mortality (5q0).* The probability of dying before the fifth birthday.

Source: NFHS-3.

A surprising feature to note in Table 5 is that the Neonatal Mortality Rate is higher in the SCs as compared to the STs. The STs outdo all the other categories in case of Peri-Neonatal Mortality Rate. But again the SCs have higher incidences of infant mortality than in the STs. However, the STs again score the highest points in the case of child mortality and under five age mortality.

Yet again a very surprising observation is that the rate of still births, early neonatal deaths and perinatal mortality rate among the STs is not just the lowest but also remarkably far behind the rates recorded for all the other castes/categories. This trend poses severe contradictions in the context of the very bleak picture which emerges regarding certain factors associated with the tribals like the age at conception, antenatal care, place of delivery, etc.

The scenario regarding the antenatal care received by the tribals projects a very mixed picture. Anti-Natal Care (ANC) received at the hands of the doctors is the minimum for the STs while the same provided by the nurses is the highest for this community. The score of the STs in receiving ANC through Other Health Personnel (OHP) again exceeds those of the SCs and the Other Backward Classes (OBCs). On the other hand, as can be expected from the high percentage of deliveries at home in the tribal community, the ANC received from the Dai is the maximum for these people. Nevertheless, it is heartening to note that the availing of the ANC under the governmental efforts like the Integrated Child Development Scheme (ICDS) is again the maximum by the tribals. However, the STs again top in the category of no ANC.

Table 6 Perinatal Mortality Rate

Caste/Tribe	**Still[1] Births**	**Early[2] NND**	**Perinatal[3] MR**
SC	247	409	55.0
ST	70	153	40.6
OBC	467	676	49.3
Other	309	438	45.3

[1]*Still births* are foetal deaths in pregnancies lasting seven or more months.

[2]*Early neonatal deaths* are deaths at age 0–6 days among live-born children.

[3]*Perinatal mortality rate* is the sum of the number of stillbirths and early neonatal deaths divided by the number of pregnancies of seven or more months' duration.

Source: NFHS-3.

Table 7 Antenatal Care

Caste/Tribe	Doc	Nurse	OHP	Dai	ICDS	None
SC	42.0	28.1	0.7	1.5	1.8	25.9
ST	32.8	28.3	1.0	2.3	5.9	29.4
OBC	48.4	23.1	0.8	0.7	1.3	25.5
Other	63.6	17.7	1.6	1.1	0.7	15.2

Source: NFHS-3.

Table 8 shows that any kind of institutionalized place of delivery whether public sector, private sector, or an Non-Governmental Organization (NGO) for a place of delivering a child is preferred the least by the STs as against the highest preference shown by them for home deliveries.

It is evident from Table 9 that the tribal women face all the problems in accessing existing health care to the highest degree as compared to all the other castes due to many reasons. These problems vary from personal problems like seeking permission at home to accessing health care, non-availability of money, physical distance, transportation, lack of mobility to external problems like absence of female health care provider or no provider at all or lack of drugs, etc. Thus, it is evident that the attitudinal problems outweigh the availability of the already meagre health care facilities.

Table 8 Place of Delivery

Caste/Tribe	Public Sector	NGO	Priv. Sector	Home
SC	19.4	0.2	13.4	56.8
ST	11.6	0.3	5.8	70.9
OBC	16.1	0.5	21.1	51.8
Other	21.8	0.6	28.7	40.5

Source: NFHS-3.

Table 9 Problems in Accessing Health Care

Caste/ Tribe	Permission	Money	Dist.	Trans.	Can't Go Alone	No Female Provider	No. Prov	No. Drug
SC	7.0	20.4	27.3	25.3	12.8	19.7	23.9	24.2
ST	9.5	31.2	44.0	42.0	20.1	28.4	35.2	35.8
OBC	6.9	16.4	26.0	23.6	12.2	19.7	23.2	22.8
Other	5.5	12.9	18.5	15.9	8.4	14.3	18.2	18.7

Source: NFHS-3.

NOTABLE ISSUES (NFHS-3)

Certain observations regarding tribal health can be identified as notable issues.

- *Birth Weight.* It is noteworthy that despite the lowest access to health care and negative trends like early motherhood, the percentage distribution of births with a birth weight less than 2.5 kg is higher for SCs (23.7 per cent) as compared to the STs (22.3 per cent). While, the percentage distribution of births with a birth weight more than 2.5 kg is higher for STs (77.7 per cent) as compared to the SCs (76.3 per cent). However, this comparison, although very alarming, cannot be treated in absolute terms as there is a huge gap in the number of births for both the categories owing to the under-reporting of ST deliveries taking place at home.

- *Still Births*[1] *and Neonatal Deaths*[2]. It is strange to note that the number of still births is the lowest for the tribal community (70) as compared to that for the SCs (247), OBCs (467) and others (309). Similarly, the number of neonatal deaths is again the lowest for the STs (153) in comparison to the SCs (409), OBCs (676) and others (432).

- *Acute Respiratory Infections versus Smoking.* The prevalence of symptoms of Acute Respiratory Infections is also surprisingly the least among the STs (4.6 per cent) as against that in SCs (5.3 per cent), OBCs (5.5 per cent) and others (7.0 per cent).

- *Tuberculosis versus Tobacco.* Use of any kind of tobacco is the highest among the tribals, yet the percentage of both men and women who have heard of tuberculosis (TB) is the minimum among all the categories. So it can be deduced from this combination that either the STs suffer from undiagnosed TB in ignorance or they do not become victims of it at all. In the latter case, the outcome is again surprising and unexplained.

- *Anaemia.* The percentage of children aged 6–59 months classified as having anaemia by caste/tribe shows that STs top the category of any kind of anaemia (<11.0 g/dl) and moderate status of anaemia (7.0–9.9 g/dl), but again they score points lower than the SCs in the category of severe anaemia (<7.0 g/dl). On the other hand, the percentage of men aged 15–49 with anaemia shows that ST men also top in the categories of mild, moderate and any kind of anaemia. Broadly, this reflects upon the poor nutritional status of the community as a whole.

- *Fever.* The percentage of children under age five with fever shows that the incidences are found to be the least among the STs (12.2 per cent) as against the SCs (14.6 per cent), OBCs (14.6 per cent) and others (16.2 per cent).
- *Diarrhoea.* The STs (8.8 per cent) suffer from diarrhoea less frequently than the OBCs (9.5 per cent) but more than the SCs (8.7 per cent) and others (8.5 per cent). However, they lag behind all in case of knowledge of Oral Rehydration Salts (ORS) packets as only 61.4 per cent of tribal women seemed to have this awareness as compared to the SCs (71.4 per cent), OBCs (70.8 per cent) and others (79.4 per cent).
- *Use of Antibiotics.* The tribal community (8.8 per cent) is ahead of SCs (8.7 per cent) and others (8.5 per cent) in the use of antibiotics but lag behind the OBCs (9.5 per cent). Use of antibiotics for fever among children has shown an increase with increasing education of the mother and increasing wealth status of the household. However, antimalarial drug use during fever varies little by age of child and is highest among Buddhist/Neo-Buddhist children and children belonging to the STs.
- *Alcohol.* The tribal community surpasses all other castes in alcohol consumption. The striking feature is, however, that the gap in the case of women is phenomenal while that in the case of men is moderate.
- *Food Consumption.* Both women and men from STs have a relatively poor diet that is particularly deficient in fruits and milk or curd. They lag behind in the consumption of almost all the food items like the pulses or beans, dark green leafy vegetables, eggs and non-vegetarian foods; however, the difference between the STs and the other categories becomes less striking in the case of non-vegetarian foods.

Thus, a very hybrid picture emerges regarding the health status of the tribal women which poses many contradictions and reflections. These findings of NFHS-3 reveal the fact that the STs face the maximum constraints on the levels of exposure and awareness, receiving of health care, facing problems in accessing health care facilities, food consumption and nutrition, and attitudes and practices in self-health management. They follow tobacco and alcohol consumption as a way of life. Contrarily, the health parameters for this community exhibit certain unexpected revelations as the childhood and perinatal mortality rates, and morbidity rates do not project as bleak picture as is expected in the backdrop of the constraints.

IMPACT OF SHGS ON TRIBAL MINDSET

The primary survey shows the following:

- Prior to SHG association, only 4 per cent of the women respondents had a say in decision making in the household, but later 29.3 per cent of the respondents reported a role in the decision-making process.
- Earlier 26.7 per cent of the women respondents supported child marriage but after SHG membership only 12.7 per cent of the respondents expressed their opinion in favour of the custom.
- Before SHG membership, 12.7 per cent of the women respondents favoured family planning, but after SHG association 64.7 per cent of the respondents supported it.
- Before associating with the SHGs, none of the women respondents had a positive view regarding girls' education but after SHG membership 61.3 per cent of the respondents advocated female education.
- After SHG membership, access to credit or involvement in income generation triggered a change in the food consumption pattern of 6.7 per cent of the respondents but none of the respondents was motivated to initiate a change in their clothing or housing.
- The attitude of the tribal women towards *purdah* system, *manauti*, *mrityu bhoj*, alcoholism and smoking did not undergo any change even after associating with SHGs.
- As against 100 per cent of the respondents supporting dowry system prior to SHG association, 80.7 per cent of the SHG members later stood in favour of the system.
- Prior to SHG membership, 100 per cent of the respondents believed in magico-religious practices (*jhaad phoonk*) for treatment of diseases but after SHG membership 93.3 per cent of the respondents advocated these.
- About 86.3 per cent of the respondents supported delivery in hospital or under medical supervision after SHG association, whereas earlier 100 per cent of the respondents favoured delivery at home.

Thus, it is evident that where the social and financial intermediation of SHG mechanism cannot cast impact on certain very deeply rooted social customs and practices, nevertheless the association plays a potential role in influencing certain crucial factors related with female autonomy, awareness, attitude, and health in general and reproductive health in particular.

RECOMMENDATIONS

There is no denying the fact that amidst the dearth of health facilities in the country as a whole, the tribal community is automatically bound to suffer from a more severe setback on this front. Moreover, the problem is aggravated by the physical distance that the tribal dwellings pose, the financial distance that the tribal poverty generates and the mental distance that the tribal mindset creates. Therefore, the community-specific problem of tribal health too has to be addressed in a peculiar manner. The medical practitioner cannot approach the tribals, particularly tribal women, like routine doctors and have to assume the roles of care giver, decision maker, communicator, community leader, manager, educator, investigator and policy maker.

Above all, looking at the not so worrisome health parameters on some levels of mortality and morbidity, it is essential to trust the inherent immunity power, sturdy and strong built of the tribals emanating from the tough life they happen to lead, the indigenous remedies and the strong linkages between environment and the community. So, the health care policies should be framed specifically for tribal women, which should aim at balancing between traditions and modernity.

- ❖ Improving equitable access to quality public health care service
- ❖ Adequacy of financial allocation and effectiveness of expenditure on health care
- ❖ Accountability of staff
- ❖ Organizational development
- ❖ Human resource management
- ❖ Monitoring, accounting, reporting and correction
- ❖ Global health partnerships to leverage funds, technology and knowledge
- ❖ Public private partnerships
- ❖ NGO participation
- ❖ Treat disease, provide preventive measures and promote life styles in individuals and communities
- ❖ Impart health education
- ❖ Strengthen the matriarchal system

FOCUS AREAS

- ❖ Scientific verification and patenting of indigenous knowledge
- ❖ Empowerment and enlightenment through *aanganwadis*, SHGs, integrated child development services, reproductive and child health, etc.
- ❖ Preserve and strengthen the environment linkages

Hence, it should be recognized that the tribals have certain peculiarities attached with their traditions like matriarchal system, bridal price (extracting dowry from the bridegroom), strong environmental linkages, indigenous remedies for diseases and inherent physical well-being and immunity power. Moreover, they have their own languages, lifestyle, perception and constraints. So, mere provision of health facilities will not be sufficient to address their health problems. Instead preserving their useful practices, a vibrant SHG mechanism should be used to tactfully inculcate awareness, attitudinal change and health modernity in the mindset of tribals, particularly tribal women, so that they voluntarily adopt a healthy lifestyle and absorb the provisions. Simultaneously, vigorous attempts should be made to facilitate availability and accessibility with regard to subsidized health care.

NOTES

1. Still births are foetal deaths in pregnancies lasting seven or more months.
2. Early neonatal deaths are deaths at age 0–6 days among live-born children.

REFERENCES

Abel-Smith, B. (1990). 'The economics of health care', in T.A. Lambo and S.B. Day (eds.), *Issues in Contemporary International Health*. New York: Plenum Press.

Das Gupta, M. and L.C. Chen (1998). 'Introduction', in M. Das Gupta, L.C. Chen and T.N. Krishnan (eds.), *Health, Poverty and Development in India*, New Delhi: Oxford Publications.

Draft National Policy on Tribals (2005). Ministry of Tribal Affairs, Government of India.

Gwatkins, D., S. Rustein, K. Johnson, R. Pande, and A. Wagstaff (2000). *Socio-Economic Differences in Health, Nutrition and Population*, Washington, DC: The World Bank. Available online: http://www.worldbank.org/poverty/health/data/index.htm.

International Institute for Population Sciences (IIPS) and Macro International (2000). *National Family Health Survey* (NFHS-2), 1998–99. India.

International Institute for Population Sciences (IIPS) and Macro International (2007). *National Family Health Survey* (NFHS-3), 2005–06, Volume I. India.

Krishnan, T.N. (1999). 'Access to health care and the burden of treatment in India: An inter-state comparison', in M. Rao (ed.), *Disinvesting in Health: The World Bank's Prescriptions for Health*, New Delhi: Sage Publications, pp. 208–230.

Planning Commission of India (2008). *Eleventh Five Year Plan*, New Delhi: Oxford University Press, p. 113.

Registrar General of India, Census of India, 2001.

Wagstaff, A. (2001). *Poverty and Health*, CMH Working Paper Series. Paper No.WG1:5. Commission on Macroeconomics and Health.

Wagstaff, A. (2002). 'Poverty and Health Sector Inequalities', *Bulletin of the World Health Organization*, 80: 97–105.

CHAPTER 12

EMPOWERMENT OF TRIBAL WOMEN THROUGH JOINT FOREST MANAGEMENT: AN ANALYSIS

Debashis Debnath and Lolita Pradhan

The concept of empowerment became very important in the field of development studies during sixties. Nowadays, women are the centre of development studies and their empowerment is a crucial issue because gender discrimination and disparities are generating the multiple forms of exploitation in the socio-cultural system. Women empowerment is a burning subject in the present day world, especially in the developing country like India. The meanings of women's empowerment in a nut-shell are women's sense of self-worth for their right to have access to opportunities and resources to control their own lives, both within and outside the home to influence the direction of social change nationally and internationally. A number of incidences of physical violence, mental torture, discrimination in employment opportunities and family disharmony due to hostile attitudes of the in-laws occur every day.

The objective of women empowerment is to create an enabling environment where women can freely exercise their rights both within and outside the home as equal partners along with men. The international indices of empowerment of women as the Gender Empowerment Measures (GEM) developed in the United Nations Development Programme (UNDP) Human Resources Development (HRD) involve the extent of woman's

1. Power over economic resources as depicted through per capita income;
2. Access to the professional activities and participation in decision making based on share of jobs on the professional, technical, managerial and administrative categories; and
3. Political opportunities and decision making reflected by the share of parliamentary seats.

In Indian Constitution, the principle of gender equality provides the first guidelines to empower the women and simultaneously to adopt measures of positive discrimination in favour of women. In recent years, empowerment has been recognized as the central issue in determining the status of women. The National Commission of Women was set up by an Act of Parliament in 1990 to safeguard the rights and legal entitlements of women. The 73rd and 74th Amendments (1993) to the Constitution of India have laid a foundation stone for their participation in decision making at the local levels. In consequence, Indian women are leading 72,120 village Panchayats out of a total 2,34,676 village Panchayats in India and are representing 36.87 per cent of the 28.18 lakh elected Panchayat representatives. India has ratified various international conventions and human right instruments committing to resume equal rights of women. However, there still exists a wide gap between the goals enunciated in the constitution, legislation, polices, plans, programmes and related mechanism on the one hand and the situational reality of the status of women in India on the other. Gender disparity manifests itself in various forms. The most obvious being the trend of continuously declining female ratio in the population, violence against women at the domestic and societal levels, discrimination against girl children and so on. The underlying causes of gender inequality are related to social and economic structure, which is based on informal and formal norms and practices. Consequently, the access of women belonging to weaker sections especially scheduled castes and scheduled tribes to development programmes, i.e., education, health and productive resources, is inadequate. Therefore, they remain largely marginalized, poor and socially excluded.

The objective of this paper is to show the implication of Joint Forest Management (JFM) policy and programmes in India in gender development and equality, involving the tribal women in the process with the analysis of the primary data collected in JFM villages.

TRIBAL WOMEN STATUS

In tribal society, women, and nature are inseparable from each other as nature is governed by feminine principle – life-supporting, sharing and diversity – and the women's support and contribution in upholding the society are immense. From the various studies on the tribal women in India (Mann, 1987; Chauhan, 1990; Ghosh, 1987; Majumdar, 1973; Rivers, 1973), the tribal women are shown as a valuable human resource for contribution in domestic, social, cultural and aesthetic life. In tribal society, a woman supports the whole family from dawn to dusk starting from cleaning of house and utensils, fetching water, collection of fuelwood, vegetation, cooking, nurturing children and so on. In their activities, they are found as collectors, users, protectors, conservers, sellers and managers of the available resources. Such multi-variant roles always give the better status to the womenfolk in comparison to non-tribal counterparts. In the social institutions, we find some social liberalization. For instance, there is no child marriage, no stigma on widowhood. She enjoys the right to decide about her marriage, etc. Instead of dowry there is bride price indicating high social status of the tribal women. A tribal woman can divorce and marry easily. She earns and is, therefore, to a great extent economically independent. However, there are many facts which indicate the low status of the tribal woman. For example, she does not have property rights except in a matrilineal society (here also in a limited way), which is small portion of tribal population. In matrilineal society, the descent is traced through female lines, but political power generally rests with men. Land and other property are inherited through women, but its management is done by men (Dube, 1990: 97). In Meghalaya, there is a Khasi saying, 'War and politics are for men, while property and children are for women. Among them, the rulers, chiefs and power-wielding "elders" are all male, but women have important economic roles.' The tribal women are paid less wage in comparison to their male counterparts for the same work. Several taboos discriminating against tribal women exist in certain tribal groups, implying impurity and the low status. The tribal women cannot hold the office of priest. There are taboos related to menstruation as in non-tribal communities.

The status and position of women is still subordinate due to the patriarchal socio-cultural structure of the society. Existing socio-cultural characteristics like caste, marital status, economic condition, level of education and access to information are the determining factors of the status or position of women in society

In the context of empowerment, the status of tribal women is reflected in the lower educational status, lower literacy rate, lower enrolment rate and higher dropouts in the schools. The literacy rate among the tribal females is 34.76 per cent as written in 2001 Census, which is comparatively lesser than general females, that is 53.67 per cent. A very large majority of tribals (almost 90 per cent) are engaged in agriculture; their other economic activities being food gathering (including hunting and fishing), pastoral, handicrafts, trade and commerce, and industrial labour. Rarely are they engaged in one occupation. The employment status of tribal women may be considered in terms of their work participation, agriculture, forests, non-agricultural activities and impact of development programmes.

Their work participation is 33 per cent in comparison to males who have 52 per cent. From the comprehensive analysis of the health status of tribal women (Basu, 1993), it has been found that they have higher infant mortality rate, low nutritional status, lower life expectancy and higher fertility rate.

Still in the modern era the impression of the tribal society in the minds of other people comes from the women sections. Since the earliest form of livelihoods, i.e., gathering-foraging activities, their role and responsibilities are still prominent as found among the Primitive Tribal Groups (PTGs), a special category having pre-agrarian occupation developed in the Fifth Five Year Plan, which has been categorized as Particularly Vulnerable Tribal Groups (PVTGs) in the Tenth Five Year Plan. In the pre-agrarian tribal communities, the equity is observed among tribal men and women. In many conservation movements (Chipko), ethos of tribal women is very much prominent and reflected. Further, in the follow up of National Forest Policy in 1988, the tribal women have been considered as key stakeholder in participatory forest management. Considering their symbiotic relationship, they have been brought in the decision-making process in natural resources management and community development. A number of measures have been adopted to meet up the daily requirement of fuelwoods, fodder, Non-timber forest products (NTFPs) and medicinal plants. In planning and implementation, their involvement has been emphasized as they face large number of problems. In employment and income-generating activities, the capacity building and skill development programmes have been organized. In the community mobilization, the local non-governmental organizations and community-based organizations have taken significant role. It has been found that formation of Self-Help Groups (SHGs) of tribal women is the best organizational process to generate livelihoods as well as provide equity and sustainability.

CONCEPTUAL DEVELOPMENT OF EMPOWERMENT

Empowerment means in terms of knowledge and awareness of one's own life and society including legal status with regard to the human lives. The term 'empowerment' implies change: enhancing people's capacity and propensity to influence decisions that affect them (in their locality and in other aspects of their lives). McArdle (1989) defines empowerment as the 'process whereby decision is made by the people who have to wear the consequences of those decisions. The process is more important than the achievement of goals.'

Community empowerment is about allowing people to take control of the decisions that influence their lives and health. Empowered community is one which is

- Confident
- Inclusive
- Organized
- Cooperative
- Influential

These five dimensions provide a framework for planning work which is empowering for communities. Real community empowerment is the result of putting community development values into action. These values are learning, equality, participation, cooperation and social justice which help in achieving the five respective dimension of empowerment.

In other words, empowerment is probably the totality of the following or similar capabilities (Das, 2012):

- Having decision-making power of one's own.
- Having access to information and resources to make proper decisions.
- Having a range of options from which you can make choices (not just yes/no, either/or).
- Ability to exercise assertiveness in collective decision making.
- Having positive thinking on the ability to make change.
- Ability to learn skills for improving one's personal or group power.
- Ability to change others' perceptions by democratic means.
- Involving in the growth process and changes that is never ending and self-initiated.
- Increasing one's positive self-image and overcoming stigma.
- Increasing one's ability in discreet thinking to sort out right and wrong

Participation is a vital component of self-help and empowerment process. People must be involved in those decisions that effect their lives, thus gaining confidence, self-esteem and knowledge and development of new skills. The process is cumulative; the more skills, the more the person is able to participate and the more he can gain. Participation must facilitate learning action and the achievement of goals (Onyx and Benton, 1995). Studies reveal that the achievement of personal goals may require at least the following steps:

- Identification of need
- Identification of options and strategies
- Decision or choice of action
- Mobilization of resources
- The action itself

In other words, 'empowerment' require that the steps for the achievement of personal goals are completed by the person themselves with minimal outside intervention

The need for involving community in developing forest/environmental management plans has been advocated in many studies, which revealed that plans formed only by inputs given by technical experts have been a failure in long term and the community has not readily accepted them. It is generally perceived that this approach has led to a number of failures as these managers rarely had the benefit of detailed local indigenous knowledge and failed to generate community support for policy changes. So there is an urgent need for involving the community members in planning and decision making, and for that indicators need to be developed to measure progress towards sustainability (Fraser et al., 2006).

It may be understood as enabling women, especially tribal women, to acquire and to possess power and resources, in order to make decision on their own or resist decisions that are made by others which affect them. A person may said to be powerful when he/she has control over a large portion of power resources in society (Gowda and Yogesh, 2006). The extent of possession of various resources such as personal wealth, assets, land, skilled education, information, knowledge, social status, position held, leadership traits, capabilities for mobilization of resources, etc. indicate the level of empowerment.

WOMEN EMPOWERMENT

Woman empowerment is a multidimensional process which intersects the woman's personal, family, social, cultural, economic and political space. Empowerment is defined as the process in which women challenge the existing norms and culture of the society in which they live to effectively improve their well-being (Swain and Wallentin, 2008). Thus, although economic interventions are important, other development initiatives such as education, political quotas, awareness generation, property rights, etc. are also essential for empowering women (Kabeer, 2005; Malhotra and Mather, 1997; Deshmukh-Randive, 2003).

The Beijing Declaration 1995 (section 13) presents women's empowerment as a key strategy for development: It states that

> Women's empowerment and their full participation on the basis of equality in all spheres of society, including participation in the decision-making process and access to power, are fundamental for the achievement of equality, development and peace.

Gender Empowerment Measurement (GEM) developed by UNDP focuses on the women's political and economic power at the aggregate level. Beteta (2006) further recommends incorporating broader representation and including activities such as voting, demonstrating and getting involved in political organizations, as well as participating in informal organizations to solve community problems.

The women's empowerment has the following five components:

1. Women's sense of self-worth.
2. Their right to have and to determine choices;
3. Their right to have access to opportunities and resources;
4. Their right to have the power to control their own lines(both within and outside the home); and
5. Their ability to influence the direction of social change, to create a move just social and economic order, nationally and internationally.

DIMENSIONS OF WOMEN EMPOWERMENT

Women empowerment is not an outcome, but a process (Johnson, 2005). The factors that lead to women empowerment include economic factors and financial confidence (economic), managerial power (manage), networks, political and social awareness and participation (politics), and behavioural changes within the respondents and household members (behaviour) and education. It is well established in literature that an economically active woman with her own independent savings and greater income share within the household has higher bargaining power within the household, thereby making her more empowered and likely to challenge the prevailing norms that restrict her ability to make choices (Asraf et al., 2006; Swain and Wallentin, 2007; Swain and Wallentin, 2008; Duflo, 2003; Browning and Chiappori, 1998; Blumberg, 2005).

Behavioural changes in the woman within the household to improve her own well-being are also a crucial component of empowerment. A wider range of factors such as legal and regulatory framework, women's social and economic rights and societal attitudes are also important. The factors that lead to women empowerment include economic factors and financial confidence (economic), managerial power (manage), networks, political and social awareness and participation (politics), and behavioural changes within the respondents and household members (behaviour), and education (Beteta, 2006).

Women empowerment is also measured by the indicators that cover the decision-making on family planning, on children's marriage, on buying and selling of property, on sending daughter to school and use of birth control. It is also provided by the following indicators: respondent's income as a share of the total household income, primary activity that the respondent is engaged in, her own independent savings that she controls and her contribution to her household's assets.

Financial confidence in meeting a family financial crisis and/or the ability to arrange credit also improve a woman's bargaining power within a household, thereby further empowering her. Women participation in social and political activities, their legal status in terms of marriage, divorce and inheritance of property, and seeking health care should be taken into consideration.

POLICIES AND LEGISLATIONS FOR WOMEN EMPOWERMENT

In Indian Constitution, the principle of gender equality provides the first guidelines to empower the women and simultaneously to adopt measures of positive discrimination in favour of women. India has ratified various international conventions and human right instruments committing to resume equal rights of women. However, there still exists a wide gap between the goals enunciated in the constitution, legislation, polices, plans, programmes and related mechanism on the one hand and the situational reality of the status of women in India on the other. Gender disparity manifests itself in various forms. The most obvious being the trend of continuously declining female ratio in the population, violence against women at the domestic and societal levels, discrimination against girl children and so on. The underlying causes of gender inequality are related to social and economic structure, which is based on informal and formal norms and practices. Consequently, the access of women belonging to weaker sections especially scheduled castes and scheduled tribes to development programmes, i.e., education, health and productive resources, is inadequate. Therefore, they remain largely marginalized, poor and socially excluded.

Thus, women empowerment means women's full participation on the basis of equality in all sphere of society, including participation in the decision-making process, awareness of development policy and programmes and enhancement of economic capacity and access to power constitute the fundamental conditions for achieving the objectives of equality and development. Hence, the objective of women empowerment is to create an enabling environment where women can freely exercise their rights both within and outside the home as equal partners along with men.

The state enacted several women-specific and women-related legislations to protect women against social discrimination, violence and atrocities and also to prevent social evils like child marriages, dowry, rape, practice of Sati, etc.

The National Policy for Empowerment of Women 2001 has as its goal bringing about advancement, development and empowerment of women in all spheres of life through creation of a more responsive judicial and legal system sensitive to women and mainstreaming a gender perspective in the development process.

The objectives of this policy include

1. Creating an environment through positive economic and social policies for full development of women to enable them to realize their full potential;
2. The *de-jure* and *de-facto* enjoyment of all human rights and fundamental freedom by women on equal basis with men in all spheres – political, economic, social, cultural and civil;
3. Equal access to participation and decision making of women in social, political and economic life of the nation;
4. Equal access to women to health care, quality education at all levels, career and vocational guidance, employment, equal remuneration, occupational health and safety, social security, public office, etc.;
5. Strengthening legal systems aimed at elimination of all forms of discrimination against women;
6. Changing societal attitudes and community practices by active participation and involvement of both men and women;
7. Mainstreaming a gender perspective in the development process;
8. Elimination of discrimination and all forms of violence against women and the girl child; and
9. Building and strengthening partnerships with civil society, particularly women's organizations.

The international commitments and conventions and the Millennium Development Goals (MDGs) has identified 12 critical areas of concern for women which are as follows:

1. Women and poverty
2. Education and training of women
3. Women and health
4. Violence against women
5. Women in armed conflict
6. Women and economy
7. Women in power and decision making
8. Institutional mechanisms for the advancement of women
9. Human rights and women
10. Women and media
11. Women and environment
12. Girl child

WOMEN EMPOWERMENT IN JFM

JFM is a collaborative forest management regime for sharing of products, responsibilities, control and decision-making authority over forest lands between forest departments and local user group based on formal agreement. In this management regime, there is a paradigm shift from centralized, custodial, controlled, timber harvesting and revenue earning forestry to decentralized, participating community forest management. This process envisaged the involvement of the tribals in protection, management and development of forest in India. Till date all the 28 states have declared their JFM resolutions and consequently 1,200,000 JFM communities have been formed that brought 17 million hectare of forest areas under JFM activities.

The JFM process started in 1990 with the declaration of resolution at the national level following the National Forest Policy of 1988, which also envisaged women's participation in the protection of forests. The rules of the Government of India (GOI) Order 1991 specified that at least two women should be on every village management committee in the JFM programmes. In 1998, an advisory committee to promote the involvement of women in the forestry sector was constituted by the Ministry of Environment and Forests. It submitted a number of recommendations which would increase women's participation (GOI, 1999). Following these recommendations, it was decided that 50 per cent of the members of the JFM General Body

(GB) should be women and the presence of at least 50 per cent of women members should be requisite for calling a GB meeting. Besides the JFM resolution of 2000 has emphasized on 33 per cent representation of women in executive committees also. In the official JFM committees in all states, established for the implementation of the programme, there is a provision for compulsory participation of a certain number of women from the concerned communities

Thus, policy has given due consideration to the important role played by tribal women as resource users and has been instrumental in empowering women. JFM can play an important role in achieving the four dimensions of empowerment, i.e., social, political, economic and psychological. The following measures need to be taken for making JFM movement more women-friendly.

Providing an Enabling Environment to Realize Their Full Potential and Self-Worth

In most of the state JFM resolution, although the members of Joint Forest Management Committees (JFMCs) have been given usufruct rights on NTFPs, in most cases major economically beneficial NTFPs are nationalized as a result of which the JFMC members do not get the full autonomy over the resource in the JFM areas. In most of the areas, women are the primary collectors of Non-Wood Forest Products (NWFPs), an effective measure of empowerment is to give them rights to collect, sell and retain the revenues from the sale of all the major NTFPs. In tandem with giving rights to collection of NWFPs from a community managed forest, the government should allow women to sell them in the open market instead of restricting sale to government agencies such as the Girijan Cooperative Corporation (Andhra Pradesh). Exclusive rights of collection and processing should be given to the women NTFP collectors and their organizations/SHGs, and monopoly leases should be cancelled. These SHGs should be trained about sustainable harvesting of the NTFPs resources and should be levied fines on exploitation or improper maintenance of the resource. The State of Madhya Pradesh has moved in this direction by recently granting the ownership rights of NWFPs to tribals. The state should also make provision for storage to primary collectors' organizations on rent.

Women SHG federation should be formed within the JFMCs where women collectors can sell and buy their NTFPs in present rates. Effective institutional platforms of the women NTFP collectors should be established for improved access to finance. The women NTFP collectors should also be given training on value addition and processing techniques so that they can sell the collected NTFPs profitably in higher value.

In addition to this, species that yield locally preferred NWFPs should be promoted instead of fast-growing varieties. In the long term, this will ease the burden on women to meet both the subsistence and income needs of their households. Women's multiple use of forests is sustainable only with species that yield NWFPs. Fast-growing species that yield timber and construction poles might generate revenues for forest management but will not alleviate the burdens of women.

Providing a Conducive Environment for Enjoyment of All Human Rights and Fundamental Freedom

In the JFM programme, the JFMC helps them to develop their potential, ensures freedom of thought, participate in decision making and work without feeling of being deprived. Special attention needs to be given for capacity building and education of the women through trainings and awareness generation programmes so that women are aware of their fundamental rights. In JFM meetings, equal weightage should be given on women-related issues, and JFMC should provide them the opportunity to express their concerns and views.

Disparity in the ownership and control over resources relative to gender responsibilities places women in a subordinate and disempowered position relative to men as they are forever dependent and run a greater risk of being excluded from their homes and livelihood (Sarin et al., 1996). Despite the shortcomings, women are involved and benefiting from various aspects of the programme, particularly in NTFP collection and trade, micro-credit, vegetable gardening and forest wage work. In more than 80 per cent of the cases studied by Indian Institute of Forest Management (IIFM), Bhopal, women have been found seemingly active in programme implementation (Singhal et al., 2000).

Equal Access to Participation and Decision Making

The JFM activity begins with formation of village institutions constituted by at least one male and one female member from each household to keep the balance in equitable sharing of responsibility. Women sections suffer maximum due to degradation and depletion of natural resources. Considering their role significant, in many states the women belonging to landless section or backward section are given special status in executive body of the village *vana suraksha samiti* (Forest Protection Committee). The mechanisms established by the forest department to promote women's involvement need to be further strengthened, particularly with regard to representation for women on the executive body. Even in planning process women's participation needs to be ascertained compulsorily, and for doing so in the whole Participatory Rural Appraisal (PRA)-based planning, women members should be involved and for that women Non-Governmental Organization (NGO) representatives should be hired on spearhead planning teams.

Studies reveal that during the initial phase of JFM women were consulted through household surveys and interviews, but subsequently their contribution and participation in meetings and decision making has declined. A study conducted by IIFM in Madhya Pradesh states that although in 70 per cent cases women were consulted during PRA, in only 33 per cent of these they are actively involved in meetings and decision making. It further reports that in 25 per cent of the cases women complain that they did not have time to attend meetings and so their husbands and children informed them about the groups' decisions made in the meetings (Singhal et al., 2000). So in order to enhance women participation in meetings and planning the venue, time and date of these meeting should be fixed after consultation with the women members, and prior intimation of these meetings should be given so that it is convenient for them to attend meetings.

The Forest Protection Committee is an all women team in the Jahana Village in Ranchi District, Jharkhand. In the biodiversity conservation, the women's knowledge of species diversity among trees, shrubs and herbs are valuable. In the resource mapping, the women's involvement has been strengthened to assess the resource potentiality with variability of species. As part of the learning environment, significant changes in practice to broaden participation in forest committees have been put in place. For example, development of SHGs that target women's participation has increased in leaps and bounds over the years. The Government Resolution has been amended twice to reflect the need for greater representation by women and also by NGOs.

Another important contribution (although again difficult to quantify) that women can make to forest improvement is through their knowledge of how certain forest products should be extracted when the forest is opened periodically, or which products to promote in planting efforts. Their knowledge about the products that they typically collect require particular skills, such as how tree fodder should be plucked (excessive plucking can reduce growth) and at what stage of its development – some fodder leaves are best when young, others are poisonous when young or how ground grass should be cut, or medicinal herbs and wild vegetables procured, can also prove significant in forest conservation efforts.

Changing Social Attitudes and Community Practices

A gender perspective can uncover patterns of resource control with implications for refining JFM policy. For example, in a study of women and forests in Jharkhand, it was observed that women play an important role in gathering forest produce. Thus, it may be concluded that within the family the income from sale of forest produce tends to be counted as the income of the individual who gathers and sells the produce. Increasing the income from forestry will thus also help strengthen the position of women within the family. Here is an instance where women have the same rights as men vis-à-vis control of income from the sale of forest products. JFM policy initiatives, to begin with, should capitalize on such gender equal opportunities, wherever they are present, to improve the social and economic standing of women.

With the implementation of Panchayat Extension in Scheduled Area (PESA) 1996, the quorum of the Gram Sabha is formed with the presence of 50 per cent of the women members. In the JFM committees, the guidelines have been followed in the tribal states, such as Jharkhand, Madhya Pradesh and Chhattisgarh, that is, 33 per cent reservation for the women in village institution and 30 per cent reservation for women in heading the village committee

Mainstreaming a Gender Perspective in the Development Process

In the JFM programme, the financial support has been given for upbringing girl children and subsidiary food support to the pregnant and lactating mothers for nutrition. In the Harda Village, it was found that under *Vatsalya Yojana* from Block Development office Rs. 500/- was given to the households for bringing up their girl children and provided 'dalia' (cereal) to the pregnant and lactating mothers for nutrition under ICDS project.

Building and Strengthening Partnerships with Civil Society, Particularly Women's Organizations

JFM is itself a partnership-based community forest management enlarging the collaboration of not only village people and forest department, but also a number of stakeholders which are informal groups and formal organizations. We find the role and responsibilities of a number of civil society organizations and community-based organizations. Among them the women's organizations like Mahila Chetana Manch in Bhopal and informal women groups like Mahila Mandal in Chhattisgarh and Bairani Kuldis in Jhabua in Madhya Pradesh can be cited as examples. The group is local SHG starting from a group of 15 to 20 women on the thrift saving of meagre amount. Women's SHG is one of the successful indicators of women empowerment. These SHGs have been working effectively in poverty reduction and environmental management. Through SHG the women get employment in nursery raising, seed storing, pit-digging, plantation, water-harvesting structures and so on. In many divisions, Madhya Pradesh Forest Department (MPFD) staff has introduced women's self-help savings groups to provide a venue and focus for women's involvement (there are about 2,000 SHGs). This has resulted in their participation in these savings group activities, but rarely are the links built back to the aims of forest management. The MPFD recognizes the weaknesses in women's involvement in the programme and is trying to address this through local training for staff, village leaders and women's groups, through collaboration with NGOs and in promoting leadership within the villages of more educated women but a great deal more work is required to this end.

In Vellore forest division in Tamil Nadu, under the Tamil Nadu Afforestation Programme (TAP), a JFM programme funded by Japan Bank of International Cooperation (JBIC), many number of local NGOs started to develop the capacity of women SHGs to produce vermicompost as non-chemical organic fertilizers used for raising medicinal plants in the community and forest lands. To mobilize the people along with the confidence building, the forest department organized various training programmes for the women SHGs in alternative economic sources for the income generation with the help of local NGOs and some skill-development units of the line department, which are involved in livelihood interventions. These alternative economic pursuits are candle making, plastic bag making, tailoring, etc. Some SHGs were also encouraged to produce guava in the leased land and many women SHGs raised 'Kasini Keerai' (*Cichorium* sp.) in their agricultural fields, which they marketed to raise their income level (Debnath, 2005).

WOMEN EMPOWERMENT IN JFM VILLAGES

A study was conducted in two villages, i.e., Jalikheda and Bamnai in Hoshangabad and Raisen districts in Hoshangabad and Obdullahgunj Forest Divisions, respectively to assess the process of empowering women in JFM activities on the basis of the criteria and indicators of the women empowerment. The methodology and approaches were the questionnaire techniques and informal discussions to get the input from the respondents on the major four dimensions of employment, i.e., social, economic, political and psychological.

Jalikheda is a forest village located in Hoshangabad Division. It is situated in Suktava Range of Hoshangabad Division. It is about 20 km form Itarsi. The Forest Protection Committees of Jalikheda were formed in 2001. The village is predominantly inhabited by the Gond tribe, besides the Korkus and Katias are also found. The village Bamnai is having Eco-development Committee (the JFM committee in National Park/Wildlife Sanctuary in Madhya Pradesh Forest Policy) coming under Ratapani Sanctuary in Obdullaganj Forest Division, situated about 30–35 km away from the division headquarters and near the Bhopal–Itarsi main road. The brief profile of the village is given in Table 1.

Table 1 Socio-Demography and Socio-Economy of the Women in Two Villages

Characteristics/ Items	Jalikheda	Bamnai
Total population	398	355
Population of male	162	
Population of female	105	
Population of children	131	
No. of households	29	79
Occupational types of women	Wage labour – 40% NTFP collection seasonal – 60%	Wage labour – 65% NTFP collection – 20–30%
Female literacy	40%	40%
Female educational status	Mostly up to 5th standard	Mostly up to 5th standard
Female annual income	2,000–7,000	1,500–5,000
Female landholding capacity	Nil	Nil

In the Jalikheda Village, the women members of the JFMC have formed SHGs and are engaged in poultry activity. This initiative has been collaboratively undertaken by an NGO, which is PRADAN and forest department. These women members were provided 40 days training and were taught how to raise the chickens. Poultry farms have been constructed in their houses in subsidized rates. These women SHGs are provided with the chickens and chicken feed. After these chicken hatched in to hens, they are paid on the basis of the weight of the hen/fowl developed. They earn approximately Rs. 7,000 to Rs. 8,000 per month from poultry. This activity has not only provided the JFMC members a source of income but also reduced the dependence of women on forest for fuelwood. Due to the trainings and exposure, women have become economically independent.

In Bamnai under the initiation of the MDFD and Ecotourism Board women members have grouped themselves into an SHG and are engaged in making toys and handicrafts from paper mesh/waste paper. The forest department imparted training for this activity through some NGOs/institutes. These toys are sold at herbal *melas* or fair (*van melas*) organized by the forest department, which are held regularly at different places of the state. These are also exhibited in Delabadi Ecotourism Centre. This is a very cost innovative marketing mechanism initiated by the forest department. The forest department provides them raw materials like waste paper, gum, etc. which are required for making toys. Their products are sold by the forest department and women members engaged in this activity get about Rs. 80/day.

RESULT AND DISCUSSION

Table 2 gives a glimpse of the responses provided by the women SHG members of the two JFMCs involved in various forestry activities.

In both the JFMC under the initiation of the forest department the women SHG have undertaken two activities. Poultry raising and paper mesh handicraft-making activities in Jalikheda and Bamnai villages, respectively. These women members participating in different income livelihood activities have savings account in the banks, i.e., 80 per cent of them save their money. The income-earning capacity has increased the family income and status in the society. Women now spend money on buying things for themselves as well as education for their children. There is no discrimination on the basis of payment or work against male and female in any activities undertaken under JFM/FDA. This fact was accepted by all the women being interviewed. But property rights on land is still under males

Table 3 shows JFM has given opportunities for political empowerment of women in both the villages. Women have been given the right to vote, women members are well-represented in the general and executive committee as per the norms mentioned in the state resolution. In both the JFMCs, 60–80 per cent of the women members have accepted that they get equal opportunities to express their views and opinion in the JFMC meetings. But 40 per cent of the women complained that due to inconvenient timings of meetings and time constraint they failed to attend the meetings. Due to continuous trainings, capacity buildings activities and exposure visits, women in both the JFMCs have become more confident and enterprising.

Table 2 Assessing the Economic Empowerment

Items/characteristics	Bamnai (Percentage of Women Responding)		Jalikheda (Percentage of Women Responding)	
	Yes	No	Yes	No
Extent of opportunity in participating in income-generating activities	70	30	80	20
Extent of opportunity to access to saving and credit	80	20	80	20
Control over income and expenditure	70	30	80	20
Income spent on self and education of girl children	60	40	60	40
Control and ownership over other productive assets, e.g., land, business and industries	Nil	100	Nil	100
Equal payment for plantation, nursery tending operation etc undertaken under JFM equal payment for work	100	0	100	0
Discrimination of work distribution under JFM activities between men and women	Nil	100	Nil	100
Equality in wage increment in comparison to men	100	Nil	100	Nil
Ability to increase support to family income	60	40	75	25
Opportunity to be involved or represented in local trade associations and access to markets	Nil	100	Nil	100

They now play an important role in major household decision making. Of them, 60–80 per cent of women members have accepted this fact. But for technical matter in forestry activities like selection of species, time of plantation, etc., women are rarely consulted. But no work is imposed on them. They have been given the freedom to choose the activity they are comfortable with.

Table 4 clearly shows that of all the respondents, about 60–70 per cent of women members, have accepted that they have no hesitations in interacting with their senior forest officers and discuss about their problems.

Table 3 Assessing the Political Empowerment

Items	Bamnai (Percentage of Women Responding)		Jalikheda (Percentage of Women Responding)	
	Yes	No	Yes	No
Women representation in the general body and executive committee	100	Nil	100	Nil
Attendance in the GB and EC meetings	40	60	60	40
Opportunity to express and share their views	60	40	80	20
Awareness about the intuitional structure of JFM/FDA and means of access to it	40	60	40	60
Domestic support for political engagement; exercising the right to vote	20	80	40	60
Participation in selection of the president and other members of the JFMC	60	40	80	20

Free and compulsory primary education for girls is available in both the JFMC, and girls go to school regularly. But in terms of availability of proper health care facilities for girls and women, the situation is not up to the mark. Regular awareness programmes dealing with women and girl health care are rarely conducted. Although women have become economically independent, there has been no improvement in the nutritional level, they hardly spend on their food and there has been no improvement in the diet of the women.

When the responses for psychological empowerment were collected and analysed, it was found that 60 per cent of women of Jalikheda felt that they are given more respect in the society because of their financial independence. They get more respect in their family and outside because of their successful venture. People from outside come and visit their area and give them recognition for their work. In Bamnai, the craft work made by women SHG members have been appreciated by the senior officials; this has given them due recognition and in turn increased their confidence. But only 40 per cent of women have been empowered to choose their own activity.

Above analysis clearly shows that income-generating activities have enhanced the decision-making capacity of women. Exposure and trainings conducted through the JFM activities have enhanced the confidence of women,

Table 4 Assessing the Social Empowerment

Items	Bamnai (Percentage of Women Responding)		Jalikheda (Percentage of Women Responding)	
	Yes	No	Yes	No
Involvement in major household decisions, i.e., large purchases (house, household appliance), agricultural decisions	60	40	80	20
Accessibility to information and communication technology made available to them	0	100	0	100
Consultation during the time of plantation	0	100	0	100
Consultation about the species to be planted	0	100	0	100
Consultation about the works to be undertaken	70	30	70	30
Opportunity to interact with the outside world/ more exposure to the society	60	40	70	30
Availability of free and compulsory education for girls	60	40	50	50
Availability of proper health care system for girls	40	60	40	60
Ability to speak with authorities about their problems and concerns	40	60	60	40
Participation in trainings, exposure visits under JFM	40	60	70	30
Free mobility in the forest areas and other places with or without permission or assistance	80	20	80	20
Provision of women adult education in the region.	20	80	20	80
Improvement in the nutritional level of women	40	60	40	60

and tribal women are able to express their views and concerns more freely. They are becoming economically independent today.

CONCLUSION

Effective and democratic institutions of governance like JFM require representation of all segments of the population specially women. Inclusion of women can lead to a more efficient and equitable outcomes. After the span of more than 15 years since the declaration of JFM resolution at the national level, on the one side the women have been empowered by various activities of JFM programme, and on the other side various issues have been identified. These are as follows:

1. Due to lack of awareness and cultural hindrances the tribal women are not involved much in the decision-making process.
2. Though women have the vast indigenous knowledge, the forest department has not given much in the conservational values of the bioresources, rather than it gave emphasis on revenue earning from commercially valued trees.
3. In the executive committee of village institution, they have been given positions, but have not got the equitable sharing of responsibility and benefits.
4. In the implementation process of JFM programmes, women had to tackle a number of emerging problems in connection with the availability of natural and environmental products.

For community and state partnerships in forest management to be successful, it is imperative that tribal women are involved in decision making in the forest protection committees. In addition, JFM cannot be viewed as another new scheme or project. Co-management strategies, such as JFM, constitute a paradigmatic shift in state, people and forest relations. JFM should truly devolve authority to forest dwellers and make them empowered stakeholders in protection, management and use of forests. JFM should strengthen community-based institutions, which requires innovative ways of making women and other vulnerable segments of a community in the process of crafting rules and regulations for community forest management. In this regard, rigid guidelines and policies which impose uniform structures and management prescriptions seldom motivate and energize local communities. It is also important not to impose numerical targets as they lead to hastily formed forest committees by forest department officials, without any consideration for local traditions and forest use patterns (Poffenberger, 1995). Such targets shift the focus of JFM away from their real intent, to form representative community institutions that are capable of protecting and managing forests for the long-term benefit of its members. As mentioned before, JFM is about ensuring the long-term viability of forests through a set of community-based institutions that regulate the behaviour of its members vis-à-vis forests.

REFERENCES

Ashraf, N., D. Karlan and W. Yin (2006). 'Female Empowerment: Impact of a Commitment Savings Product in Philippines', Center Discussion Paper No. 949, Economic Growth Center, New Haven: Yale University.

Bali Swain, R. (2007). 'Impacting Women through Microfinance', Dialogue, *Appui au Développement Autonome*, 37: 61–82.

Basu, S.K. (1993). *Study on Fertility and Mortality Trends among Tribal Population of India – A Review* (Monograph), New Delhi: Indian Council of Social Science Research.

Beteta, H.C. (2006). 'What Is Missing in Measures of Women's Empowerment?' *Journal of Human Development*, 7(2): 221–241.

Blumberg, R.L. (2005). 'Women's Economic Empowerment as the "Magic Potion" of Development?' *Paper Presented at the 100th Annual Meeting of the American Sociological Association*, Philadelphia, August.

Browning, M. and P.A. Chiappori (1998). 'Efficient Intra-Household Allocations: A General Characterization and Empirical Tests', *Econometrica*, 66: 1241–1278.

Chauhan, A. (1990). *Tribal Women and Social Change in India*, Etawah: A.C. Brothers.

Das, S.K. (2012). 'An Analysis of Constraints in Women Empowerment in Tribal Area: Evidences from Assam', *Asian Journal of Research in Social Science & Humanities*, 2(4): 61–74.

Debnath, D. (2005). 'Conservation, Cultivation of Medicinal Plants in Livelihood Intervention – A Case Study of Tamilnadu', in *IIFM Communiqué* (A newsletter of IIFM), Vol. VII, March.

Dube, S.C. (1990). *Indian Society*, New Delhi: National Book Trust.

Deshmukh-Ranadive, J. (2003). 'Placing Gender Equity in the Family Centre Stage: Use of "Kala Jatha Theatre" ', *Economic and Political Weekly*, 26 April.

Duflo, E. (2003). 'Grandmothers and Granddaughters: Old Age Pension and Intra-Household Allocation in South Africa', *World Bank Economic Review*, 42: 1–25.

Fraser, E.D.G., et al. (2006). 'Bottom Up And Top Down: Analysis of Participatory Processes for Sustainability Indicator Identification as a Pathway to Community Empowerment and Sustainable Environmental Management', *Journal of Environmental Management*, 78: 114–127.

Ghosh, S. (1987). 'Women's Role in Health and Development', *Health for the Millions*, Vol. XIII, No. I&II.

Gowda N.K. and S.N. Yogesh (2006). 'Vision of women empowerment in India', in O'deyar D. Heggade, L.D. Vaikunte and Ravi N. Kadam (eds.), *Empowering Women in India: March towards Gender Equality*, Vol. 1, Mysore: Arjun Publishing House, pp. 13–23.

Kabeer, N. (2005). 'Is Microfinance a "Magic Bullet" for Women's Empowerment?: Analysis of Findings from South Asia', *Economic and Political Weekly*, 29 October.

Malhotra, A., and M. Mather (1997). 'Do Schooling and Work Empower Women in Developing Countries? Gender and Domestic Decisions in Sri Lanka', *Sociological Forum*, 12(4): 599–630.

McArdle, J. (1989). 'Community Development Tools of Trade,' *Community Quarterly*, 16: 47–54.

Johnson, S. (2005). 'Gender Relations, Empowerment and Microcredit: Moving on from a Lost Decade', *The European Journal of Development Research*, 17(2): 224–248.

Majumdar, D.N. (1973). *A Glimpse of Garo Politics in North-Eastern Affairs*, London: Longman.

Mann, K. (1987). *Tribal Women in Changing Society*, Delhi: Mittal Publications.

Onyx, J. and P. Benton (1995). 'Empowerment and Ageing: Toward Honoured Places for Crones and Sages', in G. Craig and M. Mayo (eds.), *Community Empowerment: A Reader in Participation and Development*, New Jersey: Zed Books.

Poffenberger, M. (1995). 'India's Forest Keepers', *Wastelands News*, Aug.–Oct., pp. 65–79.

Rivers, H.H. (1973). *The Todas*, London: Macmillan.

Sarin M. (1996). 'From Conflict to Collaboration: Local Institution in Joint Forest Management', JFM Working Paper No. 14, SPWD, New Delhi: Ford foundation.

Singhal, R., D. Debnath, et al. (2000). *Process Documentation of Joint Forest Management and Eco-Development: Consultancy Report*. (Mimeo) Bhopal: Indian Institute of Forest Management, for Madhya Pradesh Forestry Project.

Swain, B.R. and Wallentin, F.Y. (2007). 'Does Microfinance Empower Women? Evidence from Self Help Groups in India', Working Paper 2007:24, Department of Economics, Uppsala University.

Swain, R.S and F.Y. Wallentin (2008). 'Economic or Non-Economic Factors – What Empowers Women?' Working Paper 11, Department of Economics, Uppsala University.

CHAPTER 13

IN BETWEEN DEPRIVATION AND DEPENDENT ECONOMIC DEVELOPMENT: THE CASE OF TRIBAL WOMEN OF MADHYA PRADESH

S.N. Chaudhary

Deprivation refers to negation or near exclusion of a section of population from available resources, both animate and inanimate, material or non-material, largely on subjective and primordial considerations. With reference to tribal women, it refers to negation or near-negation of their access to and control over the local level available natural resources. And this negation is caused by the historical forces mainly managed by the state, its capitalistic model of development and the vested interest groups. There is continuous degeneration of forest and forest-based resources since the establishment of the British Raj. This ongoing process has made forest resource scarce over the time which has further led to exclusion of social groups that are local and otherwise marginalized. Tribal women are the first and worst victims of this process. During free India, efforts have been made by the state and civil societies to improve quality of life of tribal women. Many of them have received benefits out of this process. But this development is dependent-prone. Its continuation and sustainability is doubtful if there is apathy and reluctance on the part of dominant change agents. Here dependent economic development refers to the process which is extraneous, unsustainable, limited and relatively less productive. This process contributes to development among a small section, but the process is neither tenable nor equitable. This process of development discontinues once the support mechanism is withdrawn by the concerned change agents.

So far as tribes are concerned, they are victims of both these processes, i.e., deprivation and dependent economic development. The reason is mainly acculturation; over the time its intensity have increased manifold. The history of acculturation is very old among them. This process is both functional and dysfunctional. It is functional only for those few who avail the benefits and dysfunctional for many, especially those who are failed to avail its benefits. Over the time, since the inception of British rule, attempts have been made, especially by the rulers and change agents, to continue this trend. After independence, however, on the one hand the trend of deprivation is continuing unchecked, in spite of constitutional measures and development schemes, but on the other hand a section of them have availed some benefits of development. But as expected, the ongoing process of development has made beneficiaries dependent-prone. Hence, the pertinent question is how the ongoing process of development can be retained even if there is apathy and reluctance on the part of the state in the welfare sector under the dictates of globalization and market forces which is in principle, anti-welfare?

In the light of these broader issues, the paper is an attempt to examine dynamics of social status of tribal women in Madhya Pradesh in the historical perspective. The paper is divided into two parts. Opening part deals with status of tribes of Madhya Pradesh, in general, and tribal women, in particular, in the past. The second part examines dynamics of economic status of tribal women in the light of some of the initiatives taken in the recent past.

I

In spite of more than 65 years of independence, the socio-economic status of most of the tribal women is pitiable in comparison to even tribal men in Madhya Pradesh who themselves are historically marginalized. During the pre-British days, women's access to and control over the sources of livelihood was almost equal in comparison to their male counterparts. Source of their livelihood was primary which largely consisted of collection, processing and marketing of Minor Forest Produce (MFPs), domestication and grazing of cattle in the local forests, collection of fuelwood, participation in the decision-making process, agricultural activities and so on. The local natural resources, especially forest served as a source of their economic and non-economic life. Their need and requirement was also limited. Forest was also a source of clean environment, health and nutrition and custom and tradition. There was symbiotic relation between tribes and forest. Restrictions imposed by external forces relating to the use of forest resources were limited and bearable. But subsequently with the expansion of different non-tribal dynasties in the tribal world an alien culture was imposed in tribal villages. Generally, the degree of interaction between tribal and non-tribal society increased. This process directly or indirectly contributed to deforestation which, in turn, affected tribal culture–material and non-material – in a negative manner. According to one observation, the rise of the *Marathas* from the mid-seventeenth century onwards for the first time led to serious inroads into the Bhils homelands in the western Madhya Pradesh. In order to develop trade and settled agriculture so as to boost their revenue, the Marathas carried out sustained campaigns against the Bhils who refused to agree to this incursion into their lifestyle. Peasants and traders from Gujarat and Maharashtra were encouraged to settle in the Bhil regions and forests were cleared to bring land under the plough. Thousands of Bhils were massacred when they rose in revolt against this policy (Manohar, 2001). Many more studies may be cited to support and validate the argument pertaining to exploitation of tribal masses by non-tribal rulers during the pre-British days.

With the establishment of the British rule, the situation in the tribal world turned from bad to worst. Besides continuing and retaining the process initiated by dynasties, the British introduced a number of schemes to manage forest and other natural resources. The Forest Act and Policy (1865 and 1927) divided forest into different categories such as protected forest, reserved forest, etc., which on the one hand restricted entry of tribals into the forest and on the other hand promoted deforestation by the vested interests at the wider level. Tribal women were the first and the worst victims of this process. Collection of minor forest produce, firewood and drinking water, grazing of goat, etc. were badly affected. According to Luard (1908), the British followed the policy of the *Marathas* and brought in *Kunbi*, *Patidar* and *Jat* farmers from Gujarat and Rajasthan, respectively, and settled them on the Bhil lands in the plains so as to both increase the earning from land revenue and commercial agriculture and also to tame the militant Bhils. While some of the Bhils withdrew into the hills, most others were converted into serfs or bonded labourers of these non-*adivasi* farmers. Hence, British Raj deprived and excluded tribes, in general, and tribal women, in particular, in their homeland with the help of newly introduced and capitalism-driven forest management practices.

According to Ghurye (1999), tribals are poor not by accident, rather they have been systematically deprived of their lands, homes and livelihood by the state since the British days. To quote him (op. cit.), 'The acuteness of discomfort was very often so great that it led to apathy, indifference, moral deterioration and even a decline in population'. More or less similar observation was made by Hutton. According to him (1931),

> Far from being of immediate benefit to the primitive tribes, the establishment of British Rule in India did most of them much more harm than good.... It may be said that the early days of British Administration did very great detriment to the economic position of tribes through ignorance and neglect of their rights and customs .... many changes have been caused incidentally by the penetration of the tribal country, the opening up of communications, the protection of forests and the establishment of schools, to say nothing of the openings given in this way to Christian Missions. Many of the results of these changes have caused acute discomfort to the tribes.

Some of the micro-level social movements took place in different areas against the Raj and its anti-tribal activities, but such movements were either suppressed or they were socio-cultural in nature. These movements could not stop the ongoing anti-tribal natural resource/forest management practices in a meaningful manner. Even the freedom struggle could not address these issues, because the movement was mainly concentrated in the plain area and most of tribes were living in hill and forest areas. Even today about 93.56 per cent tribes of Madhya Pradesh live in villages which are in the so-called forest and hilly areas (2001 Census Report).

Needless to mention that the net result of acculturation process of different varieties between tribal and non-tribal traditions during both pre-British and British period was near breakdown of the autonomous character of tribal culture. A new and alien way of life was gradually imposed on tribes and a significant part of it gradually became elements of their culture. Due to their specific cultural heritage, tribes could not adjust with the newly introduced alien culture for long period. But gradually they became the victims of assimilation. Dealing with one of the implications of acculturation relating to age at marriage among girls of Hill Marias of Bastar, Grigson (1991) observed 'Pre-puberty marriage never occurs among the Hill Marias, who look upon it as an utterly abhorrent custom of the Kosor or Hindus. Unfortunately a few Bison-horn Marias are beginning to ape their Hindu neighbours in this as in other matters; but even now probably only three in a hundred Bison-horn marriages are child marriages.'

On this basis, it may be said that the process of ruinization which started during the pre-British days among tribes by non-tribal rulers and kings became common in both economic and non-economic life, without any concerted and successful effort to stop this, during the British period. Initially the Raj maintained social distance with socio-cultural practices in tribal areas in principle, but in practice its natural resources management policies and schemes were designed and implemented in such a fashion that it contributed to erosion of tribal social and cultural heritage along with economic deprivation and marginalization, and tribal women who are the backbone of tribal culture and economy were the worst victims of this process.

II

Historical marginality and exclusion of tribes was realized by the Constitution makers. Their inclusion with the wider society was given top priority by the macro-level change agents. Hence, a number of provisions were made and acts were passed in order to discontinue their marginalization and to improve their socio-economic status. In principle, all these provisions are equally applicable for men and women. It seems that while formulating laws social and economic variations among tribes living in different regions as well as the question of gender discrimination was not taken into account. All these acts and provisions can be grouped under four broad categories:

1. *Protective Provisions* – Articles 15, 16, 19, 23, 29, 46, 164, 330, 332, 335, 338, 339, 342 and 371.
2. *Developmental Provisions* – Articles 15, 16, 19, 46, 275 and 399.
3. *Administrative Provisions* – 344 for fifth scheduled areas. It covers 2.5 million tribes of different states and 6th schedule for north-east states under Articles 338 and 339.
4. *Reservation Facility* – Articles 330, 332, 334, 335 and 334 for reservation in Parliament/state assemblies/government jobs and admission.

To actualize these provisions and Articles of Indian Constitution, a number of development projects and schemes were formulated and implemented at the national level. Important among these are Integrated Rural Development Programme (IRDP), National Rural Employment Programme (NREP), National Rural Landless Employement Guarantee Programme (NRLEGP), Training of Rural Youth for Self Employment (TRYSEM), Jawahar Rojgar Yojna (JRY), Self Help Group (SHG), Indira Awas Yojna (IAY), Jeevandayi Yojna (JY), District Poverty Alleviation Programme (DPIP), Integrated Wasteland Development Project (IWLDP), Nehru Rojgar Yojna (NRY), Self Employment Scheme for Educated Unemployed Youth (SEEUY), Swarna Jayanti Gram Swarojgar Yojna (SGSY), Antayodaya Yojna (AY), National Old Age Pension Scheme, Integrated Child Development Scheme (ICDS), International Nutrition and Health Programme (INHP), Literacy Mission, Watershed Mission, Sarva Shiksha Abhiyan, Pre and Post Matric Scholarship, Ashram School, Tendu Patta Policy and so on.

All these institutional interventions, which are highly influenced by improvement approach of development, aimed to bring change in the quality of life of the tribal masses without challenging the existing constraints. The state assumed that by introducing development and welfare projects, it will ensure human rights of tribes. This thinking was purely logical with having no legitimacy from history and felt experience.

However, as a result of these institutional interventions, social and economic changes have taken place in the tribal world. The process of class formation is going on, although the speed is very slow. There are few from among them who have availed benefits in different walks of live. There are thousands of political representatives both men and women from Gram Panchayat to parliament level from tribal community. But many more have been left out. In the secondary and tertiary sector occupations, their presence is insignificant. It is largely because they do not have required inputs and skills like education, capital, risk taking capacity, faith in long-term investment and so on. Even among those few who have availed benefits, there is wide gap between men and women. Women lag far behind men in all spheres of life. In short, not only there is a wide gap between tribes and non-tribes, but also within tribes there is gap between general tribes and primitive tribes and within each tribe there is gap between men and women. Tribal women are far behind tribal men in terms of land ownership, literacy and education, bureaucracy, representation and say in formal political process, number of passbook and bank accounts holders, life longevity and so on. In spite of broadly having equal number, tribal women lag behind tribal men if we see the number of workers, main workers, cultivators, in household industries, etc. But if we see the number of women suffering from different forms of anaemia and female non-workers, they outnumber their men counterparts. This is obvious from Table 1.

Today there are three primitive tribes in Madhya Pradesh: Saharia in Shivpuri area, Bharia in Patalkot area of Chhindwara District and Baiga in and around Mandla District. The pattern of development along with the increasing gap between men and women found among the non-primitive tribes is also gradually appearing among the primitive tribes as their interaction with outside is increasing. Specifically, they reside in 15 districts. Besides other ongoing development and welfare schemes, there are 11 development authorities to ensure development of these three primitive tribes. Among them too, although the process of development is slow, gender disparity is found in every element of development. Level of literacy may be taken as an example.

Table 1 Classification of Tribal Population of Madhya Pradesh on the Basis of Some Development Indicators

Variables	
Total population	12,233,474
Male (%)	50.64 (6,195,240)
Female (%)	49.35 (6,038,234)
Total literacy rate (%)	41.20
Male (%)	53.50
Female (%)	28.40
Percentage of anaemia 2005–2006 (NFHS-3)	
Mild (male) (%)	20.4
Mild (female) (%)	44.8
Moderate (male) (%)	18.1
Moderate (female) (%)	21.3
Severe (male) (%)	1.1
Severe (female) (%)	2.4
Any anaemia (male) (%)	39.6
Any anaemia (female) (%)	68.5
Male workers (%)	53.40 (6,173,431) 50.46
Female workers (%)	46.59
Main workers (male) (%)	64.00 (4,186,896) 34.22
Main workers (female) (%)	36.00
Male cultivators (%)	64.94 (2,324,501) 19
Female cultivators (%)	35.05
Male agricultural labourers (%)	58.16 (1,338,230) 10.93
Female agricultural labourers (%)	41.83
Male in household industries (%)	57.15 (42,508) 0.34
Female in household industries (%)	42.84
Male marginal workers (%)	31.07 (1,986,535) 16.23
Female marginal workers (%)	68.92
Male non-workers (%)	47.82 (6,060,043) 49.53
Female non-workers (%)	52.17

Source: A-11 state Primary Census Abstract for Individual Scheduled Tribes-2001, P.59.

Table 2 Level of Literacy among Primitive Tribes

	Population	Total Literate	%	Male Literate	%	Female Literate	%
Baiga	332,936	85,706	26	59,266	69	26,440	31
Bharia	152,472	43,604	29	30,205	69	13,399	31
Saharia	450,217	96,724	21	70,934	73	25,790	27

Source: A-11 State Primary Census, 2001 as above.

Absence of feminization of development projects is the root cause behind this. The prime root responsible for this state of affair is expansion of patriarchy and Hindu tradition among them due to acculturation. The near absence of indebtedness among relatively more isolated Bharia tribe and the presence of indebtedness in Saharia tribe, which is more exposed to outside world including Hindu tradition, may be taken as an example to explain negative implications of acculturation process.

One of the important institutional interventions for tribal development was initiated under the banner of Tribal Sub-Plan (TSP) during mid-seventies. This plan strategy was developed by an Expert Committee set up by the Ministry of Education and Social Welfare in 1972 under the Chairmanship of S.C. Dube for the rapid socio-economic development of tribal people and was adopted for the first time in the Fifth Five Year Plan. The strategies adopted continue till date. Guidelines of TSP stipulated that 30 per cent of the funds shall be kept apart for women component and have to be spent for income generation activities of women beneficiaries.

Besides institutional intervention, some new developments have taken place during last couple of decades. There is rapid increase in men headed seasonal outmigration, establishment of large-scale development projects in the tribal areas, displacement of tribes due to development projects, expansion of extremism in tribal-dominated area, popularization of NGOs, expansion of transportation and communication networks, spread of consumer culture, etc., which have influenced tribal world both functionally and dysfunctionally. There is massive change in the world view of tribal masses. However, from development and empowerment point of view the picture is mixed. The gap between tribal men and women is yet to be reduced. In many cases, it is rather increasing. Introduction of dowry system, Hindu rituals and festivals and other forms of Hindu patriarchy are contributing to the existing gender gap.

In short, if we critically examine all these institutional and social interventions, as stated above, it is obvious that these were mainly addressed to the problems of tribal masses. These schemes are seldom exclusively directed to the concerns of tribal women. It was assumed that with overall development of tribes, development of tribal women will automatically take place. Even if some provisions are exclusively available for women, these are seldom implemented in the true sense of the term; the reasons are many more.

During an era of globalization, since July 1991 some specific efforts have been made to develop vulnerable groups, especially women. Broadly, it also covers tribal women. These efforts are given in the following sections.

Madhya Pradesh Policy for Women

This policy was enacted in 1995. Its broad purpose was to improve socio-economic status of cross section of women. Extension of land right to women and making them joint or single *pattadharini* is also one of the objectives of policy for women. However, its specific purposes are the following:

1. Ensuring the survival and protection of female life.
2. Ensuring the fullest participation of women in civil society, and strengthen their role in decision making.
3. Increasing self-confidence and enhancing the status of women.
4. Empowerment of women to enable them to take the fullest advantage of development efforts in all fields.
5. Affirmative action to ensure women's full participation in economic activity.
6. Ensuring the visibility of women in all walks of life.
7. Bringing about sensitization and attitudinal change in the larger society on the women question.
8. Prevention of atrocities and acts of violence against women.

Women policy of Government of Madhya Pradesh is innovative in principle. It is directed to the overall empowerment and development of women. But specifically it is not directed to the concerns of tribal women. It is needless to mention here that majority of tribal women are confronting with their day-to-day problems which are basic and primary in nature. How can one ensure his/her development and empowerment until and unless he/she is freed from day-to-day struggle relating to drinking water, basic health facility, food security, illiteracy, corruption, dependence and so on? All these issues have not been covered by the women's policy.

The Provisions of the Panchayats (Extension to the Scheduled Areas) Act 1996 (PESA)

In the light of the 73rd Constitutional Amendment, a committee was constituted in June 1994 by the Government of India under the chairmanship of Dilip Singh Bhuriya. Purpose of this committee was to examine issues relating to extension of the provisions of part IX of the Constitution to the Scheduled areas and to make recommendations on the salient features of the laws for extending the provisions of this part of the Constitution to the scheduled areas. Broad features of the recommendation of Bhuriya Committee (also known as Panchayat Extension to the Scheduled Areas Act, 1996) are as follows:

1. All the villages must have *Gram Sabha* and it shall be competent enough to safeguard and preserve the traditions and customs of tribes.
2. *Gram Sabha* shall approve the plans, programmes and projects for its development and implementation.
3. *Gram Sabha* shall be held responsible for the identification of persons as beneficiaries under the poverty alleviation and other programmes.
4. Every Gram Panchayat shall obtain from *Gram Sabha* a certificate of utilization of funds for the plans, programmes and projects.
5. The reservation of seats in the scheduled areas in every Panchayat shall be in proportion to the population of the communities in the Panchayat. The reservation for scheduled tribes shall not be less than one-half of the total number of seats. Further, all seats of chairpersons of Panchayats at all levels shall be reserved for the scheduled tribes.
6. Planning and management of small water bodies in the scheduled areas shall be entrusted to concerned Panchayats.
7. Recommendations of the *Gram Sabha* shall be mandatory in granting of licence by the Gram Panchayats, for mining lease, for minerals and concession for the exploitation of minor minerals by auction in the scheduled areas.
8. The state legislature shall endow Panchayats and the *Gram Sabha* specifically with: (1) Power to enforce prohibition or regulate or restrict the sale and consumption of any intoxicant; (2) Ownership of minor forest produces; (3) Power to prevent land alienation in the scheduled areas;

(4) Power to manage village markets; (5) Power to control money lending to scheduled tribes; (6) Power to control local plans and resources for such plans, including tribal sub-plan; and (7) The state legislation that may endow Panchayats with powers and authority, as may be necessary to enable them to function as institutions of self-governance, shall contain safeguards to ensure that Panchayats at the higher level do not assume the powers and authority of any Panchayats at the lower level or of the *Gram Sabha*.

The states are directed to implement PESA and transfer resources and functions to *Gram Sabha*. Since its enactment in 1997, PESA has remained by and large a law on paper. As per PESA guidelines, the power to transact business of MFPs (including nationalized items like *Tendu Patta*, *Lakh*, *Sal Seed* and *Gum Karaya* in Madhya Pradesh) was to be transferred to the Gram Panchayats so that the tribal could receive more than the collection charges. Since collection and marketing of NTFPs is largely the domain of tribal women and they are supposed to avail maximum benefit out of PESA Act, they could not avail the benefits primarily because the Act was not honestly implemented.[1]

Even if certain rights have been extended to the Gram Sabha, these rights are properly not exercised due to near non-functioning of Gram Sabha primarily due to apathy, ignorance, lack of assertiveness, increasing individualism, manipulation by Panchayat representatives, massive corruption at the Panchayat level, reluctance on the part of local level tribal elites and so on.

In many cases, meetings of the Gram Sabha are organized only on the paper by the Gram Panchayat president and secretary, and some of the like-minded members are asked to put signature on the decision as and when required. Following case from a tribal Panchayat of Madhya Pradesh may be cited as an example.

> "During the tenure of Rajni Dhurve, Sarpanch (2005-2009) of Pathai Panchayat of Betul district altogether 21 *Gram Sabha* meetings were organized. In actual sense 17 meetings were held and for want of quorum[2] 4 meetings were cancelled. Whether this was a *gram sabha* meeting which was most often participated by very small number of villagers or not it is another story because, in most of these meetings there was no presence of villagers. Only the key persons such as Sarpanch, Up-sarpanch and couple of panches participated in the meeting. The data reveal that of all 17 meetings hardly in 5 meetings large number of villagers were present. It is said that actually many such meetings were formally not

> at all organized but all formalities were made on paper only, the paper work was done by Sarpanch and Secretary of the panchayat and some panches were asked to put their signature once the so- called meeting was over. Hence, it is difficult to say that all the agendas presented in the so-called meetings and its approval by the same committee was really based on mass based participation and decision. During the course of study it was observed that villagers do not know about the concept and importance of gram sabha and its meetings. They only assemble in large number at the Panchayat Bhavan when they are directed by the Sarpanch/Secretary especially at the time of visit of some high officials." (Chaudhary, 2010: 143–144)

It is needless to mention that because of variety of reasons such as the ongoing process of deforestation and land alienation in the name of national development and entrance of the market forces, either availability of NTFPs is getting reduced on constant basis or these are not easily accessible to tribal women. This development has reduced women's economic contribution to the family. Even if they are engaged in the collection of items like *Mahua* flower and firewood, it is not sufficient enough to meet even their basic requirements. In addition, the changing patterns of consumer behaviour especially in favour of consumerable items like detergent powder, cosmetic, ladies garments, cold drinks, etc. are compelling women to spent whatever they earn on these consumerable items. Most of them are hand to mouth. In case some of them have savings, usually in an informal way, they spent it on consumerable items. The increasing number of modern household assets in many tribal households may be taken as an example (for detail information see Chaudhary, 2010, op. cit). They are largely unaware of the importance of modern saving mechanism.

In short, the tall claim of PESA is totally failed to meet the requirement and extend justice to tribes in a wider perspective. Heavy reliance of PESA on sick institution like *Gram Sabha* is one of the grassroot level reasons responsible for this state of affair.

The Scheduled Tribes and Other Traditional Forest Dwellers (Recognition of Forest Rights) Act 2006

This act is commonly known as the Forest Rights Act 2006. This Act was introduced to repair historical damage caused to tribal masses by alienating them from land by both the state and other vested interests. This Act intends to extend ownership rights to tribes on the land which they are tilling since long with ownership right. Special features of this act are as follows:

- Recognizes and vests the forest rights and occupation in forests lands in forest dwelling scheduled tribes and other traditional forest dwellers who have been residing in such forests for generations but whose rights could not be recorded.
- Recognizes the responsibilities of the Forest Dwelling Scheduled Tribes (FDST) and other traditional forest dwellers for sustainable use, conservation of biodiversity and maintenance of ecological balance and thereby strengthening the conservation regime of the forests while ensuring livelihood and food security to them.
- Recognizes the forest rights on ancestral lands and their habitat which were not adequately recognized during the colonial period as well as in independent India.
- Addresses the long standing insecurity of general and access rights by RDST and other traditional forest dwellers including those who were forced to relocate their dwelling due to state development interventions.

The Forest Rights Act 2006 recognizes 13 rights of tribes and other forest dwellers. These are as follows:

1. It extends rights to hold or live in the forest land under the individual or common occupation by forest or self-cultivate for a livelihood by a member or members of a forest dwelling people.
2. It extends community rights or *nistar*.
3. It extends rights of ownership/access to collect, use and dispose of minor forest produce.
4. It permits to hold other community rights or entitlement such as fishing or grazing.
5. It extends rights, including community rights, terms of habitat and habitation for primitive tribal groups and pre-agricultural communities.
6. It holds rights in or over disputed lands.
7. It provides rights for conversion of *pattas* or leases or grants issued by local authority.
8. It provides rights of settlement and conversion of all forest villages into revenue villages.
9. It legalizes rights to protect or conserve or manage community forest resources.
10. It accepts rights which are recognized under any state law or laws of any autonomous district council or rights of tribal under any traditional or customary law of the concerned tribes of any state.

11. It facilitates right of access to biodiversity and customary right to intellectual property and traditional knowledge related to biodiversity and cultural diversity.
12. It acknowledges any traditional right which are not mentioned above.
13. It extends rights to *in situ* rehabilitation including alternative land in the cases where they have been illegally evicted or displaced from forest land prior to December 13, 2005.

This act is supposed to confer landownership titles on *Adivasis* and others. Names of both men and women are supposed to be on land *Patta* distributed under this scheme. But if we see the achievement, the picture is frustrating. For examples, in Madhya Pradesh, till March 2010, altogether 4,04,591 claims were received from both individuals and community, but only 1,09,000 (about 25 per cent) claims were cleared. Altogether 3,59,502.09 acres of land were allotted under 89,035 titles. It is also claimed that the *Pattas* distributed are not accepted as negotiable instruments for receiving subsidies or accessing bank loans.

Dalit Agenda and Distribution of Grazing Land to Tribals

Under the Bhopal Declaration, popularly known as *Dalit Agenda*, around 5,23,645 hectares of grazing land was distributed among landless and near landless dalit and tribal households in Madhya Pradesh during 2002. About 2,22,289 hectares of land was distributed among tribes. One of the provisions that entitlement of land rights shall be shared jointly by husband and wife was largely followed. One-time incentive was also provided to ensure proper farming. Besides economic gain, although in a limited sense, this scheme enhanced morale of both men and women, and the feeling of having land ownership had also social implications (Chaudhary, 2006).

Besides these, other institutional interventions like 33 per cent reservation for women in the Panchayat, formation of large number of tribal women dominated Self-Help Groups, etc. have benefited large number of tribal women both economically and socially. Today there are thousands of tribal women as Panchayat representatives at all the three levels of Panchayat. It has wider socio-political implications from empowerment and development of tribal women. These are examples of social mobility among women.

But this is one side of the coin. The other side is not so shining. Their development is totally dependent on state. It is neither automatic nor autonomous. And if there is apathy and reluctance on the part of the state, and if operations at the village level remain corrupted and manipulation unchecked, then the functioning of these change agents working for the cause of tribes are likely to suffer.

So far as the role of these women representatives, as a change agent, is concerned, it is not praiseworthy. Women Panchayat representatives have even failed to address the problem of tribal women. These agents have imitated roles of both tribal and non-tribal-established elites. In addition, they are equally and most often insensitive to the issue of *Gram Sabha* meetings like their men counterparts.

Self-Help Groups have also failed to empower even the women members in social and economic terms. Many of such Self-Help-Groups of all varieties are functional only on papers. Whatever achievements have been made by few organizations, some of these are bound to suffer and these are likely to disappear once the institutional support is withdrawn.

Schemes of the Ministry of Tribal Affairs (GOI)

Out of 16 schemes of the Ministry of Tribal Affairs, Government of India, 7 schemes are specifically addressed to the development of tribal women. These schemes are (1) construction of educational complex in low literacy pockets for development of women literacy in tribal areas, (2) support to National Scheduled Tribes Finance and Development Corporation, (3) scheme of PMS, book bank and upgradation of merit of ST students, (4) scheme of hostel for ST girls and boys, (5) exchange of visits by tribals, (6) special central assistance for tribal sub-plan and (7) scheme under provision to Article 275 (1) of the Constitution (Ministry of Tribal Affairs, 2007–2008).

There are a large number of tribal women who are away from the scope of these development initiatives. They are either wage workers or engaged in farming or both. The new scheme like MNREGS has given seasonal employment to many of them at the local level, and the result is encouraging in many cases. But here also the trend of development is not sustainable. They do not know how to link success in one sector with success in other sector. They do not know how to manage their income in a beneficial manner. They do not know about their future once scheme like MNREGS ends. In the absence of required inputs including skill and market linkage, the farming work is gradually becoming non-economical.

Needless to mention that during 20 years of the formal history of globalization, a number of new initiatives have taken place to promote primary and middle education. Important among these are *Sarva Shiksha Abhiyan*, Education Guarantee Scheme, free uniform and free bicycle to a section of them, Mid-Day-Meal (MDM) and so on. As a result, most of the tribal boys and girls have been enrolled in primary schools. This is a success story. But gradually as one moves from middle education onwards the number of girl students decreases and hardly few of them are able to enrol themselves in colleges and universities. The second problem is related to the quality of education which they receive. It is much below the average. And in the absence of required level of education as well as specific quality of education, tribals in general and tribal girls in particular are unable to avail globalization initiated benefits of development. Only a section of tribal girls from the middle class or those who have urban linkages are capable of availing such benefits. As a result, hundreds and thousands posts reserved for tribals are lying vacant for want of suitable candidates, and in this way globalization is hardly functional for most of tribes.

In short, it may be concluded that majority of tribal women have experienced exclusion and marginalization, especially in economic term, during the British and post-British period. This development is an outcome of the external forces, especially the state and the market forces. It has largely snatched their century-old sources of livelihood. Globalization is also enemical to them. It has forced them to remain at the receiving end. Many of them have been forced to become pauper by damaging their community-old support base. It has failed to make them partner in the development process. Attempts have been made to encounter the process of exclusion and marginalization initiated by both the state and globalization forces, individually and collectively, but the outcome is not encouraging. Only few of tribal women have been able to avail benefits of development. In addition, there are only few who are able to improve their economic life due to their own effort. There is some improvement in physical and social quality of life of those who have availed benefits of development even in a limited sense. But this development is very slow, selective and totally dependent-prone. It is not tenable without institutional support. It contributes to individualism and self-centeredness among many of them. Until and unless there is social capital formation among all categories of tribal women and need based as well as area-specific development approach is not followed, change agents are sensitized on regular basis, tribal women are made aware, corruption is reduced, if not eradicated, their development is not possible in a sustainable manner under the given socio-economic and political context which is democratic in principle and more on paper and less in practice especially from tribal development point of view. It may be assumed that Draft National Tribal Policy which contains 15 issues, including gender equity, if passed and implemented with catholic spirit in a holistic manner may become a milestone for the development and empowerment of tribal women.

NOTES

1 According to one observation (Chaudhary, 2008–2009), tribal women face problem at the level of collection, processing, storage and marketing of NTFP. Reasons are both macro and micro. Unemployment, poverty, population growth, macroeconomic policy and forest management strategy which is capitalistic in nature are the macro factors, and lack of awareness, alternative source of income, infrastructure and support from state and civil societies are the micro-level problems. These two set of problems create conditions against the interest of tribal women who are engaged in the collection of NTFP. As a result their human rights pertaining to freedom from discrimination, want, torture, injustice and exploitation are denied by all the concerned. They do not have power to take decision, work decently without exploitation and have no capacity to form association to escape exploitation. Under the given adverse situation, the forces of globalization have also added fuel to the fire.

2 As per the revised Adhiniyam (6) 2005, of the total voters of the Panchayat, who are members of Gram Sabha either 1/10th of them or 500 members, whichever is less, fulfil the quorum. But of 1,154 inhabitants of Pathai alone, and there are two other villages in Panchayat, about half of them (586) are above 20 years of age and 1/10th of them will be around 58. On this parameter, of 17 meetings organized by Pathai Panchayat, only 5 meetings and its decisions may be perceived as valid.

REFERENCES

Chaudhary, S.N. (2012). *In Search of Sustainable Development: Scenario in a Tribal Village of Madhya Pradesh*, New Delhi: Serials.

Chaudhary, S.N. (2008–2009). 'Human Rights of Tribal Women Engaged in Collection of Non- Timber Forest Produce in Madhya Pradesh', *Journal of Gender Equality and Sensitivity*, 3(1).

Chaudhary, S.N. (2006). 'Grazing Land to Dalits in Madhya Pradesh: Social Opportunity and Political Cost', *The Indian Journal of Social Work*, 66(3).

Ghurye, G.S. (1999). *The Scheduled Tribes* (2nd edition), Bombay: Popular.

Grigson, S.W. (1991 Reprint). *The Maria Gonds of Bastar*, New Delhi: Oxford University Press and Vanya Prakashan (Bhopal).

Hutton, J. H. (1931). *Census of India*, Delhi: Gian.

Luard, C.E. (1908): *Central India Gazetteer Series: Western Series* (Malwa), Vol. V. Bombay: British India Press.

Manohar, D. (2001). *Bagh Ke Bacche Hai Hum* (We Are the Children of the Tiger), Hoshangabad: Dishasamvad.

Ministry of Tribal Affairs, Govt. of India (2008). *Annual Report* (2007–2008), New Delhi, p. 119.

CHAPTER 14

PARTICIPATION OF TRIBAL WOMEN IN GRASSROOTS POLITICAL INSTITUTIONS: EVIDENCES FROM TRIBAL REGIONS OF MADHYA PRADESH, RAJASTHAN AND GUJARAT

Yatindra Singh Sisodia

The 73rd Constitutional Amendment Act and State Conformity Act, which were modelled on the lines suggested by the 73rd Amendment Act, provided respectable spaces to the tribal people in the working of the Panchayat Raj system, but such legislations cannot make the tribal communities the sole masters of their socio-political destinies in their homelands. The need was always felt that the institutional structures within the scheduled areas were to be in consonance with the tribal needs and ethos; tribal institutions had to be shaped in a manner with which these people were familiar for ages. In addition, many of such areas, which were once freely managed by the tribal people, for example, the management of their forests, lands and water resources, were unfortunately out of their purview as they were under the authority of external institutions/agencies.

Added to such disgruntlements were the voices of the friends of Panchayat Raj system as well as of the tribal people themselves who pleaded for more powers to the Panchayats under scheduled areas in a way that their institutions, while enjoying decentralized status and functioning as units of self-government, could at the same time preserve and safeguard the traditions, customs and cultural identities of their people. As a result of such demands and felt needs of the tribal communities, Union Government passed a legislation known as 'Panchayat (Extension to the Scheduled Areas) Act, 1996'.

A perusal of the powers and functions of the Panchayat Raj institutions (PRIs) of scheduled areas indicates that the Panchayats of the scheduled areas have been equipped with special powers and functions, which are in consonance with the ethos of the tribal people/communities. Such provisions bless these bodies with some preferential powers and functions. At the foundation level is the 'Gram Sabha', as the tribal people live in a scattered manner in the *phalias* or hamlets/group of hamlets. The Act defines a village in the scheduled areas as 'which shall ordinarily consist of a habitation or a group of habitations or a hamlet or a group of hamlets comprising a community and managing its affairs in accordance with its traditions and customs'. Reservation of seats for scheduled tribes in every Panchayat of the scheduled areas shall be in proportion to their respective population in that Panchayat area. In addition, all seats of sarpanch/chairperson of Panchayats at all levels in the scheduled areas are reserved for members of the scheduled tribes.

The Panchayat Raj system in scheduled areas has empowered *Gram Sabhas* with all such powers and duties to become the real unit of self-governance. As a result, there has been a growing concern for the speedy development of tribal areas.

If we look at the background of decentralization, after Independence, persistent efforts have been made to make rural local self-government viable and self-sustainable on the lines portrayed by Mahatma Gandhi. Unfortunately, the response of the state governments was of very different nature and thus the pace and pattern of establishment of rural local political institutions were not very enthusiastic in the initial phase. The state governments showed very little interest to empower these institutions, and transfer of power to the representative institutions was almost negligible. Although political leaders of some Indian states like Kerala, Karnataka, Maharashtra and West Bengal came forward to establish Panchayats at local level, on the whole the pace of development was restricted which left much to be desired. Champions of local self-government debated and argued that the development planning was faulty, that the results did not reach the people concerned despite plethora of schemes and massive investments in rural sector. It was also realized that the infrastructure at the local level was in a very bad state and one of the obvious reasons was poor delivery system through local bureaucracy. People's participation was rarely seen and the development model was of 'top down approach'. Accountability of the delivery mechanism was nominal as it rested with the bureaucratic hierarchy that viewed rural masses as mere recipients.

Almost after 45 years, the Central Government realized this hard truth that the delivery system in the tribal/rural area was not effectively operational; it realized at last that without making people's direct and responsible participation through Panchayats purposeful development in the desired manner was not possible. As a result, the introduction of 73rd Constitutional Amendment Act was enacted in 1993. The execution of the Act was made mandatory for all the Indian states, and Panchayats have been provided a constitutional status. A special chapter has been added to the Indian Constitution on Panchayats. The 73rd Amendment has provided uniformity and formal structure to these traditional institutions of self-governance for the sake of their effective functioning. The 73rd Amendment has initiated a fundamental restructuring of governance and administrative system of the country based on the philosophy of decentralization and power to the people. Policy planners have realized by now that the new PRIs have the potential to usher in a new era of change and development in accordance with people's needs and priorities, and to revitalize a deeply troubled system of democracy (Behar and Kumar, 2002).

The idea that produced the 73rd Amendment Act was not a response to pressure from the grassroots, but it was due to an increasing recognition that the institutional initiatives of the preceding decades had not delivered that the extent of rural poverty was still much too large and thus the existing structure of government needed to be reformed. It is interesting to note that this idea evolved from the Centre and the State Governments. It was a political drive to see PRIs as a solution to the governmental crises that India was experiencing. The institutions of Panchayat Raj in its rejuvenated form seek to achieve the objectives of democratic decentralization to accelerate socio-economic development and usher in equity and social justice.

The enactments of the 73rd Constitutional Amendment Act and the subsequent state-wise Panchayat Raj Acts in India have brought to frontline the significance of grassroots democratic processes. This change in the Indian political system is the result of a growing conviction that the big and distantly placed government cannot achieve growth and development in a society without people's direct participation and initiative. This experience has brought the lesson that the success of the new Panchayat Raj system largely depends on the congruence of perception and commitment of the people, their leaders and the officials, about the role to be played by them in the new system. Contextually and theoretically too, the new Panchayat Raj system has been created as a model of self-governance (Sisodia, 2002). The objectives of decentralization are to execute and implement schemes and programmes to meet the local needs, to mobilize people, to channelize their energies towards socio-economic reconstruction and to involve them in all the activities of the communities through the new institutions. Its objectives include also reducing the size of work of the higher level government and leaving the responsibility to the local people to decide their destiny as per the new dispensation. Decentralization is now a much-debated issue in India and other countries with federal system of governance. Although there are various arguments for and against decentralization, arguments in favour of decentralization far outweigh those against it because of the inherent potential of democratization in the decentralized federal system through proper empowerment of people at the grassroots level.

A decade and a half of Panchayat Raj in India has been a matter of debate and speculation about its performance and impact. All the major states have completed at least one round of Panchayat elections and in majority of cases at least two successive rounds. Almost three million people including one million women and a sizeable number of SCs/STs took part in these elections. The sizeable presence of underprivileged and the poor as representatives through reservations for the grassroots political institutions is a landmark development in the rural politics of the country. This significant development has special meaning because a decade earlier in most parts of rural India these groups were excluded from public life and political participation. This is also a matter of serious debate as how this excluded lot after their inclusion in active politics at grassroots level would effectively participate and tackle local power equations and set the agenda for development. Yet the fact remains that these backward and so far ignored classes have heralded their arrival on the political stage of the country in the countryside.

The responses of the state governments to the implementation of Panchayat Raj varied significantly and it is very difficult to generalize about this issue on the basis of their functioning for the last one decade or so. Only a few states like Maharashtra, Gujarat, Kerala, Karnataka and West Bengal have had a track record of Panchayats since 1950s, and the exemplary lead taken by the state of Madhya Pradesh after 1993 brings together a total of six states only that took steps to strengthen PRIs. On the other hand, states of Bihar, Jharkhand and Jammu & Kashmir are considered prominent examples among states where little or no progress had taken place over the last decade; even regular Panchayat elections were inordinately delayed in these states.

A perusal of state profiles would show that Panchayat Raj reforms have certainly taken place with vigour and zeal in some western and southern parts of the country that are relatively sound from the point of view of economy, are vibrant socially and have active civil societies. On the contrary, the northern states with the greatest degree of poverty, inequality and deep schisms of caste and low pace of governance resulted in weak Panchayats (Robinson, 2005).

In this mixed scenario of development, exemplary reforms have taken place in Kerala and Madhya Pradesh due to the strong political will of the political leadership of these states after the implementation of the 73rd Amendment Act. In Kerala, the people's planning campaign was predicted on a high level of popular mobilization that was made possible by high level of literacy and professional support with a mass base social movement (Issac, 2000). In Madhya Pradesh, the then Chief Minister Digvijay Singh had introduced a series of reforms and amendments in Panchayat Raj system to strengthen the grassroots institutions, specially the *Gram Sabha*. The example of West Bengal is well known where the CPM government used the PRIs as a political support base in rural areas with a significant degree of success. The land reforms in West Bengal could take place due to Panchayat Raj (Webster, 1993).

II

73rd Amendment and Implementation of PESA

Tribal communities are most marginalized section of the Indian society. They have remained comparatively isolated from the mainstream development process and maintain an uninterrupted long tradition of well-knit cohesive social structure and value system backed their own custom and traditions. They also have several indigenous traditional institutions to resolve their conflict and manage their resources and socio-political life. When the institution of new Panchayat Raj was planned to be introduced in the tribal areas, it was felt that there is an urgent need to protect the tribal from the marginalization in the age of globalization. The working group (1996) of the Ninth Five Year Plan suggested participatory planning as a necessary prelude for growth and equity in tribal areas which have not gained significantly from the development process since independence. In order to strengthen the grassroots level local bodies and to provide self-rule of tribal, the Part IX of the Constitution, which deals with Panchayats, has been specially extended through an Act of Parliament called Panchayats Extension to Scheduled V Areas (PESA) Act 1996. Prior to this Act, a committee was constituted under Shri Dilip Singh Bhuria to examine various dimensions of self-rule of tribal and the constitutional requirement for extension of the Panchayats provision in the scheduled areas. The suggestions made by the committee assimilated various provisions of scheduled V and scheduled VI areas and 73rd Constitutional Amendment. Under PESA, special treatment has been given to the social, political, cultural and economic aspects of tribal life.

One of the highlighting features of PESA is its suggestion that 'every Gram Sabha shall be competent to safeguard and preserve the traditions and customs of the people, their cultural identity, community resources and the customary mode of dispute resolution'. In addition to this, the Central Act of 1996 provides extensive powers to Gram Sabha in the scheduled areas in the following sectors: (1) approval of plans, programmes and projects for social and economic development prior to their implementation, (2) identification of beneficiaries of anti poverty programmes and (3) certify utilization of fund spent by the Panchayat.

PESA after giving the above exclusive powers to the lowest unit of grassroots democracy has further provided that the Gram Sabha or Panchayats at appropriate level shall have the following powers: (1) to be consulted on matters of land acquisition and resettlement, (2) grant prospecting licence for mining lease for minor minerals and concessions for such activities, (3) planning and management of minor water bodies, (4) the power to enforce prohibition or to regulate or restrict the sale and consumption of any intoxicant, (5) the ownership of minor forest produces, (6) the power to prevent alienation of land and to restore any unlawfully alienated land of a scheduled tribe, (7) the power to manage village markets, (8) the power to exercise control over money lending to scheduled tribes, (9) the power to exercise controls over institutions and functionaries in all social sectors and (10) the power to control local plans and resources.

While prescribing such wide ranging powers to 'Gram Sabhas or Panchayats at appropriate level', PESA has further warned that 'the State legislation that may endow Panchayats with powers and authority as may be necessary to enable them to function as institutions of self government. It also contains safeguards to ensure that Panchayats at higher level do not assume the powers and authority of any Panchayats at the lower level or the Gram Sabha'. The states were suggested to amend their respective GP acts to extend the provisions of the Panchayat to scheduled areas of their respective states within a year keeping in mind the letter and the spirit of the Central Act of 1996.

Three different forces are influencing the process of decentralized governance – the state, the civil society and the community. The interaction between these forces and its intensity governs the pace and pattern of implementation of PESA. Although at surface the state aims to decentralize the governance, the political economy of decentralization restricts intense interaction between the state, the civil society and the community.

Efforts have been made to empower people through legislation in scheduled areas, but there are indications that the level of participation of people at grassroots level is very low. The grassroots institutions like Gram Sabhas are almost a formal institution with no role in various development works at the level of village. It is unfortunate that both the grassroots leadership and grassroots bureaucracy have not been able to strengthen the *Gram Sabha* in scheduled areas. The responsibility of natural resource management (land/water/forest) lies with village level institutions, but there still exists discrepancies regarding minor minerals/minor forest produce and therefore the direct control of the tribal community over natural resource management is far from reality. All the plans including tribal sub-plan are to be implemented through grassroots level institutions but lack of information is a major bottleneck in this regard. Decision making at grassroots level is of typical nature where elected representatives are more genuinely involved in the process of decision making whereas the community is at large ignorantly out of this process.

So far as financial status of Panchayats is concerned, it is completely dependent on the grants from government. Revenue generation at local level could not become possible because of lack of resources to generate revenue in tribal regions; taxation is also not possible because of the lack of basic amenities needed for day-to-day life; majority of the people live in acute shortage of livelihood bases which in turn lead to a situation where basic survival is a major question among majority of people. The grants and funds percolating to grassroots institutions through governments are mainly for welfare programmes and development works and hence the Panchayats lack total control over such resources and local planning; prioritization of such funds for the community is ignored.

In tribal regions, there is a stronghold of traditional leadership which creates hindrances to the smooth functioning of Panchayats. Nevertheless, there are examples where the traditional and Panchayat leadership is the same, and in such a situation the functioning of Panchayat is much better. Low level of people's participation can be mainly attributed to a strong and invincible social and economic stratification existed in villages. Sarpanch and other influential people tend to dominate the decision-making process. There are generally two prominent and sharply contrasting groups leading the Panchayats: (1) the traditional influential representatives and (2) the other of new entrants. The performance and efficacy of Panchayat members is strongly influenced by the social stratification and class distinctions. Moreover, Gram Panchayats are not adequately accountable to Gram Sabha. The Gram Sabha is not aware of the Gram Panchayat functioning. The idea of participation as an important part of Panchayat Raj has rarely been observed in practice. In fact, in retrospect, it seems inevitable that persons of influence would look at larger community participation with hostility.

In scheduled areas of Madhya Pradesh, Rajasthan and Gujarat, the village level situation is different from the high expectations created by PESA. State Acts are also confronting with the provisions of PESA. The issue of tribal non-tribal leadership in scheduled areas has created new political equations. The political dynamics at grassroots level has different dimensions; it has many players in the circles and they throw their weight according to their influences in the local power dynamics. As a matter of fact, it can be argued that despite the specific provision provided through PESA, there is a gap between macro-level decisions and grassroots level reality. Tribal regions have their own peculiarities. The main actors in Panchayats are traditional leader, new entrants, local bureaucracy, non-tribal society and government departments like forest and revenue. The traditional leadership generally looks at the decentralized process as a rival parallel institution and challenge to their natural stronghold and in this circumstance need for awareness generation and sensitization of people regarding new Panchayats Raj very much necessary. The new entrants to Panchayats are not fully acquainted with the provisions of PESA and therefore their understanding of this aspect needs to be broadened. Planning and management of minor water bodies is entrusted to Gram Sabha but there are other institutions as well like watershed mission to look into this matter hence it is necessary to create coordination among traditional systems with new schemes. Amendments have been made in Acts for mining lease, exploitation of minor minerals and minor forest produce, to prevent alienation of land, but still there are dilemmas of sharing the stronghold in implementation process. Non-tribal leadership has been very strong in tribal regions; they work as middleman/agents for development schemes. They have established good network with local bureaucracy and influence decision-making process in their favour negating the tribal leadership at the grassroots level.

Against this backdrop, the research paper is a humble attempt to find out the participation of tribal women in grassroots political institutions in Madhya Pradesh, Rajasthan and Gujarat.

III

Fieldwork: Methodology and Context

The issue of women Panchayat representatives was considered for observation within the study so as to comprehend the dynamics of its working, nature of changes and development. The study also planned to understand the interplay, inter-linkages and conflict between these actors. The study focused on the conditions for the implementation of the Panchayat Raj in tribal regions of Madhya Pradesh, Rajasthan and Gujarat. The major concern of the study was to comprehend the implementation of PESA in Madhya Pradesh, Rajasthan and Gujarat. Western tribal belt of Madhya Pradesh, southern tribal belt of Rajasthan and northern tribal belt of Gujarat have many social and cultural similarities. The political and social movements in these regions have also been very close in these parts at times. Looking into these similarities one district from each tribal belt of the states was selected for the micro-level study. The selected districts were Jhabua from Madhya Pradesh, Banswara from Rajasthan and Dahod from Gujarat. Ten villages were selected from each district and the total number of villages included in the sample was 30. A representative sampling framework has been adopted for this. Women Panchayat representatives were the units of observation. Interview schedule was structured and administered to the respondents.

IV

Women Panchayat Raj Representative's Participation, Attitudes and Perceptions Regarding Implementation of PESA: An Analysis

Exposure towards PESA

It is indeed a matter of concern that overwhelming majority of the respondents has no exposure towards special status of Panchayats in the fifth schedule areas. Broadly very superficial information is available with the respondents. If we look at the data in terms of specific states, the scenario remains more or less the same.

Operationalization of Gram Sabha

There is almost no change in the perception of respondents regarding Gram Sabha. This is also because the level of exposure among the tribal women is very low who have hardly any understanding of these issues. Overwhelming majority of the respondents who are Panchayat representatives have no exposure to special rights and this situation remains almost similar in all the three states. Only some prominent issues are known to a few respondents regarding special rights of Gram Sabha.

It is a very negative situation to note that overwhelming majority of the respondents does not know the right quorum required for Gram Sabha meetings. This situation is almost similar in all states.

It is indeed very important that in majority of cases the information is made available about the Gram Sabha meetings. The availability of information significantly varies and it does not have state-specific phenomenon. It is interesting to note that overwhelming majority of the respondents do know about one or another very important work of Gram Sabha.

The major reasons for the participation are related to make the tribals aware about the problems of the village and appraise them regarding different schemes and solutions for their problems. It is indeed very important that a sizable number of respondents have negative point of view for attending Gram Sabha meeting knowing the fact that it is of no benefit to them, hence nobody listens in the meeting.

Operationalization of Gram Panchayat

Gram Panchayat is the main executing institution of all the work at the grassroots level. Overwhelming majority of the respondents do participate in Gram Panchayat meetings regularly which is very significant from the point of view of tribal situation. Non-understanding of the proceedings and the husband representing women representatives are the main reasons of irregularity in meeting. Proposal discussion is most important task in Gram Panchayat meetings. Decisions are rested either with unanimity or with recommendation of Gram Sabha. Overwhelming majority of the respondents inspect the ongoing construction work in the village. The respondents do visit different offices for inspection purposes; however, the schools and *anganwadies* are mostly under inspection of respondents. Villages are still in demand of basic amenities like drinking water, electricity, road/bridge, etc. on priority basis.

Almost half of the respondents present a very negative picture as Gram Panchayat has no role in solving village problems whereas a large number of them are of the opinion that they do forward the proposal. This is because the respondents are Gram Panchayat members who have already aired the problems in Gram Panchayat meetings repeatedly.

Natural Resource Management

This is one of the main activities under PESA. Less than half of the respondents do know one of the very important tasks assigned by PESA Act for the management of natural resources (land, water and forest) through Gram Sabha. Fifty per cent tribal villages have the availability of forest and minor forest produce. As far as control over forest is concerned, all the respondents are categorically of the view that government/forest department has control over it.

Conservation and Protection of Traditions and Rituals

Overwhelming majority of the respondents do believe in local traditions and rituals. Gram Sabha has the responsibility of conservation and protection of traditions, rituals and cultural identity. Surprisingly, this fact is not known to majority of the respondents. Issues of conservation and protection of traditions, rituals and cultural identity in Gram Sabha are discussed by a limited number of respondents. Knowledge about traditions and rituals is confined to very superficial issues and no specific details are discussed in terms of traditions and rituals to be protected by the Gram Sabha like traditional pattern of dispute resolution, worshiping natural resources, traditional method of natural resource management, livelihood patterns, etc. In majority cases, Gram Sabha/Jati Panchayat looks after the question of dispute resolution.

Gram Sabha and Jati Panchayats are considered as most effective institutions in conservation and protection of traditions, rituals and cultural identities. The respondents who have made their point of view in favour of Jati Panchayat for the conservation and protection of traditions and rituals have supported the acceptance of the role of tadvi/patel in all these matters. Social evils in tribal society are plenty which ultimately leads the life of many to miserable conditions. The PESA Act has provision of including this matter in discussion of Gram Sabha; a large number of members endorse this fact which is indeed good for the tribal society.

It is interesting to note that there is a very constructive role of the Gram Sabha in many important aspects related to village development work; however, the number of persons having this opinion is limited. Even then, this is definitely a positive indication that involving women members in the Gram Sabha has raised the status of this institution.

Candidature for Panchayat

Tribal society is a relatively close society where selection of a candidate for elections is usually determined by a variety of considerations. The nomination is usually decided by the villagers in many cases whereas sub-caste and socio-economic elites also have their dominant role as well. These considerations become more pertinent when the candidature for a woman is involved. Of late political parties too have penetrated in local elections to establish their hegemony in decision-making process of the local candidates. Overwhelming majority of the respondents opine that the village community decided their candidature. It is indeed a pointer that village community has a hand in deciding as to who would represent the village in its Panchayats.

Women Leadership and Family

The question of the 'proxy women' in Panchayats is repeatedly argued. It is alleged that since many of the women are beginners and illiterate, they depend on their men folk for conducting the Panchayat activities. In other words, the women surrender their powers to men folk without understanding the implications of the surrender. Hence, they are termed as 'proxy women'. The reasons shown by the respondents for not taking into hands the reins of administration of Panchayats are as follows: husband participates on her behalf; other family members participate on her behalf; busy with agriculture and labour work; and illiteracy and lack of knowledge of rules and regulations of Panchayat affairs. Unauthorized intervention of male members extends even up to the issues including putting signatures, allotting benefits, attending meetings, etc. on behalf of women representatives.

In some cases, the secretaries of the Panchayats tried to implicate the inexperienced women by asking them to sign on blank cheques for which some of the women sarpanch had to face legal suits and embarrassing situations.

Women's dependence on husbands or male relatives was often found to extend to their functioning as public figures. In many cases, a woman sarpanch acted as a rubber stamp or played a subservient role while her husband or male relative played the official role. This dependence is because of their illiteracy, lack of confidence, awareness or experience and a general isolation from public life. The prevalent norms of the village also make a woman's independence and political participation difficult. Usually women representatives visit Janpad Panchayats with their husbands or male relatives. This also meant a loss of earning days for the later.

Additionally, the interaction of a woman sarpanch with front-line government officials remains distanced and only a 'courtesy'. Panchayat-related matters are discussed with their husbands. This situation has made the tribal women leadership subservient to their men folk.

On the contrary, there are many examples, which strengthen the argument that the men folk have really become a source of strength for the women at the grassroots level. Sizeable respondents argue that they could manage the Panchayat affairs only because of the positive and inspiring support of male members of their family. Since the functioning of Panchayat involves multifaceted tasks, the women need the help of family and other male members. Such are the examples where husbands and male members have played a supportive role, which enabled women representatives to become more effective.

There are also cases where women sarpanches are found to be active without the assistance of their husbands. Particularly the educated tribal women have better exposure from this point of view. The decision to contest elections, in most cases, has not been that of the women but of their husbands, who are usually either an ex-panch or sarpanch of the Panchayat. This situation is witnessed in majority cases. Unless supported by husbands or male relatives in powerful positions, women sarpanches found it difficult to function and take decisions.

Women Leadership in Traditional Socio-Cultural Setup

Women in tribal societies have remained isolated from political activities. Even tribal women believe in the dogma that as women they should lead their lives very differently and be subordinate to male wishes. This makes women insecure, lacking a sense of self-worth and are thus incapable of assuming decisive control over their milieu, social or political. The process of generation of political and cultural socialization has also been very slow in the tribal society. Thus, when tribal women cross over their traditionally assigned private space and take on leadership roles in the public realm, hostile social attitudes take various forms in tribal society. The widespread view in the tribal community is that women are neither capable nor interested in attending Gram Sabha and Panchayat meetings.

Moreover, women are portrayed as submissive. They are not meant to be active and outspoken, particularly in the presence of men and elders. When respondents were asked regarding their working in the presence of men and elders, overwhelming majority admitted that it was difficult for them to cross the traditional barrier and be outspoken to have their say.

Although the PRIs are based on democratic values of equality, the attempts are rare by tribal women to go against male dominance to assert their right to equality.

Leadership Pattern

For many women to be called a sarpanch is not only novel but also new experience of having an independent identity as a public figure with respectable status. The larger picture is still not very encouraging, and the elected tribal women representatives acquire position due to their husband's status. The reason lies in the economic and cultural background of the family in many cases. After the elections, these women are often relegated to the background by their active male relatives. Issues of discussion amongst women representatives primarily revolved around improving their domestic roles. Discussions among tribal women Panchayat representatives tend to be confined to issues such as drinking water, infrastructure development (school, community hall, road construction), setting up of Anganwadi centres, etc. The more important political issues, such as women's education and economic self-sufficiency, alcohol abuse or issues/plans favouring the poor, are hardly discussed or rarely raised. Women not only feel incapable of dealing with these issues, their awareness about these issues has also remained low.

Harassment Faced by Women Representatives

Man-dominated tribal socio-political scenario has been a major hurdle in smooth and independent functioning of tribal women-headed Panchayats in villages. Direct or violent harassment is low so long as women accept established male dominance. Tribal women in elected positions of power are still largely unaccepted and patriarchal forces often in combination with traditional mindset resort to all possible means including violence and oppression to block the effective functioning of elected tribal women representatives.

The cases of harassment against tribal women representatives are prominent where women are vocal, extrovert and dare to take decisions on their own. The harassment is in the form of verbal assault and in few cases it is in the form of physical assault as well. Although evidences available from the field suggest that it is not a generalized phenomenon, rather the occurrences of incidents are aberrations. The cases conform that these situations are evident where the fragmentation within the tribal society is deep rooted to anti-establishment forces are very aggressive to maintain the status-quo and adamant for the hegemony over all the decision-making process with vested interests.

If this power equation is challenged by the tribal women representatives without adequate support system, the chances of harassment are most certain. It is therefore urgently needed for the administration to handle such situations keeping in view the honour of the office of Panchayat. At the same time, the tribal women representatives should also create the situation in favour of them to corner and alleviate such disturbing elements.

Effectiveness of Support to Women Representatives

Tribal women are poorly informed about the nitty-gritty of Panchayat meetings and Panchayat functioning. Sometimes husbands attend the meetings and share discussions with their wives. Although women sarpanches are supposed to be informed about meetings in an official manner, in practice information reaches them via the male members. Cut off from information, women are more susceptible to manipulation and domination. Most women representatives sign various documents but they have little knowledge about their content.

It appears that the major chunk of male relatives willingly and knowingly hide the important issues. Women representatives are deliberately avoided in informing the day-to-day functioning of the Panchayat. In the name of supporting women representatives, they are effectively kept in dark about Panchayat affairs. This situation needs to be changed urgently. The support structure required for performing and discharging the duties, the women capacity building is of paramount importance.

IV

Conclusion

Systematic awareness building and training is needed for enhancing tribal women's capacity to take up their new responsibilities as decision makers under Panchayat Raj. The local government bureaucracy is also in urgent need of sensitization to tribal women's problems and issues linked to gender bias in local development planning. The panel responsible for formulating the training agenda should include elected women representatives besides local development personnel. The training of tribal women Panchayat members should be based on their own local experiences and elicit their involvement in preparing a framework that will enable them to analyse and understand their roles and responsibilities as envisaged under the PESA Act.

Training should be both for trainees and trainers. Training module should have a focus area and relevant content areas. Framework should not be rigid;

it must accord with active capabilities of tribal women members and their viewpoint. Process of training should not be fluid but tailored to the needs and expectations of the tribal women trainees. The content should not be lecture-oriented, but based on interactions and discussions along with PLM techniques. Resource persons should function as facilitators/catalysts to help tribal women leadership to understand roles and responsibilities. Local experts should have working knowledge of the local language and training methods and material should take into account sensitivities of tribal women members. Trainers should use participatory training methods and tools, which meet tribal women trainees' expectations in the area of decentralized rural local governance, both in method and design. Field visits should be an integral part of the training programme for women members.

It has been evident from the working experience of PESA and also as the above-mentioned responses of respondents indicate that the level of participation of people at grassroots level has been relatively low. Despite knowing the procedural aspects, Gram Sabhas are almost a formal institution. The state governments did not transfer all the powers through conformity acts. There is an urgent need to opt for an effective device whereby maximum people can be informed, made aware and motivated to come forward for the proper implementation and execution of PESA. There is an urgent need to break the culture of silence and to strive for capacity building, sensitization and orientation to improve the tribal self-rule scenario. It cannot, however, be denied that as a result of reservation for tribal women their participation in the political process has been ensured. There should also be a change in the attitude of their men folk and the administration. Women's empowerment through the Panchayats requires a sustained campaign and vigorous efforts for creating awareness about their rights and duties. With the passage of time and gaining of experience, it is believed and hoped that women leadership will become more mature and effective. Regular training of this class and cooperative attitude of males and government officials will definitely provide strength to the leadership to work and to create a gender-sensitive society at the grassroots level.

References

Behar, A. and Y. Kumar (2002). 'Decentralisation in Madhya Pradesh, India: From Panchayati Raj to Gram Swaraj (1995 to 2001)', Working Paper 170, ODI, London, UK.

Issac, T., M. Thomas and R.W. Franke (2000). *Local Democracy and Development: People's Campaign for Decentralised Planning in Kerala*, New Delhi: Leftword.

Robinson, M. (2005). 'A Decade of Panchayat Raj Reforms: The Challenge of Democratic Decentralisation in India', in L.C. Jain (ed.), *Decentralisation and Local Governance*, New Delhi: Orient Longman.

Sisodia, Y.S. (2002). 'Decentralised Governance in Madhya Pradesh: Experiences of the Gram Sabha in Scheduled Areas', *Economic and Political Weekly*, October 5.

Webster, N. (1992). 'Panchayat Raj in West Bengal: Participation for the People or the Party?' *Development and Change*, 23(4).

CHAPTER 15

EMPOWERMENT OF TRIBAL WOMEN: A SOCIOLOGICAL ANALYSIS OF SAHARIYA IN MADHYA PRADESH AND KHASI IN MEGHALAYA

D.K. Verma

PERSPECTIVE

The most affecting social institution for women's status, role and power in the society is marriage and thereby inheritance of power-yielding factors and social relations. As free India's first law minster, Dr. Babasaheb Ambedkar drafted and introduced the Hindu Code Bill on February 24, 1949. Through that Bill, Ambedkar wanted to ensure high status and dignity to women by putting an end to various marriage systems prevailing in India[1] and legalize only monogamous marriage.

Ambedkar considered most importantly that the Bill sought to confer on women the right to property and also sought to give equality to women in all legal matters. But caste Hindu 'leaders' and 'intellectuals', Ambedkar commented that, 'were not prepared to respect women as equals, opposed that Bill calling it an attack on their religion'. Parliament debated on the Bill[2] divided the house on the issue and leaders like Rajendra Prasad, Govind Vallabh Pant and Madan Mohan Malviya opposed the Bill and Sarojini Naidu even threatened to go on a hunger strike if the Bill was not dropped.

On September 22, 1951, Jawaharlal Nehru, fearing a caste Hindu backlash, dropped the Hindu Code Bill. Ambedkar considered that that was a lost golden opportunity to remove all the constraints imposed on Hindu women by the patriarchal brahminical social order based on the dictates of Manu. Ambedkar was of the opinion that 'as was commonly known, women in Hindu society had historically been denied political, social and economic rights. Brahminical texts denied women education. Sati, child marriage, widow ostracization were cunningly used to deny women their rights to property.'

Ambedkar was heavily criticized for standing in favour of women's rights. Hurt by the lack of commitment to positive change and Nehru's backtrack, Ambedkar resigned from the Union Cabinet. Later on and in due course, the Indian National Policy for the empowerment of women was made to bring about the advancement, development and empowerment of women, as was aspired by Ambedkar.

The policy also provided for economic empowerment through poverty eradication, micro credit programmes and training of women to facilitate them in playing efficient role in agriculture and industry. Elimination of all forms of violence against women, physical and mental, whether at domestic or societal levels, including those arising from customs, traditions and accepted practices were ensured through various acts and legislations.

In fact, participation has become an essential component for empowerment now. Although the term 'participation' entered into mainstream vocabulary of development in last decade of the previous century, since the beginning of this century that term is largely used for empowering beneficiaries to take development in their hand (Willis, 2005) together with state intervention (Mosse, 2005; Coelho, 2007).

Although approach towards confounding participatory development and social exclusion has been criticized (Sen, 2000), for tribes that approach is considered most suitable. Participatory development approach is considered most suitable, particularly for tribal women in the present context too where aspirations of tribal women (what they need) get priority over their development target (what we extend). Currently, the social empowerment of women is being facilitated through effective provisions of education, health, nutrition, drinking water and sanitation, gender sensitization through their participation along with state intervention.

The forgoing discussion on women's identity, status and empowerment approaches world over and in the Indian society in particular converges on similar aspects for the tribal women too. The difference is that of adjective of 'tribal' identity with the women. It is irony that the majority of the academic discourse believes that the word 'Tribe' denotes a group of people living in primitive or barbarous conditions. The problem is with the perspectives: how we (non-tribals) look at them, understand them and also project them (tribals) but with our (non-tribal) standards as superior one?

Against the majority of scholarly but traditional writings on tribals, it would be a gross misconception in the present context, if the word 'tribe' still denotes a group of people living in primitive or barbarous conditions or considering tribe as a social group living in isolation within territorial affiliation, endogamous with no specialization of functions. From the current policy and planning perspectives also, it would be an anomaly if 'tribal' development is still considered based on Nehruvian model.

Further, the problems of scheduled tribes could also be seen emerging from the policies adopted and laws enacted during British Raj and in Independent India too. Certain tribes were notified as criminal during British period.[3] The tribes 'notified' under the Criminal Tribes Act (CTA) were labelled as *Criminal Tribes* for their so-called criminal tendencies. As a result, anyone born in those communities across the country was presumed as a 'born criminal', irrespective of their criminal precedents. That gave the police sweeping powers to arrest them, control them and monitor their movements.

Once a tribe was officially notified, its members had no recourse to repeal such notices under the judicial system. When they tried to make a living like everybody else, they did not find work outside the settlement because of public prejudice and ostracization. The 'criminal tribes' were denotified in 1949 but another act 'Habitual Offenders Act' (HOA) continues till date since it came into existence in 1952[4] and ironically in present time also police in various states still follow the list of CTC, and whenever and wherever there is any act of crime, the first suspects are from denotified tribes. The stigma of first notified and then denotified still haunts them. Making their condition worse, the Ministry of Social Justice and Empowerment has set up a National Commission for Denotified, Nomadic and Semi nomadic communities in 2003.[5]

Customs, tradition and practices among tribal communities reflect that tribal women are socially empowered within their respective communities in terms of their high social status and equal gender role, equal work share with their male counterparts. They enjoy a higher sex ratio, freedom of expression and movement, choice to marry and remarry, higher social and family status due to bride price, and thus they enjoy a higher social-empowered status as compared to their non-tribal counterparts. These perspectives pose certain questions (Verma, 1993, 1994, 1999, 2008, 2010) like why a class (tribal women) which is socially empowered inside (intra-tribal interactions) becomes vulnerable and backward (educationally, economically and politically) outside (non-tribal social interactions) though their outside counterpart (non-tribal women) are socially less empowered inside but are forward (e.g., higher literacy rate) outside? Answer could be substantiated with theoretical discussions.

Are we becoming too sympathetic? and very less academic? when we classify certain tribes as notified and then denotified, nomadic, primitive tribes (PTG), most marginalized sections, What is the need of such classifications?

While as a member of the working group[6] and then as a chairman of its high level sub-committee, the author expressed that[7] there was a need to start a developmental terminology, for the empowerment of tribal people. The imposed graded inequality of terms that we use must be avoided like primitive, barbarous, *jungli, adimjati.* These are nothing but continued social stigma attached to their identities.

And whether and how far customs and practices of tribal communities (traditions) are responsible for unsustainability (educational and economic backwardness) in empowerment (modernization) of tribal women? Instead of answering the above question, certain issues concerning tribal women empowerment are being placed for discussion. In particular, Khasi tribal women from Meghalaya and Sahariya tribal women from Madhya Pradesh are selected for making a comparison of status and power within matrilineal and patriarchal communities.

Sahariya Women in Madhya Pradesh: Participation and Empowerment

Even after more than six decades of tribal welfare and development, the Government of Madhya Pradesh reviewed that after independence, the India Constitution adopted many provisions to provide tribals with special status and the Parliament through various protective legislations made conscious efforts to safeguard their interest. Despite all these efforts made to improve the socio-economic conditions of tribes, it is still a fact that the life situations of scheduled tribes (STs) have improved only marginally. While emphasizing the approach, it was noted that the major concern of the Tribal Development Department of Madhya Pradesh is to develop the tribal community as educated and skilled enough so that they could be able to compete with the general population, in comparison to 'ours' as superior perspective.

Under the current tribal sub-plan strategy, the problems of tribal development are broadly classified into three approaches: areas of tribal concentration, areas of dispersed tribes and particularly vulnerable tribal groups (erstwhile Primitive Tribal Groups, PTGs). There are seven primitive groups, i.e., Abhujmaria, Baiga, Saharia, Pahari Korba, Birhor, Bharia and Kamar in the undivided Madhya Pradesh, and after separation of Chhattisgarh, three tribal communities, i.e., *Baiga*, *Bharia* and *Sahariya* were declared primitive tribal groups in the reorganized state of Madhya Pradesh. Bharias are found more concentrated in Patalkot area in Chhindwara District and Baiga are found in Mandla, Dindori, Umaria, Shahdol, Anoopur and Balaghat districts. Sahariya are found in the northern part of the state largely concentrated in Gwalior, Datia, Morena, Sheopur, Bhind, Shivpuri, Ashok Nagar and Guna districts. For this study on Sahariya women, Sheopur District of Madhya Pradesh was selected.

Very poor literacy rates among tribal women place greatest hindrance in their empowerment. Non-tribal communities exploited tribal women both economically and physically because most of them are engaged as unskilled labourers that too largely in primary sector. Among all tribal women, the status and empowerment of Sahariya women is lowest. There are several research studies available on the health problems among Sahariya (Chakma et. al., 1996; Biswas and Kapoor, 2003; Mahawar and Jaroli, 2007) and survey reports by voluntary organizations have brought out the fact that the most concerning challenges were malnutrition and maternal death among Sahariya (Singh, 2006; Jain and Kumar, 2007; Sharma and Tiwary, 2007). The main reason for very low health status of Sahariya women could be easily traced to their low level of awareness, very low literacy rates and very poor and unhygienic living conditions.

In spite of their poor health and adverse living conditions, during group discussion Sahariya women demanded they need respect and dignity. They aspired for their development through participation but by excluding the exploiters. This could be understood from the context that the Saharia region (Chambal region and border regions of Madhya Pradesh–Rajasthan–Uttar Pradesh) had been dacoit and robber-infested areas. Although not admitting explicitly, Sahariya men responded that they showed little care for women for such stigmas. Some other communities which had family traditions and are traditionally engaged in human trafficking placed all tribal women in the region vulnerable to various forms of exploitation.

Sahariya women are powerless as they do not enjoy privileges that women enjoy in other tribes like Bhil and Gond and further, due to rampant and traditional forms of human trafficking in the region degrade their dignity and thus their social status is lowest. Health and education programmes are being effectively implemented, but their impact on Sahariya women are not seen. In other words, if we need to empower Sahariya Women, we need to respect their aspirations which are mainly expressed in terms of elevating their dignity.

Khasi Women in Meghalaya: Privileges and Power

One of the Seven Sisters of North-Eastern part of India (now eight), Meghalaya with its legacy of having matrilineal society holds a unique distinction in the country. Popularly known as the Scotland of India,

Meghalaya became the 21st state of the Indian Union on January 21, 1972, comprising the Khasi, Jaintia and Garo hills where Khasis are the oldest inhabitants belonging to the Austro-Asiatic family of human race being matrilineal upheld the women power at its peak commanding respect unlike rest of India where women are much weaker section in terms of their socio-economic status.

There are seven districts in Meghalaya, i.e., East Garo Hills, East Khasi Hills, Jaintia Hills, Ri Bhoi, South Garo Hills, West Garo Hills and West Khasi Hills. According to the 2011 Census, the total population of Meghalaya is 2,964,007. Previously, the total population was 2,318,822 in the 2001 Census. The male population is 1,492,668 and the female population is 1,471,339 from the entire population of Meghalaya. The sex ratio in Meghalaya is 986 per 1,000 males and has increased from 975 per 1,000 males since the last census. The child sex ratio is 970 per 1,000 males and has increased as compared to 932 in the last census. Meghalaya has a literacy rate of 75.48 per cent, with male literacy at 77.17 per cent and female literacy at 73.78 per cent. In figures, the total literates in Meghalaya are 1,817,761 out of which the males are 934,091 and females are 883,670, respectively.

It is interesting to note in words of Sen (2004) that 'despite the proverbs and the manipulation of codes to ensure hegemony of men over women there existed in the Khasi-Jaintia hills women rulers'. Christian missionaries came to the Khasi Hills simultaneously with the British colonial hegemony and were considered a challenge to the indigenous identity, thus formed a social reform association *Seng Khasi*.

Further, as in the rest of India, exposure of the tribes to the non-tribal social institutions generated among them new urges and aspirations. The major problems tribes face are due to inadequacy of the process of structural change in independent India and also due to distortion inadvertently introduced into their socio-economic life in the name of tribal welfare and development. Facing the twin challenges of Christianity earlier and democratic modernization later, Khasis went under revival and reform but keeping their matrilineality intact and rather making it more powerful as is evident from the recent agitations by Khasi men against their matrilineal system. The women are not the second sex among Khasi.

The youngest daughter inherits ancestral property, children take their mother's name and once married, husbands live in their mother-in-law's home and it was told that men are not entitled to take part in some family gatherings. Keeping the traditions intact, Khasi women have many privileges enjoyed by their men too as institutions like Khasi Hill Autonomous

District Council protect their laws and customs. It is a counterargument that men from plains (non-Khasi) marry Khasi women to take advantages of such privileges. It is said about Khasi people that their women rule the roost while men demand gender equality (Bouissou, 2011). However, during a discussion with a group of Khasi women, it was revealed that though it is widely acknowledged that Khasi women are much privileged they cannot take decision on their own, almost all crucial decisions by Khasi women become effective only when her maternal uncle (male) or a Lyngdoh (priest among Khasi, again a male) endorse them.

Although Khasi women do not perform roles like those defined under patriarchal societies, they are considered to have authority over most household decisions while Khasi husband is expected to work for the gain of his wife's family but having no important social role. Although Khasi men were the rulers, women were not in power albeit the rulers left their thrones to the son of their youngest sisters. Traditionally, social roles of Khasi men are subservient (Nakane, 1967) and that has sparked gender equality movements by Khasi men (Nongbri, 1988; Van Ham, 2000). There is matrilineal system but not the matriarchy. In men's perceptive, the family life among Khasi is organized around mother-in-law's house and the youngest daughter never leaves the family and eventually becomes the head of the household.

It was informed during the group discussion that Khasi women took least part in political affairs and almost all the political leaders were men and a very few women took part in meetings, not even in village councils. Coincidently, the period of study was also the time of recent election in the state and it was observed that in rallies and campaigns a few women were seen to take part but almost all the contesting candidates were men. Thus, when inheritance of ancestral property is considered to be one of the major social facts deciding power relations but that does not stand in consistency with the matrilineal system among Khasis. Therefore, it can be said that Khasi women have certain privileges over men but they are not equally powerful as men within their community.

This is in contradiction to what Bouissou (2011) has commented quoting by Kaith Pariat as 'men are the weak sex in Meghalaya'. Currently there is a campaign under way in the state, Syngkhong Rympei Thymai (SRT), to promote reform of family structures through which men demand more than mere equality, as Pariat says: 'Men are endowed with natural leadership. They should protect women, who in return should support them'.

It is further argued that the matrilineality protects land ownership with women, and thereby Khasi men have a poor economic status as they are unable to take part in modern economic activities where land or real estate is the legal tender or collateral for availing bank loans or to be offered as equity in lieu of cash in other businesses.

During the discussion, Khasi men also pointed out that Khasi women were not sticking to the matrilineal system and bartering away their custodial rights as they marry a non-Khasi men and because of that (*Khatduh*, in Khasi the only daughter) the outsider gains control over all their ancestral property. In fact, *Khatduh* is an institution in herself also with many responsibilities like her home is open to all; any member of the family in distress finds shelter in the Khatduh's home. Her brothers and sisters can continue to live in the ancestral home as long as they are unmarried. Thus, Khasi give power to Khatduh rather than to all women, but that too is limited when decision making is concerned. In other words, inheriting the ancestral property and thus incurring privileges *Khatduh* is powerful but in limited sense of economy and not socially as Khasi men enjoy their power and status outside their community.

Gneezy et al. (2009) explored whether there are gender difference in selecting into the competitive environment across two distinct societies, Maasai in Tanzania (patriarchal) and Khasi in India (matrilocal) where they found that Khasi women chose the competitive environment more often than Khasi men. There are also perspectives like men and women are innately different (Lawrence, 2006) to substantive heterogeneity that exists among individuals raised in similar environments but even socially constructed hierarchical, be it nurture enabling expression of nature (Turkheimer, 2004) or co-evolving nurture and nature (Boyd and Richerson, 2005). But the present analysis does not conform to such understandings. Although Khasi men do not consider themselves powerful within their community, Khasi women aspire to become as powerful as Khasi men are outside their community.

The sociological analysis of women empowerment throughout the *global society* is also reflected in the aspirations of tribal women whether they are empowered by their own community (*Khasi*) or the state is leaving no stone unturned to empower them (*Sahariya*, the most marginalized tribal group erstwhile a PTG). Khasi women have high literacy rates with low gender-gap while Sahariya women have the lowest literacy rates with high gender-gap, but both of them are in search of their empowerment in terms of privileges that reminds the advertising slogan 'why boys should have all the *fun*?'.

These aspirations for power and privilege are rooted not in educational development and related indicators but independent decision making (empowerment) and dignity about the self within the entire collectivity, both in patriarchal (*Sahariya*) or matrilineal (*Khasi*) tribal communities.

In conclusion, the analysis converge on the finding that both the tribal women Sahariya and Khasi are in search of their identity, status and power in terms of respect and dignity within their communities as well as in the outside world and in terms of gender equality (as enjoyed by the men counterparts) and individual dignity, not just becoming at par with their men counterpart but more so essential for human rights that demand and ensure social equality.

NOTES

1. As stated in the Bill: 'so far as inheritance was concerned, the Hindus were governed by two different systems of law. According to *Mitakshara,* the property of a Hindu was not his individual property. It was property which belonged to what was called a coparcenary, which consisted of father, son, grandson and great grandson. All these people had a birth-right in that property and the property on the death of anyone member of that coparcenary passed by what was called survivorship to the members who remained behind, and did not pass to the heirs of the deceased.' The Bill attempted to universalize law of inheritance by extending the *Dayabhag* rule to *Mitakshara* also.
2. Ambedkar emphasized that the Hindu Code was the greatest social reform measure ever undertaken by the Legislature in the country.
3. 'The Criminal Tribes' Act (Act of XXVII, 1871) came into force on October 12, 1871, mostly enforced in northern India and later was extended to Bengal presidency in 1876 and with the amendments to Madras Presidency as 'Criminal Tribes Act 1911'. In 1924, after enacting several amendments and converging all such acts in different areas, the Criminal Tribes Act (VI of 1924) came into existence, which notoriously stigmatized as many as 200 tribal communities as criminals.
4. The UN's anti-discrimination body asked India to repeal the Habitual Offenders Act and affectively rehabilitate the denotified and nomadic tribes on March 9, 2007. After reviewing India's 15th–19th periodic reports, the UN Committee on the Elimination of Racial Discrimination (CERD), in its concluding observation, expressed concern and stated that 'the so-called denotified and nomadic which are listed for their alleged "criminal tendencies" under the former Criminal Tribes Act (1871), continue to be stigmatized under the Habitual Offenders Act (1852) (art. 2 (1) c)'.

5. The Government of India vide Resolution No. dated March 14, 2005, constituted National Commission for De-notified, Nomadic and Semi Nomadic tribes under the Ministry of Social Justice and Empowerment, to study various developmental aspects of these tribes. A Technical Advisory Group (TAG) of 4 months duration was also constituted by the Ministry in 2006. TAG and the Commission also gave their reports in 2006 and 2008, respectively. The Ministry of Social Justice and Empowerment, Government of India, made a token provision of rupees five crores for the year 2011–2012, for the economic and educational development of DNTs.
6. With a view to formulate Twelfth Five Year Plan (2012–2017) for the Social Justice Sector, a Working Group on 'Empowerment of OBCs and Nomadic, Semi-Nomadic and Denotified Tribes' was constituted by the Government of India, Social Justice and Social Welfare Division of Planning Commission (*vide* Office Memorandum of GOI, Planning Commission, Social Justice & Social Welfare Division, No.M-12052/9/2010-2011 dated April 7, 2011.
7. The sub-group was constituted by the Government of India, Ministry of Social Justice and Empowerment, New Delhi *vide* Office Memorandum F.No. 20012/2/2011-BC-III dated June 2, 2011, which included Chairperson Dr. Deepak Verma, Professor, BANISS, Mhow, and members were Shri A.A. Naqvi, Managing Director, National Backward Classes Finance and Development Corporation, New Delhi; Shri I.K. Srivastav, Director of Employment Exchanges, New Delhi; Dr. Mahi Pal, Assistant Commissioner, M/o Rural Development, New Delhi; Shri N. Subbarayan, Director (Policy), D/o Agriculture and Cooperation, New Delhi; Dr. M.L. Mathur, Deputy Adviser, Planning Commission, New Delhi; Shri Arjun Prasad, Special Secretary & Managing Director, Bihar State Backward Classes Finance & Development Corporation, Dept. of Scheduled Castes/Scheduled Tribes and Social Welfare, Govt. of Bihar Secretariat, Patna; Shri Dhanpat Singh, Financial Commissioner & Principal Secretary, Social Justice & Empowerment and Welfare of SCs & BCs, Govt. of Haryana, Chandigarh; The Principal Secretary, Dept. of Scheduled Castes/Scheduled Tribes and Social Welfare, Government of Karnataka, Bengaluru; The Commissioner-Secretary, Tribal Development Department, Government of Manipur, Imphal; Representative of Welfare Dept., Govt. of Puducherry, Chief Secretariat, Puducherry; and the Convenor of the sub-committee was Shri A.K. Punia, DGM, National Backward Classes Finance and Development Corporation, New Delhi.

REFERENCES

Biswas, R.K. and A.K. Kapoor (2003). 'A Study on Mortality among Saharia – A Primitive Tribe of Madhya Pradesh', *Anthropologist*, 5(4): 283–290.

Bouissou, J. (2011). 'Where Women in India Rule the Roost and Men Demand Gender Equality. The Khasi People of North-Eastern India Are a Matrilineal Society and Some Men Aren't Happy', *Guardian Weekly*, 18 January 2011.

Boyd, R. and P.J. Richerson (2005). *Thc Origin and Evolution of Culture*, Oxford: Oxford University Press.

Chakma, T., P.V. Rao, S. Pall, L.S. Kaushal, M. Datta and R.S. Tiwary (1996). 'Survey of Pulmonary Tuberculosis in a Primitive Tribe of Madhya Pradesh', *Indian Journal of Tuberculosis*, 43: 85–89.

Coelho, V.S. (2007). 'Brazilian Health Councils: Including the excluded', in A. Cornwall and V.S. Coelho (eds.), *Spaces for Change: The Politics of Citizen Participation in New Democratic Arenas*, London: Zed Books.

Gneezy, U., K.L. Leonard and J.A. List (2009). 'Gender Differences in Competition: Evidence from Matrilineal and a Patriarchal Society', *Econometrica*, 77(5): 1637–1664.

Jain, S.K. and R. Kumar (2007). *The Status of Maternal Health in Madhya Pradesh*, Bhopal: Vikas Samvad.

Lawrence, P.A. (2006). 'Men, Women and the Ghosts of Science', *PLOS Biology*, 4, 13–15.

Mahawar, M.M. and D.P. Jaroli (2007). 'Traditional Knowledge on Zootherapeutic Uses by the Saharia Tribe of Rajasthan, India', *Journal of Ethnobiology and Etyhnomedicine*, 3: 25.

Mosse, D. (2005). *Cultivating Development: An Ethnography of Aid Policy and Practice*, New Delhi: Vistaar Publications.

Nakane, C. (1967). *Garo and Khasi: A Comparative Study in Matrilineal Systems*, Paris: Mount & Co.

Nongbri, T. (1988). 'Gender and the Khasi Family Structure: The Meghalaya Succession to Self-Acquired Property Act, 1984', *Sociological Bulletin*, 7: 71–82.

Rymbai, R.T. (1998). 'Social Awakening of the Khasis', in M.N. Karna (ed.), *Social Movements in North-East India*, New Delhi: Indus Publishing Company.

Sen, A. (2000). 'Social Exclusion: Concept, Application and Scrutiny', in *Social Development*, Manila: Asian Development Bank.

Sen, S. (2004). *Khasi-Jaintia Folklore: Context, Discourse and History*, Chennai: National Folklore Support Centre.

Sharma, P.R. and P.K. Tiwary (2007). 'Health Status of Sahariya Tribe of Central India', *Rural and Remote Health*, 7: 791 (Online).

Singh, S.K. (2006). *Protect Saharias from Marginalization and Exploitation*, Petition at http://www. sambhavindia.org.

Turkheimer, E. (2004). 'Spinach and ice cream: Why social science is so difficult', in L.F. DiLalla (ed.), *Behaviour Genetics Principles: Perspectives in Development, Personality and Psychopathology*, Washington, DC: American Psychological Association.

Van Ham, P. (2000). *The Seven Sisters of India: Tribal Worlds between Tibet and Bhutan*, Munich: Prestel Publishers.

Verma, D.K. (1993). 'Intergenerational Equity: Environmental Right of the Child', *AJSDJ*, 3: 163–168.

Verma, D.K. (1999). 'Sustainable Development', *Madhya Pradesh Journal of Social Sciences*, 4(2): 37–59.

Verma, D.K. (1994). 'Ecoethical Approach for Sustainable Development and Justice', *AJSDJ*, 2: 37–59.

Verma, D.K. (2004). 'Social Devolution – A Sociological Perspective Affirmed Status of Dalits in India', *The Asianists' Asia*, August 5.

Verma, D.K. (2008). 'Tribal Livelihood Options: Socio-Ecological Changes, State Intervention and Sustainable Development', in S.N. Chaudhary (ed.), *Tribal Development Since Independence*, New Delhi: Concept Publishing Company.

Verma, D.K. (2010). 'Economics and Development of Castes and Tribes', in Arun Kumar (ed.), *Dalits and Economic Reforms*, Jaipur: Rawat Publications.

Willis, K. (2005). *Theories and Practice of Development*, New York: Routledge.

CHAPTER 16

GENDER DISCRIMINATION AMONG NAGAS OF NAGALAND

J.J. Roy Burman

The State of Nagaland which represents a portion of Naga homeland is situated in the north-eastern part of India. It has an area of 16,579 sq. km. The state is bounded by Assam in the north and west, Myanmar and Arunachal Pradesh in the east and Manipur in the south. The entire state is hilly with high ranges and deep gorges and valleys. The altitude varies between 194 metres and 3,048 metres.

Almost the entire population in Nagaland is tribal. Nagas are the predominant tribal group with their own distinctive language and cultural features, each occupying different sectors of region in the state. According to the provisional 2011 Census, the population of Nagaland is 1,980,602. Out of this 82.26 per cent of the population are rural. The population ratio is 931 female per 1,000 male. The literacy ratio is 80.11 per cent (83.3 per cent males and 76.69 per cent females). The 1981–1991 witnessed a phenomenal growth of the urban population, particularly in Kohima and Dimapur which accounts for more than 50 per cent of the total population of the state.

The Nagas who are the dominant tribal group of Nagaland comprise of 14 major groups, namely, Angami, Ao, Chakhesang, Cheng, Khiamniungam, Konyak, Lotha, Phom, Pochury, Rengma, Sangtam, Sumi, Yimchungru and Zeliang. There are 11 administrative districts with 52 blocks and 1,286 inhabited villages in the state. Each district is more or less characterized by a predominant concentration of one major tribe and other sub-tribes which present distinct socio-cultural and linguistic characteristics.

NAGA PATRIARCHY

Generally, it is assumed that among the tribes in Northeast India the women enjoy a very high status and are free from any form of oppression. But among the Naga tribes, patriliny and patriarchy are ominously prevalent.

The descent of any person – male or female – is traced through the father's lineage and the authority in private or public vests with the males. Property, particularly immovable, is inherited by the males by rule.

Longkumer (2009) writes that man has complete control over property rights and also over children. The women are debarred from participating in the Village Council, which is the highest decision-making body at the grassroots level. In fact, they cannot even enter into the community hall when the council meetings take place. The women cannot inherit immovable property like house sites, paddy fields and so on, either from father or her husband. She may be allowed to stay in the house where she has lived with her husband or in her father's house and to use certain portions of the agricultural land during her lifetime, but she has no control over such properties. Should the male heirs decide to take back the house or land, she will have no choice but to hand over the properties back.

It is curious to find that the Naga women often themselves seek the protection of her male relatives. Mills (1926) wrote long back, 'The Ao women are protected by the men – father, brother, maternal uncle, husband and the son and the clansmen. An Ao woman is far from being a slave and a drudge. Her position is in no whit inferior to that of a man. She always has her clan behind her, and were a bad-tempered husband to bully his wife he would soon have a swarm of angry in-laws buzzing around his ears'. Shimray (2004) writes that though the census returns the household work for the women as non-economic contribution, in reality this has lot of financial implications. Among the Nagas, the women are extremely industrious and they do work tirelessly at the household level.

Longkumer (2009) states that in the case of a divorce, the father, brother, maternal uncle and clansmen stood beside her. They supported her during the divorce proceedings and in times of need they spoke for her. Were a woman to be abandoned by her husband, she found a place in her paternal home. In a village, when an old widow needs repairs for her house, it was her clansmen who raised the funds among themselves and took a day off from their personal works to repair the house, for she had no one to help as her husband was dead and her children had left the village. But these reflect some sort of charity rather than a matter of right.

There are only exceptional cases when an Ao woman could inherit property. If the father is of considerable wealth and means and if he so wishes he can give landed property to his daughter, provided that the property has been acquired by him and does not belong to the clan or is an ancestral property. Such land is usually outside of the village in other towns. But he can give his daughter the property only during his lifetime and in acknowledgement the daughter will have to make a token payment to her father to seal the deal. With this payment, the property is considered to be hers to do as she wishes.

A woman gaining property can dispose it off as she wishes. She can equally distribute it to her children. But there are cases in which her clan members have demanded a share of the property. If a spinster acquires property on her own, the immovable property goes to her eldest brother, and even if he has died before her, the eldest son of the brother inherits the property rather than being inherited by her younger brothers. The younger brothers can inherit the property only if it is distributed by the rightful heir.

SOCIALIZING INSTITUTIONS AND THE POSITION OF WOMEN

Traditionally, in the past, the Nagas were marked by head hunting practices as inter-village feuds were common. Consequently, the village communities were extremely regimented. The young boys were trained up in youth dormitories called Morung or Ariju among the Ao Nagas. The girls were similarly trained up in the girls' dormitories called Tsuki in Ao. The trainings for the boys were more rigorous as they were to prepare to make the raids or defend the village. 'It was necessary to have a disciplined band of young warriors ready for any emergency. The Morung thus functioned as a guardhouse to warn the villagers in times of war. It also served as a recreational club for the youth of the village.'

Evidently, the Morung played a more pivotal role in the village polity as against the Tsuki. The primary reason for its relative importance derived from the fact that besides the obvious social functions performed by this institution, it also served as the centre of most policy decision-making in the village. Every strategic policy formulation such as for the defence of the village, or offensive strategies against other villages for raids, for development of the village – in a nutshell, most political decisions were taken at the Morung. There was a taboo for the women to be near it as it was feared that women could not be trusted to maintain secrecy needed for the welfare of the village. The Tsuki, on the other hand, remained, for all purposes, merely a socio-cultural training institution. The girls were encultured to believe that they are solely responsible for housework, which includes washing, cleaning, cooking, looking after children, collecting firewood, collecting water, kitchen gardening, caring for the sick at home, etc. Once its inmates are matured and get married, they leave the dormitory and were inevitably consigned to the domestic drudgeries of everyday life. The graduates of the Morung, on the other hand, became prepared to become members of the

Village Council – the highest decision-making body of the village. Thus, the traditional institutions for males and females in Naga society socialized their respective members based on a strict sexual division of labour. The Naga social structure is reflected by notions such as the birth of a male child being auspicious, man as a breadwinner and protector of society, and woman being subordinate to their husbands. In traditional Naga society, the status of a woman was derived in relation to her family as a daughter, wife, sister and mother.

NAGA WOMEN'S POSITION IN THE ECONOMIC AFFAIRS

Naga women play a predominant role in the household economy. They play an equal role in the jhum or shifting cultivation. While the men do the clearing of the forest and firing them, it is mainly the women who do sowing, weeding and harvesting. In the settled terraced wet rice cultivation, it is the men who do the ploughing. However, the decision about selling the produce mainly vests with the men.

Longkumer (2009) states that the Village Council plays a major role in the economy by way of enforcing the rates of wages, prices of paddy and rice, pigs, pork, etc., as well as setting the date for releasing the people for *Inkho Mapang* (the time for men to work outside the village) from all village works and also recalling them back. The Village Council acts as the arbiter in the economic sphere so that there is uniformity in the business transactions as far as controlling wages and prices are concerned. But the final decision is made after the *Ayim Mungdang* (Village General Assembly) where the people discuss and debate the issues and come to a consensus on the prices.

STATUS OF WOMEN IN THE RELIGIOUS LIFE

Traditionally, a Naga woman could not be the religious head of her family, clan or the village and was debarred from performing religious rites and sacrifices. Women were not even allowed to come to the village common altar. The women were even religiously prohibited to touch the arms and weapons used by the men in wartime (Shimray, op. cit.).

According to Horam (1975), a woman in Naga society could not become the village chief as this was considered a breach of the divine law. The rationale behind this was that a village ruled by a woman is cursed in the sight of God as this is against his will. This view was particularly stressed by the village priests and was accepted without questioning. The Ao Nagas believe that a man has three souls and three spirits while a woman has two souls and three spirits. This difference was applicable in all the performance of ceremonies during birth, sickness, death, etc.

The majority of the Nagas have now been converted to Christianity and they follow the faith very rigorously. The women too equally worship in the churches along with the men. Jamir (2012) writes that Christianity brought about a great deal of change in the social outlook providing greater mobility to the women. Church provided them with a self-worth and dignity which helped to enhance their perception of self in the patriarchal social set-up. However, this is not to say that they acquired leadership roles because under the new ecclesiastical order women were still assigned a subordinate role. They are excluded from most decision-making bodies in the church. In fact, traditional patriarchal structures resembling that of the larger society can be seen reflected in the structure of the church ministry, in which women are consigned to primarily assisting roles. From the very beginning, it appears that Christianity has not encouraged women's leadership, except in the fields of education and health services. Christianity to a large extent was conditioned by traditionalism of Naga society. Even qualified and experienced women were denied of top leadership roles, such as pastoral work or to be head of the various mission fields. Women were inducted only up to the position of associate pastors. Further, the Deacon Boards of the churches which supposedly were the highest decision-making bodies within the church were overwhelmingly comprised of only male members.

Jamir, a school teacher in Eastern Theological College, Jorhat, too alleges the churches to be discriminating against the women. She writes that pastors who are the ordained priests are the top officials of the local churches. Only licensed or ordained persons have the authority to administer the sacraments. Women are hardly appointed as pastor. So far only two Ao women have been ordained and one of them has become a pastor. One of the two ordained priests serves in the Christian education department and the other is in charge of women's department. In other churches, women perform those functions, but under different names. There they are referred to by such names as women's leader or director of Christian education. But the women in these positions do not play a pastoral role in relation to the congregation as a whole.

The other office in the local church that carries authority is that of a Deacon. Together the Deacons constitute the Board of Deacons, which is the main governing authority of the church according to the Baptist polity. While the claim is made that the deacons are appointed in accordance with the New Testament principles, it is more correct to say that they are chosen as the village councillors. Thus far, with the single exception of the Ao church in Kohima, women are not represented on the Board of Deacons of Ao churches in Nagaland. No woman has been elected to the office of deacon or church secretary or the church treasurer. Women are thus excluded from the decision-making processes in the church, even as they were in the traditional Village Councils.

NAGA WOMAN'S POSITION IN THE POLITICAL INSTITUTIONS

The Nagas have a supra tribal political institution or parliament called 'Hoho'. The Hoho exists at tribal and village levels as well. The Naga Hoho represents the entire Nagas and is considered the apex traditional decision-making body in the state, constituted by representatives from various tribes. In line with the traditional practice, no woman representatives are included in the Naga Hoho. At the village level, the Village Council is the apex decision-making body, which is represented by all the clans in the village. However, only a male member could represent a clan. Thus, customary laws do not allow women to be part of decision-making institutions, nor participate in public debates or meetings. Such exclusion of women from public forums serves effectively to render them politically incapable. Sometimes even to the point of ignorance, even in matters that affect them such as policy decisions for development of the village and community.

Since 1980 a new form of development institution has been introduced in Nagaland at the villages by the name village development board (VDB). The board is formed under the aegis of the Village Council in every recognized village of Nagaland with tenure of five years, unless dissolved by the council earlier. The VDB comprises a secretary and other members of which two members mandatorily have to be women. The VDB is entrusted to assist the Village Council in implementing the development schemes for which funds are channelized by the state government. Grant in aid is provided by the government yearly, the quantum of which is assessed by multiplying the number of total households in the village into the allocation per household. In order to avoid any discrimination, 25 per cent of the grants are earmarked for the women. The programmes for the women included income-generating schemes such as piggery where the women were given loan to buy a pig ling each. The loan was repaid after a year when the pig was sold off at a profit. The women's schemes also include weaving, knitting, etc. Other income-generating programmes include money lending with interest. These have become quite popular in villages.

Though the functioning of VDB has been acclaimed quite a lot, it is still considered to be a male's domain. The participation of the women is very little and even the two members are totally dictated by the Village Council. It is reported quite often that the quota for the women too is not channelized regularly. Mukhim, an editor with *Sikkim Times*, points out that during her visit to Mon and Tuensang districts of Nagaland, she found the native tribal women involved in jhum cultivation to be very naive and ignorant about the VDB schemes for women. The women are included in the Village Employment Council because unless it happens the schemes cannot be implemented.

Jamir (2012) states that apart from the traditional system, modern democratic system of governance has been introduced in Nagaland. But since the first election to the State Legislative Assembly conducted in 1964, not even a single woman has been elected to the State Legislature. Starting from the first General Assembly election in 1964 to the 10th Assembly Election held in 2003, there has been only 9 women candidates (two of whom contested twice) out of a total of 1,729 candidates. This accounted for a mere 0.5 per cent of the total candidature. Further, an analysis of the performance of the women candidates with regard to the votes secured in the elections suggests that the attitude of the Naga electorate towards women in governance was not favourable. Jamir (op. cit.) further states that in a study conducted about the role of women in political institutions of Nagaland revealed that the family members of women in active politics did not support them in any way and were not keen about their joining to politics. The study also showed that the role of the women in political parties was confined to their serving tea and snacks or cooking food and running errands for the male members during the meetings. 'Therefore, despite their entry into political parties it was to be seen that for the Naga women, far from being elevated to positions of decision making processes, their conventional role of domesticity was actually transferred into the political arena. Ultimately, mere membership in political parties did not guarantee the Naga women a place in decision-making'. Mukhim (Internet) points out that apart from the State Legislature no woman from the State of Nagaland has even been elected to the Parliament. Only Rano Shaiza coming from an affluent political family background was nominated to the Rajya Sabha. 'She (too) was unable to make interventions in the conflict because hers was a solitary voice' (Gill, 2005).

Since the British days, the Gao Bura (GB) institution was introduced in the villages of Nagaland. The village chiefs were usually appointed as the GB to manage the village administration. These days each Naga village has a number of GBs as even the clan heads are appointed as GB. Till very recent no woman was appointed as GB. Very recently one woman has been appointed so in the outskirts of Dimapur.

In consonance with the 73rd and 74th Amendments of the Constitution of India, the Nagaland State Legislature passed the Municipality Act in 2006 for reserving 33 per cent of the seats for women in the municipalities and town committees. But this was vehemently opposed by the Naga men. The Naga women's groups then moved the Gauhati High Court in this regard. But the Court turned down their plea by stating that it must be looked at from the point of view of Article 371 (A) of the Constitution (Applicable to the State of Nagaland) which states that 'notwithstanding anything in this Constitution (a) no Act of Parliament in respect of (1) religious and social practices of the Nagas, (2) Naga Customary Law and procedure, (3) administration of civil and criminal justice involving decisions according to Naga customary laws, (4) ownership and transfer of land and its resources shall apply to the State of Nagaland unless the Legislative Assembly of Nagaland by a resolution so decides'.

Mukhim a renowned journalist and activist based in Shillong criticized this move by stating, 'In 21st Century India, it is a matter of great regret that the judiciary is banking on some archaic tradition as a way of supporting the Nagaland government and going against the aspirations of women to be fully involved in civic administration. Is this a reflection that the judiciary, too, is still a male-centric territory and that patriarchy and its abusive sting is alive kicking in our courts?' She also states Naga society is deeply entrenched in patriarchal values and while these do not necessarily mimic the Indian model they are all pervasive and do not give women their rightful space in society and politics. Mukhim further notes that even in the Naga underground movement the women play very little role. They may be shown in the khaki fatigues in the photographs, but in reality they matter very little. Preeti Gill (2005) writes about the discriminated position of the Naga women in the Naga movement very vividly, 'Often by choice or under coercion women join the armed insurgent groups. In 1950s and 60s there were a number of women cadres in the Naga National Army and the Federal Government of Nagaland. These women worked as informers, bearers of loads and rations, cooking and sheltering men cadres et al as even among rebel groups the duties of men and women vary. Usually men take up arms and women play supporting roles. Women seldom rise to the position of commander. These groups are part of society and their value system reflects the same social values. Equality for women is not a priority; and women's issues receive importance only when some political advantage can accrue of it. But women joining these groups see themselves as empowered and as performing untraditional roles, certainly in the initial phase of recruitment. This changes later, however, when they find themselves in a minority and unable to take on decision-making roles. They often find themselves trapped into doing the same chores and household jobs that they would ordinarily take on in their homes. They find themselves confined and marginalized in the same inferior positions; sometimes it seems that they have just exchanged their traditional dress uniforms while the 'job definition' remains the same exploitative one.

It appears that the Article 371 (A) has been misused and abused with so many political agendas and socially flagitious intention. Even the Naga Hoho appears to have succumbed to pressures, 'The wisdom of Naga Hoho stands challenged when it states that the reservation Act was detrimental to the sanctity of the traditional land holding system. Everyone is aware that women's reservation in municipal councils is not about land holding system, nor is it in any way going to affect the traditional practices of the Nagas on land and ownership holdings. The Act itself is not about providing ownership status of land and property to the womenfolk but to provide opportunities for women in the decision making process. And to the end, it is very clear; thus, by bringing an unrelated issue of landholding system as an argument to counter the Act, the Hoho is tantamount to misleading the people by diverting the issue and twisting the facts.'

CONCLUSION

It may appear from the contents of this paper that the Naga women suffer from a very significant inferiority complex. They may be tortured and oppressed by their male counterparts. But in reality though they do not enjoy much space in the public sphere, they enjoy a great deal of freedom compared to the Hindu and Muslim women inhabiting the plains of India. It is of course a fact that the women's reservation Bill has not faced so strong an opposition in the 'mainstream' society as seen in Nagaland. In this regard, it is probably apt to refer to Downs (1996) who states, 'In order to understand the position of those who argue that the status of women was high, one needs to understand that their judgements are not based on an analysis of the societies themselves but upon comparisons with other societies. Their conclusions are thus relative to the models they use. On the one hand were the models of the traditional Hindu and Muslim societies in India. When compared to the position of women within zenana and purdah systems, the hills women were perceived to enjoy considerable freedom'. The women's activists of the Northeast region may be feeling it other way around.

REFERENCES

Downs, F.S. (1996). *The Christian Impact on the Status of Women in North East India*, Shillong: NEHU Publication.

Gill, P. (2005). 'Women in the Time of Conflict: The Case of Nagaland', *India International Centre Quarterly*, 32(2/3).

Horam, M. (1975). *Naga Polity*, New Delhi: B.R. Publishing Co.

Jamir, T. (2012). *Women and Politics in Nagaland: Challenges and Imperatives*, New Delhi: Concept Publishing Company.

Longkumer, J. (2009). *Change and Continuity in Tribal Villages: A Sociological Study*, New Delhi: Akansha Pub.

Mills, J.P. (1926). *The Ao Nagas*, London: Macmillan & Co. Ltd.

Shimray, U.A. (2004). 'Women's Work in Naga Society: Household Work, Workforce Participation and Division of Labour', *EPW*, April, 24–30.

CHAPTER 17

STATUS OF TRIBAL WOMEN: AN INTER-STATE ANALYSIS

Swapan Kumar Kolay and Anil Prasad Bandela

In recent times many attempts have been made to understand the status of women in the tribal society. Status is customarily defined by social scientists as a recognized social position or socially defined position of an individual or a community within a society. Some scholars perceive high status of tribal women, but others disagree. According to Sachchidananda (1978), 'it is almost impossible to depict women's roles and status in a single statement. In the tribal world of India we also meet the same difficulty.' He goes on to say that 'women's roles and status all over the world are generally determined by social institutions and norms, religious ideologies, eco-systems and class positions'. Robert Lowie (1920) has suggested four different criteria to determine the status of women in a society: (1) actual treatment, (2) legal status, (3) opportunity for social participation and (4) character and extent of work. Mujumdar and Madan (1956) state that 'expressed, some of which take a stand that primitive society" women are generally a depressed group'. For this reason, Robert Lowie has stated that any general statement regarding the relation of women to the society must be taken with caution. The Dhebar Commission Report (1961) mentions that the tribal women is not drudge or a beast of burden, she is found to be exercising a relatively free and firm hand in all aspects related to her social life unlike in nontribal societies. The tribal women in general and in comparison with castes enjoy more freedom in various walks of life. Traditional and customary tribal norms are comparatively more liberal to women.

The women in the tribal community constitute about half of the tribal population. Their role in the tribal society is even more important than in other social groups in India, because the tribal women, more than women in any other social group, work harder and the family economy and management depends on them.

In this paper, an attempt has been made to review the available literature on economic, social, political, health and religious status of tribal women in India and its correlates among tribal women, to indicate their existing actual status, to identify the gaps of knowledge and to suggest a possible plan of action besides pointing out the debatable issues.

METHODOLOGY

This article has been developed by personal field experiences of the researchers and extensive literature review. The secondary data was collected data from the government agencies, civil societies those who were engaged in promotion of women and tribal rights. In addition, the researchers have collected data from different sources like, Internet, newspapers, relevant journals and references books. Along with the objectives of the article, the researchers have also analysed and interpreted the relevant literature. The exploratory research method was used to write this article in a systematic and scientific manner.

HIGHER SOCIAL STATUS OF TRIBAL WOMEN

It was reported by Furer Haimendorf (1943), Hutton (1921), Hunter (1973) and Firth (1946) that among Tharus of Uttar Pradesh and Nagas and Garos of the North-East there is no child marriage and no stigma on widowhood. The tribal woman enjoys the right to decide about her marriage. Instead of dowry, there is bride price which indicates a high social status of the tribal women. Tribal women are independent with regards to economic status. Among the tribal society, birth of a girl is not looked down upon because they are considered as economic assets. They participate in all agricultural operations (except ploughing) and work in all sectors of indigenous cottage industries, tribal arts and production of articrafts. Tribal women enjoy lot of freedom before and after marriage. The wife may divorce her husband on the grounds of cruelty, impotency, incompatibility, poverty, infidelity or negligence. Traditionally, the practice of divorce exists and divorce is granted by the Village Panchayat. In cases of excess, the wife may even desert her husband and enter other man's house as per her choice. The tribal woman may just walk out of her husband's house with/without intimation to her husband. Although she enjoys full liberty to choose her life partner and also to break the marital bond and marry with another person, for the tribal men it is not possible to cause harm to the modesty of a married woman. Severe penalties and punishments are inflicted on man in all such cases. The women thus enjoy an almost equal status with men except in the sphere of rituals.

LOW STATUS OF THE TRIBAL WOMEN

The tribal woman does not have property rights except in a matrilineal society which is a small proportion of the tribal population. She is paid fewer wages than her male counterpart for the same work. Besides this, the women work for more time than men, they receive wages in kind which are enchased by males. The women do not have the decision-making power. The division of work is heavily loaded against the tribal woman because in addition to an equal share in the economic production process she has to take the sole responsibility of household chores. In certain tribes, only the males can participate in ancestor worship. Usually she cannot hold the office of a priest (Rajyalakshmi, 1996). A strong belief in witchcraft prevails among many tribes, even among its educated members. It is believed that a woman who practices witchcraft is responsible for unexplained misfortunes and deaths in the village. When a woman (often a widow, or a barren or old woman) is branded a witch, she is usually killed by the villagers after a public trial. The prime duty of women is child bearing. Barrenness is looked upon as a curse from heaven and is often the cause for abandonment by the husband. A barren woman may even be branded as anti-social or a witch. Discrimination between girls and boys is not obvious, but the birth of a male child is a matter of greater rejoicing. For the birth of male heirs ensures that the family lineage will be carried forward.

ECONOMIC ROLE OF TRIBAL WOMEN

Tribal women in India contribute positively towards economic pursuits by participating equally with men folk. In the nomadic hunter-gatherer tribes, men do the hunting while women collect fruits, edible roots, tubers, firewood and other household necessities. In some of these tribes, women may also be involved in supplementary occupations, like rope-making among the Birhors. Women also cook, look after the children and manage all household affairs. In the pastoral tribes, looking after the cattle is the exclusive duty of men folk. In the Toda tribe of the Nilgiris, women are not even allowed to enter the dairy as they are considered impure. The bulk of the tribal people in India subsist on agriculture. In tribes such as the Mundas, Oraons, Santals, Hos, Kharias, Gonds, etc., women look after harvesting and transplanting. Men are responsible for ploughing, levelling and watching over the crops. When relatively free from household duties and agriculture, women also prepare rice beer. Some tasks like ploughing and thatching the roof are taboo for them and may even call for social sanctions, if indulged in. The economic roles of tribal women are more significant in certain parts of the central and western Himalayas. Besides their household duties, they help in cultivation and bring fodder for the cattle. The Kinnaur women of Himachal Pradesh help their men in harvesting apples from orchards. In agriculture, they do everything except ploughing, which includes weeding, harvesting, threshing and winnowing. In the pastoral hill tribes, women are also expected to spin the wool and do the knitting. In matrilineal societies like the Khasi and Garo tribes of Meghalaya, property is transmitted from mother to daughter. Certain occupations are exclusively in the hands of women, for example, weaving and stitching and sale of fish. In these communities, we find a numerical dominance of women in trade. In a matrilineal society, it is women who are responsible for looking after children, brothers, sisters, husbands, parents, etc. They thus have to work hard to earn money. In patrilineal tribes, property is transmitted from father to son and women have no right to inherit or own property. Yet, a widow may enjoy her husband's property as long as she is alive. In the absence of a son, a daughter may enjoy the property. But her children will never inherit it and it will ultimately revert to her father's lineage. In some tribes, women are given a small portion of their fathers' land when their husbands desert them. This arrangement is to ensure their economic protection and the land reverts to the fathers' lineage after their death. However, there are some tribes where men and women are equal partners in socio-economic life and hence women are traditionally assigned an important role in the society (Singh, 1994).

CULTURAL ROLE OF TRIBAL WOMEN

The cultural life of tribal communities is very rich and music, dancing and singing occupy pivotal place in their culture. They have community entertainment with total village participating and the men, women, boys and girls all participate at equal level. They freely sing and dance with each other and joking, laughing goes on freely specially on the occasion of marriages and on festivals like Holi, Dashera, etc. Men and women of all ages dance in ecstasy on the rhythm of the drums throughout the right. It is only in the tribal rituals connected with religious practices that the men folk get a priority over the women. Alcoholism among tribals also contributes towards the misery of the women in the house. Apart from giving rise to conflict between the spouses, it also creates economic crisis in the family.

FOREST ECOLOGY AND TRIBAL WOMEN

Women made provisions for the basic necessities like food, fuel, medicine, housing material, etc. from the forest produce. The forest-based tribal economy in most parts of the world is women-centred (Menon, 1987–1991). Extractions from herbs, roots and animals were used for medicines. All these efforts incurred an excessive workload on women. In a study on the Garos of Meghalaya, Kar (1982) calculated the ratio of male or female investment in labour in shifting cultivation to be 100:136 days per year. The contribution of women was more in almost all activities like clearing (169:120), sowing (102:60), weeding (272:182) and cotton harvesting (56:6). Because of the extensive felling of trees by vested interests, the distances between the villages and the forest areas had increased forcing the tribal women to walk longer distances in search of minor forest produce and firewood. A study on the Kondhs revealed that women put in an average of 14 working hours per day as compared to 9 hours put in by men (Dasgupta, 1988). Given this additional workload, even women in advanced stages of pregnancy were required to work in the agricultural fields or walk great distances to collect fuel and minor forest produce.

EDUCATION AMONG THE TRIBAL WOMEN

The overall literacy rates and educational attainment of tribal women are significantly lower than the national average. The tribal literacy rate among women is significantly higher in the north-eastern states such as Mizoram, Meghalaya and Nagaland, where tribal groups constitute a large percent of the general population. On the other hand, tribal literacy rates are much lower in the states of Rajasthan, Orissa and Madhya Pradesh. Thus, general statistics portray the dismal state of education and literacy among tribal groups. However, the literacy rates for scheduled tribes in India have also improved substantially from 1961 (8.54 per cent) to 1991 (29.60 per cent) for both males (13.83 per cent to 40.65 per cent) and females (3.16 per cent to 18.19 per cent), respectively. This applies more to females than males both among the mainstream Hindu population and the tribal groups because girls are expected to help out with domestic chores more than boys at a very early age (Nambissan, 2000; Vasavi, 2002; Jha and Jhingran, 2002). Some unique obstacles faced by tribal women in addition to the high poverty rates are insufficient numbers of schools in many tribal areas, lack of resources in tribal schools, significant language barriers in schools where the teachers are not fluent in tribal languages (Srivastava, 1997) and the problems in social adjustment faced by many tribal boys and girls who are often discriminated against by upper-caste children. Among the scheduled tribe population, the literacy rate is highest in the State of Mizoram in north-eastern India (86.95 per cent), and the disparity in literacy between males and females is about 4 per cent. The female literacy rate is lowest in the states of Bihar (15.54 per cent), followed by Orissa (23.37 per cent) in eastern India, Rajasthan (26.16 per cent) in northern India, Uttar Pradesh (20.70 per cent) in northern India and Andhra Pradesh (26.11 per cent) in South India. Thus the 'convergence effect' of following the mainstream norm of encouraging gender inequality in education is absent among the tribal women in some of the north-eastern states of India (Dreze and Sen, 2002). The influence of Christianity in the north-eastern states also played a significant role in encouraging high literacy rates among tribal women. Tribal groups are regularly exposed to the social and cultural practices of the mainstream Hindus and their discriminatory practices against women. Among all tribal groups, the dropout rate in classes I to V was 41.13 per cent among boys and 41.91 per cent among girls. However, as the level of education increases, the gender gap becomes much more pronounced among the tribal groups. The dropout rate among tribal boys in classes I to VIII is 66.86 per cent while it is 71.17 per cent among girls. While education at the lower level is free, there are other costs, including books and learning materials, which impose a significant financial burden on low-income tribal families (Ramachandran, 2002).

MIGRATION OF TRIBAL WOMEN AND GIRLS

A large number of women and girls from tribal areas migrate to cities and towns all over India. Most of these women and girls are illiterate and unskilled. They work in inhuman conditions in cities as their living standard is extremely poor. A great number of these migrants are being exploited by middle men, contractors, construction companies and other types of employers. Many of these women and girls work as house maids where their working hours extend up to 18 hours per day. A large number of tribal women and girls become victims of sexual and financial exploitation. Their children rarely get an opportunity to go to school and learn a productive skill. Gradually, many women and girls lose contact with their kith and kins back home and become alienated from their culture and roots.

In tribal areas, land is a symbol of the organization of the community. When a transfer takes place beyond the threshold point, the community looks upon the process as alienation. It is thus obvious that transfer of land is not merely a question of exploitation of innocent tribals by cunning people, there are more complex factors involved (Chowdhuri, 1990). When land alienation takes place, migration of tribals is inevitable.

HEALTH STATUS OF TRIBAL WOMEN

Efforts have been made to collect available literature on the health studies among different tribal women in the light of several parameters, i.e., sex ratio, female literacy, marriage practices, age at marriage, fertility, mortality, life expectancy at birth, nutritional status and health, child bearing and maternal mortality, maternal and child health care practices, family welfare programme, sexually transmitted diseases and genetic disorders.

Sex Ratio

The sex composition of males and females among the scheduled tribes is 987 (1961), 982 (1971), 983 (1981), 972 (1991) and 978 (2001). This suggests that the females in the tribal society are not neglected; the social and cultural values protected their interest. However, it may he pointed out that their sex ratio (978) in 2001 census shows a definite decline when compared to the 1981 census figure of 983. The sex ratio of the scheduled tribes varied within the country, i.e., among the states it was highest in Orissa (1003) and lowest in Uttar Pradesh/Sikkim (914); among the Union Territories, it was highest in Dadra and Nagar Haveli (1022) and lowest in Daman and Diu (931).

Marriage

In many tribal communities, cross-cousin marriages were preferred and practiced. The system of cross-cousin marriage had proved to be beneficial to the females in terms of care and treatment at husband's place. It also avoided high bride price/dowry and maintained the property of the household. Consanguineous marriages may, however, result in an increased probability of abortions, miscarriage, still births, neo-natal deaths, infant and juvenile deaths, physical and mental defects, susceptibility to infectious diseases, etc. In Himalayan region, some of the tribes like Naga, Lusia, etc. practiced polygamy which was for economic reasons to protect the property and get help in agricultural activities. On the other hand, some of the tribes in India practiced polyandry because of less number of women available for marriage, e.g., Jaunsaris of Jaunsar-Bawar, Chakrata Tehsil of Dehradun and Todas of Nilgiri hills. Formerly, the Todas practiced female infanticide which resulted in less number of girls available for marriage.

Fertility and Mortality

Studies on fertility and mortality trends among the tribal population of India have been found to be fragmentary and isolated. Limited studies are available on infant mortality and hardly any study is available on maternal mortality among the tribal population. In north-eastern zone, Pandey (1990) observed high fertility and mortality in Mishmi tribal groups and attributed it to the low level of education, income and lack of knowledge of family planning method and importance of small family size, poor medical facilities, lack of proper sanitation and drinking water. In northern zone, Basu and Kshatriya (1993) while conducting research on 481 households among the Jaunsaris of Jaunsar Bawar, Dehradun, found a crude birth rate of 42.67 per thousand populations and infant mortality rate of 79.64 per thousand live births. Polyandry and polygamy were found to co-exist in the study sample. Basu (1990) found that Lepchas ate fish and a type of tuber, i.e., Diascoria, while Sherpas did not eat them. It was observed that diasoria had a fecundity-inhibiting function resulting in lower fertility among Lepchas as against Sherpas though both shared a similar physical environment. In central zone, Basu and Kshatriya (1992) studied the fertility and mortality trends among the Dudh Kharia of Sundargarh District of Orissa. They reported that the estimated total fertility, crude birth rate, crude death rate and infant mortality rate were 5.39, 38.5, 11.80 and 102.4, respectively. All these demographic figures showed higher values than the Indian national population level according to the 1981 Census. These were similar to those of the other Indian tribal populations. In western zone, Parsuraman and Rajan (1990) discussed the estimation of vital rates among the scheduled tribes. A very high proportion of 0–14 population to the total population indicated a higher level of fertility and not so high mortality. In southern zone, the study of Sirajuddin et al. (1984) among the Chenchu tribal group of Achampet Taluk of Andhra Pradesh found that the average number of children for each women. Average number of surviving offspring per married women and mortality in relation to live births were 3.67, 2.96 and 27.5, respectively. In island zone, Aggarwal (1967) found that among 45 ever married Onge women of the Andaman Islands, the mean number of children was 1.64 and the mean number of children per women was 1.13. Infant mortality was very high as revealed from the reproductive index which was 0.51.

Life Expectancy

A general indicator of the health of girl and women is their life expectancy. The expectation of life is the average number of years remaining to be lived by those surviving to that age. Basu and Kshatriya (1993) while studying the Bastar tribal groups of present Chhattisgarh estimated the average life expectancy at birth based on q5 values for Muria (males 37.56 yrs, females 40.07) Maria (males 40.26 yrs, females 45.30 yrs) and Halba (males 38.6 yrs, females 41.46 yrs) tribes and 41.1 years for all the four tribal groups combined. Although these figures were comparable to the rural non-tribal population of Chhattisgarh, they were far below the average life expectancy at birth of 58.6 yrs for the Indian population. Sex-specific mortality differentials were observed, with males experiencing highest mortality than females. The differences could only be attributed to the prevailing socio-economic, cultural and health care practices of the four tribal groups.

Nutritional Status of Mother

Good nutrition is a requirement throughout life and is vital to women in terms of their health and work. Nutritional anaemia is a major problem for women in India and more so in the rural and tribal belt. In developing countries, it was estimated that at least half of the non-pregnant and two-thirds of the pregnant women were anaemic (UN, 1984). Scanning through available data, it was observed that among most of the tribal groups the staple diet was rice or minor millets except the mompas of Assam who consumed wheat also (Basu et al., 1985). Birds, fish and other meat products were also consumed by the tribals occasionally. Diet of not a single tribal in the different states of India can be said to be usually satisfactory. Tribal diets were generally grossly deficient in Calcium, vitamin A and C, riboflavin and animal protein. Diets of South Indian tribes, in general, and of Kerala, in particular, were grossly deficient even in respect of calories and total protein. Studies carried out at the National Institute of Nutrition (1971) and Planning Commission of India (Sixth Five Year Plan, Government of India) reported high protein calorie malnutrition along the rice-eating belts. Studies carried out by NIHFW among the Gonds (Muria and Madia), Bhatras and Halba tribal groups of Bastar District, Madhya Pradesh, showed the following trends (Basu et al., 1989, 1993): (1) The average protein calorie intake was found to be much less in the Gond children as compared to the Bhattra and Halba children. (2) Higher frequencies of Bitot's spot, angular stomatitis and mottling of teeth were found among the Gond children as compared to the Bhatra and Halba children. (3) Muscular wasting was noticed to be higher among the Gond children as compared to the Bhattra children. Consumption of milk or milk products was taboo in preschool tribal children due to the fact that milking of cow was a taboo among these tribal groups.

A study among the Pauri Bhuniyas of Orissa showed those 52 women as against 17 men in a sample of 268 persons suffered from diseases related to malnutrition (Ali, 1980). This had implications particularly for the housewife who was responsible for the provision and distribution of food, in cases of shortage; she even deprived herself of food in order to feed the others. Studies in this connection have shown that tribals in general were undernourished. For example, a study had shown that over 55 per cent of Kondhs consumed less than 2,000 calories per day (Patel, 1985) and most of them as little as 1,700 calories (Sharma, 1979) compared to the ICMR stipulated requirement of 2,400 calories.

Maternal Mortality

In India, the maternal mortality was around 500 per 10,000 live births, which was about 50 times that in a developed country or in the better off segments of the India society (UNICEF, 1983). The situation was all the more aggravated among women in the tribal belt of India because of the prevailing magico-religious and socio-cultural practices. Maternal mortality was reported to be high among various tribal groups. The main causes of maternal mortality were found to be unhygienic and primitive practices for parturition. For example, it was observed that among the Kutia Kondhs (Basu 1990), the delivery was conducted by the mother herself in a half squatting position holding a rope tied down from the roof of the hut. This helped her in applying pressure to deliver the child. In complicated labour, obviously it might lead to maternal as well as child mortality.

Maternal and Child Health Care Practices

Maternal and child health care practices were found to be largely neglected in various tribal groups. Expectant mothers, to a large extent, were not inoculated against tetanus. From the inception of pregnancy to its termination, no specific nutritious diet was consumed by women. On the other hand, some pregnant tribal women (i.e., Dudh Kharias, Santals) reduced their food intake because of the fear of recurrent vomiting and also to ensure that the baby may remain small and the delivery may be easier. The consumption of iron, calcium and vitamins during pregnancy was poor. The habit of taking alcohol during pregnancy was found to be common among the tribal women and almost all of them continued their regular activities including hard labour even during advanced pregnancy. More than 90 per cent of the deliveries were conducted at home attended by elderly ladies of the household.

Maternal mortality directly related to pregnancy and childbirth was found to be appreciably high among the tribal population groups of Bastar District. In addition, extremes of magico-religious beliefs and taboos aggravated the problems.

Sexually Transmitted Diseases

Female genital tract infections were closely related to inappropriate care or poor hygiene in connection with child birth, abortion or menstruation. They included the sexually transmitted diseases which were prevalent diseases in the tribal areas. These infections were often untreated as they were difficult to diagnose and would even lead to infertility. Venereal Disease Research Laboratory (VDRL) test was observed in 4.99 per cent females and 3.91 per cent males (Basu and Kshatriya, 1993). The prevalence of Sexually Transmitted Disease (STD) was also reported to be high in the polyandrous Toda tribal group of Nilgiri hills. While conducting a morbidity study among the Kondha tribe of Phulbani District, Orissa, Swain et al. (1990) found syphilis (10 per cent) in Desia Kondhs. The presence of STDs was also reported in Andamanese and tribal groups of Chhattisgarh, Rajasthan and Mysore.

GENDER EQUITY OF TRIBAL WOMEN

The first is the greater say women have in their societies than most other women do. The combination of rights and restrictions makes their status better than that of women elsewhere. A sign of it is the division of labour and other family matters that are controlled by women. They decide what to grow and how to use the produce. This apparent social emancipation does not make them equal to men. This close link between their hold over the family livelihood and their role in agriculture makes land basic to their status. However, today agriculture and forests do not cater to the needs of many of them. Land is today bought and sold as a commodity and is not treated as livelihood. At times outsiders take control of it, thus it affects women's control over their livelihood. Both women's relatively high status and tribal identity are linked to land. Change in its use through alienation, deforestation and commercialization thus affects them negatively since by and large men control the new technology and marketing systems. With it women run the risk of losing their traditional control over their livelihood, strengthening the patriarchal ethos, weakening their equity-based culture and becoming only housewives (Barbora and Fernandes, 2002).

We have seen it in the transition of the Garo men taking decisions concerning land and Angami getting most non-agricultural jobs despite women's high level of education. Such transition to stronger patriarchy that began in the colonial age is being continued by post-colonial governments (Kekrieseno, 2002b). When that happens, the tribal tradition tends to adapt itself to patriarchy. For example, the male-dominated village councils interpret the customary law from men's perspective, as seen in the codification of the Mizo customary law or in the trend among educated men in the Garo society, to take their wives home or the fact of class formation among the Dimasa through individual *pattas* weakening women's role or the refusal of most Naga village councils to change their stand on ownership and the feminization of poverty among the Adibasi (Barbora and Fernandes, 2002). Poverty forces many of their girls in the 10–19 cohorts to go out as domestic helps (Fernandes and Barbora, 2002). In Tripura, the weakening of their subsistence economy and the changing occupational pattern marginalize women particularly in the urban and industrial sector. So men are becoming the only earners and women their dependants (Chowdhuri 1990). Thus while women's gift of managing the family economy can help them in the transition to a commercial economy (Noksang, 1997), experience shows that without steps to support the change, the result can go against them.

TRIBAL WOMEN IN POLITICAL SYSTEMS

All tribal societies are well-organized and have well-developed political and judicial systems of their own. In traditional tribal communities, women have no political role at all. They are not allowed to hold office in the village council and to participate in the council meetings. They have no direct say in matters relating to common concerns in the village. They usually convey their opinions to the village council through their husbands and other men folk. Nowadays, things are changing on this front and it is not uncommon to find a woman *manjhi* in Santal villages. There may be difference in the inheritance, marriage and conflict resolution systems but whether they are patrilineal, matrilineal or of double descent, all of them are patriarchal. The woman may take family decisions such as her children's education but social power is in the hands of men. Even in matrilineal societies, the woman who inherits land is only its custodian. Decisions concerning the resource are in the social sphere and are taken by men. Now here is the patriarchal system more visible than in their traditional political systems through which the North Eastern tribes governed themselves. In could be the village council in some cases, the village chief in a few and the clan elders in others. But in every case it was made up of men alone. The tenure of the council was hereditary in some tribes and by election in others but in every case only adult males were their members and women were denied a voice. Some change has started and some tribes have given a small voice to women. The Angami, for example, has in some villages admitted the president of the Women's Association to the village council but she cannot hope to become its president. The Garo heiress had some voice in decisions concerning their society though the village council itself was controlled by men. That voice has declined substantially with modernization. These changes have occurred because of their exposure to other value systems through education and other inputs. However, because of women's associations and other bodies and processes linked to inputs such as education and change of religion, they have become aware of their rights at least to a limited extent. Some associations have started voicing opinions in favour of women's rights. Some new bodies such as the Village Development Board, Village Panchayats and the District Autonomous Council have been set up, based on electoral politics. The law confers on men and women the right to contest elections to them as well as to the State Assembly and the Parliament. However, very few tribal women have been able to avail of the opportunities they provide. After initial resistance, some communities allowed them to contest elections but it is a slow process. For example, the Meghalaya Assembly had its first woman legislator about two decades ago and today it has 3 of them in a total of 40. This limited participation is the result both of lack of awareness of their rights among women and of resistance from men. Nagaland had a Rajya Sabha member in the 1970s and none after it. A Naga woman who contested the last State Assembly Elections was defeated badly. Before the 2004 Central elections, some women's organizations wanted to put up a woman candidate for the only Lok Sabha seat of Nagaland but they were discouraged from doing so. A major change introduced recently is the 73rd Constitution Amendment Act 1993 that reserves one-third of the seats and posts in these bodies for women. However, this legal provision does not apply to the Sixth Schedule areas of the Garo and the Dimasa. The Angami runs their civil affairs according to their customary law under Article 371A. These bodies remain almost fully male-dominated (Nongbri, 1998).

RELIGIOUS STATUS OF TRIBAL WOMEN

In most of the patrilineal tribal society, women do not have an important role in religious activities. They are not allowed to officiate in any of the ceremonies, whether at birth, death or marriage, or in other occasions or festivals. But they greatly contribute in the ceremonies. Sachchidananda (1979) observes that many responsibilities connected with worship are allotted to them. Women, for example, clean and decorate the place of worship, prepare and serve the native drink and in some tribes sing to invoke the spirit. Among the Saoras of Orissa, each village has one or two women called Kuranbois who engage themselves in divination and the spiritual treatment of illness. They play an important role in society because, in the absence of doctors, they are called to cure the sick. In Arunachal Pradesh, similar type of institution has been found among the Abors.

CONCLUSION

On the basis of overview of some of the studies and reports published at different points of time, it can be said that socio-economic status of tribal women is low. Their status is low in both public and private domain. Neither the traditional institutions nor the modern practices have been able to improve their status. Rather with the popularization of forces of modernization in the tribal regions, the status of tribal women is further deteriorated. But still they are the backbone of tribal society. If some of the suggestions presented below are accepted and translated into action, hopefully it may add to the improvement in the status of tribal women.

- Increase agricultural production through conservation to settled agriculture, where possible, with linkage to easy credit and markets and assured irrigation.
- Undertake a comprehensive survey of water resources, including surface water and groundwater, in tribal areas with the help of remote sensing to prepare land use maps. Where water levels have gone down, an integrated watershed management approach must be adopted. Ponds and tanks should be increased and renovated for optimum use.
- Promote the diversification of agriculture and non-farm sectors to create job opportunities. Train tribal women in kitchen gardening, childcare, food preservation, handicrafts and other house-based activities.
- Form and stabilize tribal women's co-operatives to take up dairy, sericulture, fisheries, handicrafts, horticulture agri-food processing and post-harvest technologies.
- Impart practical knowledge and training in modern techniques to all tribal women regularly so that their work becomes easier and crop production increases.
- Undertake research and extension to improve current practices, increase output and incomes and eliminate adverse ecological effects.

- As per the PESA 1996, the Gram Sabha enjoys the authority to decide the natural resources which include non-timber forest produce (NTFP). The monopoly restrictions over NTFP should be immediately removed while ensuring social protection through provision of support prices to tribals who should be allowed to collect, process, transport and market the NTFP.
- Low literacy, especially among tribal girls, and high dropout rates at elementary and higher levels are areas of serious concern. Focus on girls' education, inclusive of context-specific traditional and innovative interventions. Launch special and sustained education initiatives/ drives in low female literacy tribal pockets.
- Teach tribal children in their mother tongue at least at primary level. Prepare textbooks in tribal languages. Moreover, the government needs to strengthen the quality governance to deliver the best services by the teachers.
- To prevent teacher absenteeism in tribal areas, give preference to local and tribal teachers from local Panchayats, and place the teaching and non-teaching staff of primary schools under the control of the village management committee.
- Promote the synthesis of Indian systems of medicine like Ayurveda, Sidha and Unani with the tribal system.
- Strengthen the Tribal Sub Plan (TSP) strategy with an institutionalized mechanism for compliance and monitoring. Make TSP funds non-divertible and non-lapsable – develop a workable system.
- Take measures through community efforts to eliminate pernicious practices which result in the torture and oppression of women, e.g., witchcraft and superstitions.
- Discourage the migration of tribal women to urban areas, to take low paid, domestic and mental work by providing an enabling regulatory framework.
- Train tribal women to take up their responsibilities and sensitize the Gram Sabha about the new provisions.
- Inform all Gram Sabha members, including tribal women, of the functions, responsibilities and powers of Gram Sabhas.
- Encourage women's organizations working among tribals and ensure the formation, stabilization and bank linkages of SHGs to promote viable micro-economic activities with substantial support in terms of credit and market.